삶의 5대 불가사의
(The Five Mysteries of Life)
개정증보판

삶의 5대 불가사의(The Five Mysteries of Life) 개정증보판

발행일   2024년 11월 25일

지은이   강재원
펴낸이   손형국
펴낸곳   (주)북랩
편집인   선일영   편집   김은수, 배진용, 김현아, 김다빈, 김부경
디자인   이현수, 김민하, 임진형, 안유경   제작   박기성, 구성우, 이창영, 배상진
마케팅   김회란, 박진관
출판등록 2004. 12. 1(제2012-000051호)
주소   서울특별시 금천구 가산디지털 1로 168, 우림라이온스밸리 B동 B111호, B113~115호
홈페이지 www.book.co.kr
전화번호 (02)2026-5777   팩스   (02)2026-5747

ISBN   979-11-7224-394-4 03190 (종이책)   979-11-7224-395-1 05190 (전자책)

The Five Mysteries of Life

삶의 5대
불가사의

강재원 지음

심연 깊이 흩날리는 꽃잎과 가슴을 적시는 바람꽃,
삶의 찰나를 기록한 마음치유 철학 에세이

북랩

서평

이 책은 삶의 의미와 살아가는 최선의 길에 대한 것으로 인간본성, 천지만물, 철학적 성찰 등으로 엮여 있다.

이 책은 3편으로 구성되어 있으며 각 편마다 보다 나은 삶을 살아갈 수 있도록 하는 교훈, 믿음, 인간관계, 덕목 등이 담겨 있다. 또한 각 편에 음미할 수 있도록 구절마다 번호를 붙인 짧은 내용의 글들로 구성되어 있다. 그중에서 지혜로운 한 구절을 보면 "5라는 숫자는 오랜 세월 생명체가 시행착오를 거치면서 채택한 비밀의 숫자로서 그 바탕에는 안정감, 실용성, 균형, 통제력 등을 담고 있다."

이 책은 모든 사람들에 대하여 정신적인 견해를 제시함으로써 자기성찰을 통한 영적성장을 유발시키는 다감하고, 유익한 개념들의 모음집이다. 훌륭한 삶이란 정신적인 신념과 자신의 이상에 부응하여 살아가는 사람이라면 누구나 가능하다는 확신이 담겨 있으며 책 속에 담긴 시와 교훈은 읽어서 이해하고 받아들이기 쉽다. 일상적인 경험을 예로 들어 실제적인 삶의 모습들이 바탕을 이룬다. 이 책의 전체적인 분위기는 안정적이고 "이치에 합당한 목소리"로 편안함을 전해준다.

Book Review

Jaewon Kang's meditation on the meaning of life and the best way to live it, As the Wind Becomes a Flower, combines insights about human nature, the universe, and philosophy.

The book is divided into three sections. Within each, chapters explore concepts of morality, faith, relationships, and virtues that contribute to living a better life. These chapters include short, numbered entries intended to be savored. One grain of wisdom says, "Five is a secret number that life organisms choose after many trials and errors for a long time, and there is a sense of security, practicality, balance, and control in the number five."

Exemplifying the notion that spirituality is for everyone, this book is a gentle, informative collection of ideas that prompt spiritual growth through self-assessment. It includes assertions such as that a good life is available to anyone who applies spiritual principles and lives up to their own ideals, and its poetry and short sermons are easy to read, understand, and relate to.
Its real-life examples are grounded in common experiences, such as saving for retirement and caring for children. The book's tone, which is balanced and sounds like "the voice of reason," is comforting.

이 책은 일상의 일들을 자연의 법칙과 연결하고 있으며 각 구절마다 명상하듯이 천천히 음미하기를 제안하고 있다. 전체적으로 정신세계에 초점이 맞춰져 있지만, 경제활동 같은 일상생활에 대한 직설적인 교훈이나 자기 성찰 등 다양한 내용들로 엮여 있다.

시적 표현과 추상적 개념들이 혼합되어 어떤 것은 산문을 이루고 어떤 것은 시로 구성되어 있다. 한 주제가 개별적인 문구들로 구성되어 있어서 내용을 전개하는 구도와 관련된 저서 또는 인물들에 대한 참고나 연결고리가 없이 내용을 따라가기 쉽지 않다.

이 책은 어느 특정한 신앙이나 영적인 길에 일관하지 않고 본질적으로 모든 신앙을 포괄적으로 어우르는 모음집이다. 전체적인 책의 흐름은 독단적인 교리가 아닌 어떠한 세계적인 기성 종교나 신념에도 부합되는 내용들로 구성되어 있다.

바람과 꽃은 자기성찰과 개개인의 성장을 북돋우는 비유적인 묘사로서 이해하기 쉬우면서도 호기심을 자아내게 한다.

퍼워드, 클라리온 서평
(미국 미시간주 트레버스시 소재 서평전문기관, 서평일자: 2019년 7월 25일)

The book makes an effort to link everyday details with the laws of the universe. It suggests reading its entries slowly, with a group, and in contemplation. Although its focus is on spirituality, it mixes a variety of esoteric observations and mini-sermons in with its straight talk about commonsense topics like financial planning and manners.

Poetic language and abstract concepts saturate the book with mixed results. Some entries are paragraphs; others are poems. Individual pieces are organized by theme, but have no narrative arcs, references to other spiritual writings, or recurring characters. The links within them are also thematic rather than explicit, which makes chapters difficult to follow.

The book becomes essentially a catalog of ideas: inclusive, with a generic faith angle, and which don't push one particular faith or spiritual path (though the introduction focuses on Christianity). Most of the book's notions could be applied to any major religion, and principles, not dogma, guide the chapters.

Wind and flower are accessible, intriguing assortment of spiritual adages and imagery that encourages self-reflection and personal growth.

ForeWord's Clarion Review (Traverse city, MI, USA, Reviewed: July 25, 2019)

서평

저자는 서문에서 언급하듯이 "살아생전에 누구든지 알고 싶어도 아무
도 가르쳐주지 않는 불가사의한 삶의 비밀은 어떤 것일까?" 하는 의문
에 대한 해답을 찾기 위해 기념비적인 노력을 하였다.

저자는 이 책에서 거의 400가지에 이르는 철학적 성찰, 견해, 해설 등
을 한두 문장 또는 몇 쪽에 걸쳐서 제시하고 있다. 이것들은 신, 영원
성, 삶과 죽음(그 속에 포함된 모든 것), 종교, 우주에서 차지하는 우리의
위치 등 여러 가지 주제에 대한 저자의 견해를 제시한다. 어떤 것은 시
로 어떤 것은 산문으로 표현되어 있으며 대부분의 내용들이 교훈을
줄 수 있도록 비유적으로 표현되어 있다.

저자의 성찰에는 유익함도 담겨 있다. "원하는 것이면 무엇이든 즐겨
라. 그러나 부채금지, 도박금지, 마약금지, 음주금지, 흡연금지. 이 다
섯 악마에게 유혹되지 않으면 인생이 지속가능하다."
어떤 구절들은 생각을 깊이 불러일으키기도 한다. "무엇을 해야지 하
면 스트레스이고, 무엇인가 할 것이 있구나 하면 즐거움이다."

Book Review

Author Jaewon Kang has taken on a monumental task: to try to answer the question posed in the beginning of his book: "What is the secret of mysterious life that nobody teaches though everybody wants to know while alive?"

In As the Wind Becomes a Flower, Kang presents nearly 400 philosophical thoughts, opinions and commentaries—some a sentence or two, some several pages— in his attempt to bring The Big Picture into focus. They offer the author's reflections on a variety of topics: God, eternity, life and death (and everything in between), religion, our place in the universe. Some are presented in verse; others are stories, almost parables designed to impart a lesson.

Kang's reflections can be instructive: "Enjoy whatever you want. However, no debt, no gambling, no drug, [sic] no alcohol, no smoking. Regardless of any reasons, the less tempted you are to these five evils, the more sustainable your life becomes." Some provoke thought: "If you think you ought to do something, it is stressful. However, if you think there is something new to do, it is a joy."

독자들은 이 책에서 심오함에 앞서 당혹스러움을 느낄 수 있으나 색다른 철학에 관심 있는 독자라면 흥미로운 사상을 접할 수 있을 것이다.

블루잉크 서평(국제적인 수상작품 서평전문가들이 설립한 서평기관, 서평일자: 2019년 8월)

Someone with a passing interest in different philosophies might pick up an interesting thought or two here. Most readers, though, will likely find As the Wind Becomes a Flower more puzzling than profound.

*BlueInk Review (*Founded by an internationally known literary agent and an award winning book review editor, *Reviewed: August 2019)*

.

서평

저자는 이 책에서 삶과 사랑과 인성을 보여주고 있다.

제1편 「아모로스 단상」은 즐거운 감정에서부터 관료주의에 대한 견해까지 삶에서 일어나는 일상적인 일들에 초점이 맞춰져 있다.
"맥주의 청량함과 와인의 부드러움이 때로는 일상을 편안하게 해준다."라고 저자는 '즐거움'에 대해 언급하기도 한다.
장애 아이, 거지, 성폭력범 등 간결하면서도 인상적인 내용들이 단편을 이룬다. "죄악은 약자의 마음에서 일어났다가 약자와 함께 사라진다."라고 언급하기도 한다.

제2편 「바람은 꽃이 되어」는 보다 형이상학적인 내용으로 이뤄져 있다. '빛'과 '어둠'이라는 방대한 주제와 특히 저자가 한강변에 살면서 느꼈던 바람꽃에 대하여 "생명의 오고 감이 바람꽃과 같다."라고 시와 은유로서 표현하고 있다.

제3편 「삶의 5대 불가사의」는 신이란 무엇인가? 모든 존재는 어디서 왔는가? 나는 무엇인가? 죽음이란 무엇인가? 사랑이란 무엇인가? 를 다루고 있다. 저자는 종교, 역사를 두루 섭렵하여 이에 대한 해답을

Book Review

A writer reflects on life, love, and human nature in a series of brief, abstract offerings.

The first section of Kang's debut collection, "Amoros Thought," focuses on fundamental notions about life, ranging from the pleasures of the senses to his views on government bureaucracy. "Coolness of beer and sweetness of wine," the author writes on the subject of "Amusement," "sometimes both of them can make our lives comfortable."
Interwoven with these short, impressionistic passages are longer stories, which deliver snapshots in time: a young disabled girl crying because her father cannot provide her a dress, a poor foreigner begging for money, men robbing and raping a young college woman. "Vices rise from weak minds, then disappear with the weak," Kang surmises.

The second section, "As the Wind Becomes a Flower," turns increasingly more metaphysical. He explores vast subjects like "light" and "darkness," mixing in more poetry and metaphors, especially when he writes of the windflowers that he often saw living on the banks of Seoul's Han River: "The coming and going of life is like that of a windflower."

제시하고 있다.

전편에 걸쳐서 내용들이 교훈적인 성향을 보인다. 저자는 사람들이 음주나 흡연을 금할 것을 요구하고 전통적인 가치관과 성의 역할에 대해 언급한다. "가장이 가족의 생계를 위하여 일하는 것은 기본이고 아내가 가사 일을 돌보는 것은 당연하다." 이와 같은 도덕적 기준은 꽃이나 감성을 음미하는 구절들과 대치되기도 한다.

그럼에도 저자는 아름답고 놀랄만한 비유로서 내용들을 묘사하고 있다. 신세대 또는 동양사상에 조예가 깊은 팬들은 저자의 진가를 높이 평가할 것이다.

키르커스 인디 서평(미국 텍사스주 오스틴시 소재 서평전문기관, 서평일자: 2019년 8월)

The book's third section deals with the five mysteries of life: What is God?; where does all existence come from?; what am I?; what is death?; and, lastly, what is love?

The author responds to these questions, as in the other sections, with tales and poetic reflections, but uses them to further delve into religion and history.

Throughout each chapter, Kang's longer pieces tend to be surprisingly proscriptive and filled with heavy and repetitive phrasing. He commands that people should not smoke or drink and often returns to very traditional values and gender roles with statements like "It is fundamental that a husband earns a living, and it is also natural that a wife does housework." This aspect of moral judgment feels at odds with the author's shorter, wispy passages in which he ruminates on flowers or physical sensations. It's in those sparser portions that he delivers some truly beautiful and startling imagery, and it's where fans of New Age and Eastern philosophy will most appreciate his meditations.

Kirkus Indie Review, (Kirkus Media LLC, 2600 Via Fortuna Suite 130 Austin, TX, USA, Reviewed: August 2019)

독자의 소리

세상에는 여러 부류의 사람들이 신을 제각기 달리 인식하고 있다. 그러나 사람들의 인식이 제각기 다를지라도 신은 그대로 존재한다. 우리가 신을 믿을 때 중요한 것은 믿음을 선행으로 보여줘야 한다는 것이다. 신이 우리 믿음 안에 있다는 저자의 생각은 합당하다.

-교사, 리토 갈리나다

신에 대한 개념은 시대에 따라 세계의 여러 민족에 따라 다르다. 예를 들면 이스라엘 민족의 엘로힘, 이슬람국가의 알라, 인도의 수많은 신들이 그것들이다. 삶 속에서 이해할 수 없는 사건들을 규명하기 위해 신의 개념이 종종 도입되는데 선하고 섬세하고 고귀한 신의 개념이 때로는 강한 자에게는 도덕심을 일깨워주고 약한 자에게는 도움을 베풀어주기도 한다. 고대 그리스인과 인도인들은 다신교를 믿었으나 유일신을 믿는 최초의 사람들은 조로아스터교도들이었다. 또한 그리스신화는 현대사회에서 문학작품으로 축소되어 사람들이 제우스 신을 더 이상 신으로 받아들이지 않고 문학작품의 인물로 받아들이고 있다. 자연에 호기심이 많은 사람들은 신비한 현상을 추구하며 이에 열광하는 성향을 지닌다. 저자의 통찰력에 공감한다.

-기자, 마나세 마그 봄비오

Reader's Voice

———————

God is perceived differently by several kinds of people in the world, but I know that even if we perceive God differently, still God is who He is. What is important is when we believe in God, we should manifest our faith as actions for the common good. The author's idea is reasonable for us to believe God is within our faith.

-Lito Galinada, Teacher

The ideology of God may be divided by the times, and a major factor of the variation is very much connected to the many ethnicities around the world, e.g., Elohim for Israel, Allah for Muslim countries, the 10 million gods of India, etc. The idea of divine existence is often taken as human beings' effort to justify unexplainable events or circumstances in their lives. In addition, the idea of a good-hearted, watchful and rewarding God serves as a moral imperative for the strong and able to help the weak. Greece and India are two of the many ancient nations that have a polytheistic faith. The oldest monotheistic faith and the pioneer to monotheism is Zoroastrianism. In addition, Greek myths in modern society have been reduced from a form of faith to literary studies, e.g., Zeus is recognized by Greeks as no longer a god but a literary character. As humans, curious by nature, we have the tendency to sensationalize any or every claim for mystical performance. I like the author's insight.

-Manasseh Mark Bombeo, Journalist

노화 원인에 대한 연구가 깊이 진행되고 있는데 이는 사람들이 인간 수명이 영생에 근접할 수 있다고 믿기 때문이다. 환경의 제약을 극복하고 영생하려는 것은 인간의 한결같은 욕망이다. 선택은 인간 각자에 달려 있다. 우리가 지고함에 이를 때까지 자연도태와 적자생존의 법칙 속에서 투쟁을 계속할 것인지 신을 통해 영생을 얻을 것인지 모든 것은 믿음 안에 달려 있다. 오늘날 수백 수천의 기독교 교파에서 스스로 진정한 종교라고 아직도 논쟁을 계속하고 있지만 그런 문제들이 신의 존재에 영향을 미치지는 않는다. 그것은 그들 간의 오해이거나 잘못된 해석에 기인한 것일 뿐 진정한 신의 모습은 결코 변하지 않는다. 신은 언제나 사랑스럽고 자비로운 것이다. 어느 기독교 소년이 이발소에 갔을 때 이발사가 소년에게 신은 없다고 말하자 소년이 물었다.

"어째서 신이 없다고 하세요?"

그러자 이발사가 말했다. "신이 있다면 죽음도 없고 굶주림도 없고 아무도 고통받지 않고 울지도 않고 나쁜 일도 없지 않겠니."

이발을 마치고 밖으로 나온 소년은 장발을 한 사람들을 보자, 이발사를 불러서 이발사가 없다고 말했다.

그러자 이발사는 놀라며 소년에게 말했다. "조금 전에 네 머리를 깎아줬는데 이발사가 없다니?"

그러자 소년이 웃으며 말했다. "이발사가 있다면 장발머리가 없어야지요?"

이발사가 소년에게 말했다. "그 사람들이 이발하러 나한테 오지 않아서 그런 것이지."

-생물학자, 엘리자 페니톤

Genes that cause aging is now deeply studied because humans believe that there is something from it that can bring human lives on the same level of supreme individuals. It is always a desire of human beings to have immortal lives and be superior over their environment. It rests upon each member of the human race to choose: Either to struggle under the law of natural selection and survival of the fittest until we develop supremacy or to accept and believe that God is able to give eternal life. Everything lies on what is so-called faith. Nowadays, hundreds to thousands of Christian sects debate and claim to be the true religion. These issues, however, will not have an effect on what God is. It is just a misunderstanding or misinterpretation among themselves, but the picture of God will never be changed. God is known to be loving and merciful. When a young Christian boy had his hair cut in a barber shop, the barber told him that God doesn't exist.

"What made you say that He doesn't exist?" the boy asked.

"Simply because if He exists, then there are no deaths, no famines, no one will suffer and cry, and no bad things will happen" replied by the barber.

After having his hair cut, the boy went outside and saw men who had long hairs. And so the boy called the barber and told him that barbers don't exist. The barber was surprised and asked the boy, "What made you say that barbers don't exist when just a while ago I had your hair cut?"

The boy smiled and said, "If barbers exist, then there will be no long hairs." The barber said to the young boy, "That's because they did not come to me and had their hair cut."

-Eliazar Peniton Jr., Biologist

저자의 사고력에는 심오한 깊이가 있다. 철학적이면서 일반인들이 아직 경험하지 못한 신에 대한 새로운 면을 보여주고 있다. 이는 오랜 기간 인간의 내면에 대한 깊은 성찰을 통해 얻어진 결과라고 여겨진다. 신은 매일 일상의 삶 속에서 경험될 수 있는 것이지만 이러한 경험들은 수많은 물질적 제약과 혼란에 의해서 쉽게 가려져 있는 것들이다. 이런 상황에서 일반적인 사고의 한계를 초월하여 인간 상상력의 비밀스러운 영역에 깊숙이 다가선 저자의 성찰이 정말 놀랍다. 그러나 저자의 통찰력의 많은 부분들이 독실한 기독교인들이나 이슬람교인들에게는 아마도 쉽게 받아들여지지 않거나 이설이라고 간주될 수도 있다. 저자의 신에 대한 개념과 세계적인 기성 종교 간에는 분명한 대조를 이룬다. 기독교나 이슬람교의 가르침은 일상적인 의식을 통해 궁극적인 구원의 은총과 신에 대한 숭배를 신봉하는 것이지만 저자는 믿음에 의해 개체가 전체와 하나 되는 것이라고 한다. 저자의 생각처럼 믿음을 통하여 궁극에 이를 수 있다는 것은 그 또한 은총이 아닐까? 그러한 믿음이 신의 계시나 신과 소통하려는 순수한 노력의 산물과 같은 것은 아닐는지…. 이러한 믿음은 본질적으로 인간의 노력의 산물이라고 여겨진다. 그럼에도 저자는 많은 사람들에게, 특히 물질적인 세계에서 많은 유혹과 인간의 죄악 때문에 구원이 쉽게 이뤄질 수 없이 멀게만 느껴지는 사람들에게 신선한 희망을 안겨준다.

-변호사, 프로렌시오 나리도

첫째, 저자는 신을 이해함과 동시에 인간을 이해하고 있다. 신관에 대한 기초를 다른 어디에 두지 아니하고 인간이라는 우리가 공존하고 있는 가장 소중한 존재에 두고 있다는 점이다. 둘째, 완전한 하나 됨의 깊은 이해가 놀랍게 다가온다. 저자의 글 속에는 하나 됨의 갈망이 마치 하나님의 갈망을 보는 것 같다. 인간과 인간이, 인간과 신이, 신

The thoughts of the author are deep yet revealing. They are very philosophical and present a new aspect of God, yet they appeals to the ordinary experiences of ordinary mortals. His penetrating reach into God's nature must be a product of long meditation and sustained inward travel to the inner sanctum of the human mind. While God can be experienced in our everyday and ordinary lives, this experience can easily be clouded by the tremendous pull of material limitations and distractions. For this reason, I am truly astounded by the depth with which the author journeyed into the secret realm of human imagination, transcending the boundary of ordinary senses. However, to devout Christians and Muslims alike, many of his insights might not easily be accepted or even be dismissed as heresy. There is a clear contrast between and among the great religions of the world and the author's concept of the Eternal. While Christian and Muslim's teachings espouse the element of grace to achieve ultimate salvation or the worship of God according to certain daily rituals, one of the author's idea is that individuals unite with the whole through their faith. In this case, could there be an element of grace also, as the author thought that the way to eternity could be through faith? Is this faith the same as a kind of direct revelation from God or a product of pure human effort to commune with God? I surmise that this faith is primarily a product of human effort. Regardless, the author presents a very refreshing hope to many, especially to those who believe that salvation is far and unreachable due to the many temptations in this material world and man's propensity to sin.

-Florencio A. Narido Jr., Attorney

First, the author comprehends God as well as humans. He lays the concept of God on humans as a precious thing. Second, the author's profound comprehension for the perfect unification

념과 신념이 하나 된다면 그곳이 바로 천국일 것이다. 셋째, 신에 대한 이해가 형이하학을 기초로 하여 형이상학의 단계로 나아가는 깨달음이다. 저자는 주변에 일어나는 소리와 현상들을 쉽게 지나치지 않는 안목을 소유하고 있다. 인간이 지닌 믿음의 요소가 삶에 어떠한 영향력을 주고 있는지를 보고 있다. 넷째, 신과 함께하는 궁극적인 축복인 쉼과 평화를 강조하고 있다는 점이다. 마치 아이가 어머니의 품에 안겨 있을 때 그 안에 머무는 평화와 같은 것이라 생각된다. 이러한 축복을 저자는 우리 앞에 제시하고 있다. 다섯째, 인간의 한계를 넘어서는 힘을 보고 있다. 그 변화의 힘은 바로 사랑과 믿음임을 밝혀 주고 있다. 인간의 영원성은 사랑과 믿음에 있는 것이다. 믿음의 선물은 인간의 힘으로 소유되는 개념이 아니다. 믿음은 내가 무엇인가를 믿어야지, 라는 의지의 산물이 아니다. 믿음의 대상을 바라보고 이해하고 느끼고 경험함으로써 믿음이 깊어지는 것이다. 우리는 이 땅에서 선과 악을 직면하면서 살아간다. 또한 우리는 선과 악을 선택하면서 살아간다. 참된 선을 분별할 수 있는 안목이 필요한 것이다. 이것이 영적 성장이고 깨달음의 확장이다.

-목사, 안인식

이 글 속에 담긴 깊이 있고 지혜로운 내용들을 즐겁게 읽었다. 인생관과 문화가 다른 외국인으로서 나에게는 이해하기 어려운 부분도 있었다. 그럼에도 불구하고 잘 정제되고 고무적인 내용들을 이 글 속에서 발견하고 이를 간직하게 되었다. 사는 방법에 대한 주제는 내 자신의 삶에 가장 공감이 가는 부분이다. 내게 신선하게 다가온 이 주제는 나의 삶에 있어서 최고의 성취감을 향한 만족과 평화를 가져다주었다. 우리나라(미국)에서는 대부분의 사람들이 만족할 줄 모르는 까닭에 이 주제야말로 내 가슴에 깊이 다가온다. 이 글에 담겨진 철학은 정말

is marvelous. As mentioned in this book, to unite into one seems to be an aspiration for God. If human to human, human to God and faith to faith unite into one, it will be just heaven. Third, the comprehension of God is an awakening of the self, forward to the state of metaphysics from physical science. The author has discerning eyes, not allowing to pass by the sound and phenomenon arising in his surroundings, and he observes how human faith affects every aspect of life. Fourth, the author emphasizes rest and peace as the ultimate blessing together with God. It might be peace like how an infant nestles in his or her mother's breast. The author shows such peace to us. Fifth, the author observes power exceeding the bounds of humanity. He shows that the power of change is just love and faith. The eternity of humans is based on love and faith. The gift of faith cannot be possessed by human power. Faith is not to be obtained by human will but to be deepened by understanding, feeling and experiencing the subject of faith. We live confronting good and evil on earth, and we live choosing good from evil. Therefore we need discerning eyes to distinguish true good from evil. That is spiritual growth and the enlargement of awakening.

-An In-sik, Pastor

I enjoyed reading these very much as they were full of insightful thoughts and wisdom. However, I am a foreigner with admittedly much less understanding of cultures and live views of people in this country. Nevertheless I did retain some and found the writings to be both thought-provoking and well-spoken. How to live—this theme was the one that I found most relatable to my own life. The underlying theme that stood out to me was how to approach life with contentment and peace, in order to get the most fulfillments. In my own country (USA), most people are not content, and so this

유익하다고 확신한다. 이 글이 내게 특별하게 의미하는 바는 그것을 어떻게 묘사하였는가 하는 점이다. 은유적 표현이 매우 분명하여 모든 사람들이 쉽게 공감할 것으로 느껴졌다. 나는 무엇인가? 라는 주제는 나에게 시처럼 다가왔다. 아마도 철학적인 깊은 뜻을 이해하기에 내가 역부족인 듯하다. 그 내용은 삶에 있어서 공동체의 중요성과 외롭지 않은 존재를 의미하는 것이라 여겨진다. 사랑이란 무엇인가? 라는 주제는 나에게 매우 시적인 것이었다. 사랑하는 사람을 위한 희생이 잘 묘사되었고 수컷 사마귀와 암컷 사마귀의 은유적 표현이 매우 마음에 와닿는다. 사랑을 이해하려는 소망은 기독교도인 내 믿음 속에 항상 던져진 물음인데, 이 글 중에서 해답을 탐구하는 데 여러 명안들이 있음을 확신한다. 내가 궁극적으로 이해하기로는 사랑에 대한 가장 위대한 표현은 자기 자신보다 누군가를 위해서 살거나 죽어야 한다는 것이다.

-교도관, 조슈아

신성한 존재인 신을 믿지 않는 사람들에게 신이란 용어 자체가 단지 일상 대화에서 위엄을 무시하고 사용되는 속어에 불과할 것이다. 언어의 유희 외에 다른 의미가 없는 것이다. 그들은 삶에 의미를 부여하기 위하여 보고 만지고 느낄 수 있는 것을 바라는 것이다. 신이라는 용어가 그들의 욕망을 충족시키려고 주어진 것에 불과하다. 그러나 기독교인들에게 신이란 우리들의 삶에 다가와 우리들의 자유와 함께하기를 원하는 영원한 생명의 존재다. 우리가 모두 다르기는 하지만 이 책을 읽으면서 편한 마음이 드는 것은 우리가 저자와 같은 뜻이라면 견해 차이가 없을 것이기 때문이다. 신에 대한 우리의 믿음은 우리의 삶에 신을 받아들임으로써 강화된다. 신의 길이 우리보다 낫다는 것을 받아들임으로써 우리가 미래를 어찌할지 보장할 수 없는 상황으로부터

rings true to me. I believe this philosophy is most beneficial. I also believe that this particular writing spoke to me because of how it was portrayed. The metaphors were very clear and I felt that most people could easily relate to them. What am I? This theme stood out to me much like poetry. I think maybe I am not smart enough for such deep philosophical questions. I believe that part of it was speaking on the importance of community to one's life and not being a solitary figure. What is love? This theme seemed to me very much like poetry as well. The underlying theme of sacrificing oneself for those you love was well-portrayed, and I liked the metaphor of the male and female mantises. As a Christian, the desire to understand love is a common question in my own faith, and I believe there were many good thoughts in this paragraph attempting to explore the answer. The meaning I think I did understand was ultimately that it is better to live (or die) for another than for oneself as this is the greatest expression of love.

-Joshua Doak, Correctional Officer

For people who don't believe in a divine presence, God is just a three-letter word, a word that is spoken as derogatory slang, in fits of rage or casual conversation. There is no meaning other than to fill up a sentence. In their search for meaning in their lives, they look to what they can visualize, touch, and feel. The word "God" is given to the satisfaction of their desires. But for a Christian, God is the ever-living Presence who desires so much to be a part of our freedom in Him that He became Life to us. I understand we all have our differences. But while learning about this book, I feel so lighthearted because if we are just of the same mind as this book's author, we have no disagreement. Our faith in God intensifies when we invite Him into our lives. In accepting that God's ways are far better than our own, we can release that we cannot

자유로워질 수 있는 것이다. 모든 사람들 특히 신세대를 북돋아 줄 이 훌륭한 책이 출간되는 것에 박수를 보낸다. 신이란 무엇인가 하는 저자의 생각에 대하여 동료들과 의견을 나눠보았는데 모두 이 책의 내용에 기쁨을 느꼈다. 이 책은 신의 진정한 의미를 일깨우는 좋은 기념작이 될 것이다. 심혈을 기울여 갈고 닦은 저자의 선물을 함께 나눠준 것에 대하여 감사를 표한다. 이 책이 곧 베스트셀러에 오를 것이라 확신한다.

-경제학자, 존 안토니 엔더슨

manipulate or guarantee our future. I applaud the publication of this wonderful book, which is about rearing all people, specially the new generation. I have shared some of the author's ideas about God with my co-workers, and we have all found delight in them. It's a good reminder to look on the real meaning of God. Thanks to the author for sharing with us the gift that he had worked so hard to refine. I trust this book will soon be on the best sellers list.

-John Anthony Anderson, Economist

바람 불어와

남태평양과 맞닿은 필리핀군도 남쪽 끝자락 오지, 열대 꽃들이 계절도 없이 피고 지는 이곳 아모로스에는 이미 바람과 꽃들이 친구가 된 지 오래다. 그렇게 하루를 보내다 보면 남태평양에 지는 석양은 정말 아름다워 코코넛 나무들 사이로 떨어지는 낙조는 황홀하기 그지없다. 어릴 적 필리핀 우표에서 보았던 바로 그 광경이다. 경이로운 자연 속에서 미지의 설렘이 바람처럼 다가와 가슴속 심연 깊이 흩날릴 때마다 떨어지는 꽃잎을 하나둘 모은 것이 제1편 「아모로스 단상」이다. 제1편에 있는 내용들은 삶을 향해 나아가는 사람들, 특히 신세대들이 삶의 방향을 선택하는 데 길잡이가 될 것이다.

그리고 서울 한강변에서 피어난 바람꽃 중에서 세월이 흘렀음에도 아

Once the Wind Rises

It's been a long time ago since the wind and flowers became friends in Amoros, the southern part of the Philippines close to the South Pacific, where tropical flowers bloom and fall continuously regardless of seasons. While one day passes like that, the glow of the sun setting between coconut trees is really fascinating due to the extremely beautiful sunset of the South Pacific. It's just a scenery I saw on a Philippines postage stamp when I was young.

In chapter 1, "Amoros Thought," I collected petals falling whenever a thrill of joy for unknown things flutter into the abyss of my mind, coming like the wind in nature's wonder. The contents in chapter 1 will serve as a useful guide for people, specially the new generation to choose his way among the various directions in life. In chapter 2, "As the Wind Becomes a Flower," I just edited

직도 가슴을 울리는 내용들을 정리하여 새롭게 편집한 것이 제2편 「바람은 꽃이 되어」다. 제2편에 있는 내용들은 삶의 정상에 다다른 사람들에게 주변을 돌아보게 하는 여유로움과 새로운 안목을 안겨줄 것이다. 과정에서 누구나 알고 싶어도 아무도 말하지 않는 삶에 대한 의문을 가까이 다가가서 바라본 것이 제3편 「삶의 5대 불가사의」다. 제3편에 있는 내용들은 삶의 고개를 넘어서는 사람들에게 공통적으로 느끼게 되는 불가사의한 의문에 대한 오해와 편견에서 벗어나 새로운 희망을 찾는 데 도움을 줄 것이다. 이 책은 소설책이 아니다. 우리 삶 속에 반향되고 있는 사실들에 관한 것이다. 그러나 단번에 읽으려고 하면 다양한 주제들로 엮여 있어서 뜻을 놓치기 쉽다. 이 책은 12주제로 구성되어 있으니 순서에 상관없이 원하는 주제를 선택해서 가족, 친구들과 함께 한 번에 1주제씩만 읽도록 추천한다. 바람은 어디에도 막힘 없는 자유로움을 의미하고 꽃은 삶의 완성을 의미하기에 이 모든 바람이 향기로운 꽃이 되어 독자들의 가슴에 신선함과 즐거움을 안겨주기 바란다.

이 책은 2019년 『As the Wind Becomes a Flower』라는 제목으로 미국에서 첫 출간된 후 2021년 국영문 대역본으로 편집되어 『삶의 5대 불가사의』라는 제목으로 출간되었고 이후 내용을 보완하여 증보판을 출간하게 되었다.

2024년 11월 1일 양평 남한강변에서
강재원

the contents, still touching my heart even when a long time had passed since a windflower bloomed where I lived on the banks of Han River in Seoul. The contents in chapter 2 will give people who have reached the top of life, relaxation and a new perspective to look back. During this time, in chapter 3, "The Five Mysteries of Life," I observed myself moving close to questions about life that nobody has answers to, even when everybody wants to know. The contents in chapter 3 will help people look for a new hope by getting out of misunderstanding and prejudice about mysterious questions common to all while going over the top of life.

This book is not fiction but about fact resounding in life. However, if you try to read this book in one sitting, you are apt to lose its meaning due to various topics. As this book consist of twelve topics, I recommend you read one topic per session, together with your family or friends. Choose your favorite topic regardless of the order of contents. As the wind means freedom flowing without barrier, and a flower means completion of life, I hope that the wind becomes a fragrant flower, so it is new and pleasant to all readers.

This book was edited in Korean-English version with the title " The Five Mysteries of Life" in 2021 after the first edition titled "As the Wind Becomes a Flower" was published in the United States in 2019. Then it has been revised and supplemented.

From Yangpyeong, Korea in November 2024

차례

Content

Chapter 1

Amoros Thought

Chapter 2

As the Wind Becomes a Flower

제3편
삶의 5대 불가사의

Chapter 3

The Five Mysteries of Life

제1편
아모로스 단상

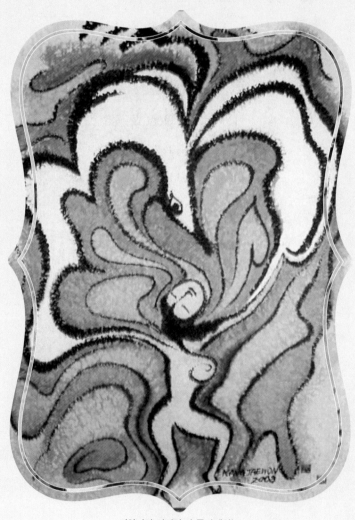

〈하나가 되리라, 수묵담채화〉

Chapter 1

Amoros Thought

1. 사는 방법

1. 땀은 일상 속에 숨겨진 행복을 일깨우는 명약이다. 진정 행복하려거든 적절한 일을 찾아서 땀을 흘려라.

2. 80%에 만족하며 인생을 즐겁게 살아라. 100% 이루려 용쓰다가 인생 거덜 난다. 80%나 100%나 1000%에 비하면 그게 그거 아닌가. 거지도 더 가난한 거지에게 나눠줄 게 있고 부자도 더 많은 부를 못 가져 안달하는 것이 세상이다. 80%에 만족하면 그것이 곧 100% 인생이다.

3. 용의 꼬리보다 뱀의 대가리를 선호하는 자는 대가리 노릇을 즐길 수는 있지만 뱀의 치졸함을 함께 감수해야 하고, 용의 꼬리를 선호하는 자는 신선놀음을 즐길 수는 있지만 언젠가 용 대가리에 물릴 것을 감수해야 한다. 그래서 용의 꼬리나 뱀의 대가리나 처지가 황망하긴 마찬가지다. 그런데 용의 대가리는 누구에게나 선망의 대상이긴 하지만 희소성만큼이나 시운을 타고나야 한다. 그런 만큼 용 대가리에 달린 뿔은 위험천만이어서 그 뿔 때문에 용 대가리도 결국 사고를 당한다. 수많은 뱀 꼬리가 뜬구름 같아서 용 대가리가 겁 없이 그 속을 헤집고 다니다가 엉켜 붙어 옴짝달싹 못 하게 되는데 결국 하잘것없는 뱀 꼬리 무리에게 용 대가리가 잡히는 것이다. 그 멋진 뿔 때문에.

1. How to Live

1. Sweat is good medicine to awaken happiness hidden in life. Try to sweat with a suitable activity if you really want to be happy.

2. Live pleasantly satisfied with 80 percent. Life will collapse if fretted to get 100 percent. Compared with 1,000 percent, 80 percent is almost the same as 100 percent. In this world, the poor can share something to those poorer, while the rich frets to get some more. If satisfied with 80 percent, it is just a life of 100 percent.

3. Those who prefer the head of a snake to the tail of a dragon must endure crudity even if they enjoy the role of leader, while those who prefer the tail of a dragon must bear suffering, bitten by the head of a dragon someday even if they enjoy elegant style in the heavens, so both of them, the tail of a dragon as well as the head of a snake, are in the same situation as a flurry. On the other hand, everybody envies the head of a dragon, but the tide should be turned to become the head of a dragon due to its scarcity. To that extent, the horns on the head of a dragon are so dangerous that the head of a dragon is in an accident due to its horns. While the head of a dragon flies recklessly into a bundle of snake tails like clouds, at last it is caught in a trap of so many snake tails thanks to its honorable horns.

4. 기대치를 낮춰서 살아라. 처음 만난 사이에는 100%를 기대하기도 하지만 살아가면서 그때마다 100%를 기대했다간 언제나 실망이다. 50%만 되어도 그러려니 생각하고 부족한 이웃을 이해하며 살아라. 네가 느끼는 이웃의 모습은 네 자신의 모습이기도 하다. 대다수 사람들의 평균 모습이 50% 정도이니 네가 만난 사람이 60% 정도라면 괜찮은 이웃이다.

5. 상대를 공격하거나 지배하려는 것은 공격을 당하거나 지배를 당하지 않기 위한 선제조치인데 이는 학교폭력에서 국가 간 전쟁에 이르기까지 폭넓게 적용되는 심리현상이다. 그러나 다툼이란 비슷한 세력 간에 이뤄지는 것이므로 진정한 강자는 상대를 두려워하지 않고 공존을 즐긴다. 공격하려는 것은 손실보다 득이 더 많기 때문인데 손실이 더 크다면 아무도 공격하려 하지 않는다. 100이 10을 공격하는 것은 10보다 적은 손실로 10을 얻으려는 것이지 10보다 많은 손실을 보며 10을 얻으려는 것이 아니다. 사자와 몽구스가 마주쳤는데 몽구스의 덩치가 사자의 발바닥에 덮힐 정도로 작다 그래도 몽구스는 굴하지 않고 죽을 각오로 으르렁거리자 사자는 어처구니가 없었던지 아니면 먹을 살점에 비해서 발바닥에 상처라도 날까 염려되었던지 몽구스를 비껴가버렸다. 만약 몽구스가 도망치려 했다면 단숨에 잡아먹혔을 것이다. 이쯤 되면 덩치만 크다고 강한 것이 아니다. 작아도 강한 것이다.

6. 아침에 떠오르는 해는 언제나 새로운 시작이다. 그러니 가슴에 해를 품고 있는 한 희망은 언제나 살아있다.

4. Live while lowering your expectations. You can expect 100 percent at first, but you will be disappointed if you expect 100 percent every moment. Live with understanding for your imperfect neighbors even if their level is only 50 percent. The features of neighbors that you feel are also your features. Considering that the average level of most people is 50 percent, whom you meet is not bad if his level is about 60 percent

5. To attack or to dominate is a leadoff offensive. Not to be attacked or not to be dominated by an opponent, that is a psychological phenomenon applied widely to school violence as well as war between nations. But the strong is really not afraid of their opponent, and they enjoy coexistence because struggles rise only when they are almost equal in power. They are tempted to attack because gains are bigger than losses. If losses are bigger than gains, nobody wants to attack. The reason why the 100 tries to attack the 10 is to get 10 at a loss of less than 10, not to get 10 at a loss of more than 10. A lion and a mongoose confronts each other, and the mongoose's body is as small as the lion's feet. But once the mongoose dares to fight and growls at the lion, the lion passes by the mongoose as if he is stunned or worried about a wound in his feet compared with the flesh of his prey. If the mongoose tries to run away, it will be captured at once. Like this, a small one, not only a big one, can also be strong.

6. As the sun rises in the morning, always making a start, so there is hope as long as you hold the sun in your heart.

7. 미혹하지 마라. 실망만 클 뿐이다. 삶은 순리적인 것이니 오직 땀 흘린 것만이 진실되다.

8. 아버지는 아이들에게 살아가는 법을 가르쳐 주고 어머니는 삶 속에 담긴 사랑을 가르쳐 준다. 그래서 아이들에겐 아버지 어머니가 모두 필요하다.

9. 노인이 될수록 이미 경험한 것들이 많고 변화에 익숙해져서 시간이 빠르게 흐르고 일 년이 금방 지나간다. 반면에 어린아이에게는 새로 경험하는 것들이 많아서 유년기의 일 년이 매우 길게 느껴진다. 나이가 들어도 어린아이처럼 새로 경험하는 것들이 많게 산다면 시간의 흐름을 늦출 수 있다. 시간은 경험하는 자에 따라 다르게 흐르므로 나이는 노인이라 하여도 생활은 청춘일 수 있다.

10. 네가 서 있는 이곳이 세계의 중심이고 우주의 중심이다. 지난 세월 정처 없이 떠돌았고 지금도 떠돌지만 그것은 망상일 뿐 바로 이곳이 너의 중심이다. 한평생 찾으려고 헤매지만 이제는 가까이 들려오는 새소리 한 호흡 숨소리를 깨우칠 때다. 더 이상 찾으려고 헤매지 마라. 지금 이곳이 바로 네가 꿈꾸던 천국이요 목적지다.

7. Don't be deluded, or you will have only great disappointments. As life is run in a rational manner, it is true to earn with sweat.

8. A father teaches his children the rules on how to live, and a mother teaches her children love in life. Therefore, both parents are indispensable to children.

9. The older a man is, the faster time flies because he has already many experiences and is familiar with variations, so one year passes by fast. On the other hand, one year passes by slowly in childhood because there are so many new things that children experience. If you live with so many new experiences like children, you can make time fly slowly. Your life can be juvenile even if you are old because time flies differently depending on the extent of your new experiences.

10. This place where you stand is the center of the world and the center of the universe. It is only an illusion to wander aimlessly in the present as well as in the past, so this place is just your center. You wandered to seek during your life, but now you have to realize the sound of birds and a breath nearby. Don't try to seek any more. This place at present is just heaven and the destination that you have been dreaming of.

11. 한 개인의 야망이 전체를 위한 것이면 이루어질 것이고 개인에 머문 것이면 망할 것이다.

12. 사람들의 마음이란 환경 따라 변하는 것으로 환경이 열악해지면 배신하기 쉬워진다. 그러므로 항상 주변 환경을 잘 다스려야 한다.

13. 행복이란 구속에서 벗어난 해방감에서 느낄 수도 있고, 원하는 바가 이뤄진 성취감에서 느낄 수도 있고, 자기완성에 도달한 일체감에서 느낄 수도 있다. 행복에는 절대적인 기준이 없다. 행복의 기준은 개인마다 다르고 개인마다의 행복도 주변의 변화에 따라 시시각각 변한다. 행복은 소리 없이 왔다가 소리 없이 가버리고 그때는 몰랐지만 세월이 지난 후에야 느끼기도 하는 것이 행복이다. 행복이 무엇이냐고 묻는다면 사람마다 여러 가지로 대답할 것이다. 한 끼 식사로 배고픔을 달랬을 때, 남녀 간에 사랑을 느낄 때, 사업에 성공했을 때, 시험에 합격했을 때, 한 송이 꽃을 바라볼 때, 고요하게 기도할 때, 편안하게 휴식할 때 등등 일상 속의 해방감과 성취감과 일체감에 따라서 각각 느끼는 행복이 다르다. 똑같은 삶을 살아가면서도 살아가는 마음밭이 어디 있느냐에 따라서 행복할 수도 불행할 수도 있다. 행복을 느끼는 요인은 자연적인 것일 수도 있고 사회적인 것일 수도 있다. 자연적인 행복감은 계절의 변화나 생체리듬에 따라서 느끼는 본래의 감정이지만 사회적인 행복감은 주변과의 관계에서 느끼게 되는 상대적인 감정이다. 사람들이 불행하다고 느끼는 대부분의 것들은 상대적인 감정에 휘둘린 것으로 이는 매우 불안정한 감정이다. 상대적인 감정에 휘둘리지 않고 본래의 감정에 자족하는 것이 행복에 이르는 길이다.

11. An individual ambition will be realized if it is for the whole, but it will collapse if it is only for an individual.

12. As the human mind is changeable according to circumstances, man is apt to betray confidence in poor circumstances. Therefore, you have to manage circumstances well all the time.

13. We can feel happiness either with freedom from restraint, with achievement from getting a goal, or with perfection of the self. Standards of happiness differ according to each personality, and personal happiness is also changeable every moment according to variations in circumstances. Sometimes happiness comes and goes silently, so we cannot feel it at a certain time, then feel it later after the moment passed. If asked when you feel happiness, you can give so many answers—that is, when you solve starving with food, fall in love, succeed in business, pass an examination, look at a flower, pray in calmness, relax peacefully, etc. Like this, our feelings of happiness differ according to freedom, achievement, and entireness. We can be either happy or unhappy according to our minds even if we live the same lives. The cause of happiness depends on natural things as well as social things. Natural happiness is an original feeling according to the variation of seasons and biological rhythm, but social happiness is a feeling relative to circumstances. Most things that people feel unhappy about are unstable things caused by related feelings. It is a way of reaching happiness, not to be involved in a related feeling but to be satisfied with an original feeling.

14. 바퀴가 지면에 붙어 있지도 그렇다고 떨어지지도 않고 굴러가듯이 인생이 살아가는 것도 부즉불이(不卽不離) 그대로다.

15. 나를 하나의 개체로만 생각하고 살다가 죽으면 천지간에 이보다 허망한 존재가 없을 것이다. 그러나 조상의 생명을 이어받아서 얼마간 나로서 살아가다가 후손에게로 다시 이어지는 생명이라 생각하면 결코 외롭지 않다. 또한 이웃에게 선행을 베풀거나 예술작품이나 가르침을 남겨서 후세에 기쁨을 준다면 자손이 없다 하여도 결코 외롭지 않은 것이다.

16. 밥 지을 때 솥이 끓어 물기가 잦아들 때까지 진불로 가열하고 그 후에는 불기운을 낮추어 뜸을 들인다. 처음 진불로 가열하는 시간이 짧으면 불기운이 밥솥 상부에까지 미치지 않아 밥 짓는 시간이 길어질 뿐만 아니라, 밥이 설익거나 뜸이 들지 않는다. 반대로 진불로 가열하는 시간이 길어지면 밥이 골고루 익기도 전에 아래 부위가 타버려서 검은 누룽지가 생기고 쓴맛이 나기 일쑤다. 인생도 밥 짓기와 같다. 과욕에 앞서 지나치게 진불로 인생을 빨리 달구려고 하면 구수한 숭늉이 되기도 전에 새까맣게 타버려서 그 인생은 요절하고 만다. 그렇다고 가슴에 혼불을 지피는 정열도 없이 약한 불기운만으로 평생을 보낸다면 그 인생은 설익은 밥처럼 인생의 진수를 맛볼 수도 없이 지루한 시간 속에서 속절없이 인생을 소진해버리고 말 것이다. 인생이 제대로 성숙하기 위해서는 혼불처럼 타오르는 정열이 필요하고 은은한 불씨로 뜸을 들일 줄 아는 인내심도 필요하다. 삶은 타오르는 혼불과 지극한 정성이 조화될 때에 비로소 향기를 발산한다.

14. As the wheel of fortune rolls while being neither attached nor detached on earth, our life is like that.

15. There is really nothing vainer in the world than if I die after living only as an individual, but I will never feel lonely if I think that my life is transferred to a descendant after living as myself for a while, since succeeding an ancestor's life. Also I will never feel lonely if I favor the coming generations with good deeds, works of art, or teachings even if I have no descendants.

16. When cooking rice, at first strong heat is applied to the rice until the hot water inside the pot boils. After, the steamed rice settles by low heat. If cooking time by strong heat is short, either it will take a long time to cook or it will not steam well because there is not enough heat to be applied to the top of the pot. Inversely, if the cooking time by strong heat is too long, the bottom of the pot will be burned before the steaming rice settles. Life is the same as cooking rice. Life will collapse with greed if you cook fast only with strong heat. Even so, if you live without passion for life, time becomes boring and life will end vainly. You need not only passion of the soul but also patience—steaming with low heat in order to mature properly in life. Life is fragrant for the first time when the passion of the soul is harmonized with wholeheartedness.

17. 준비된 자만이 기회가 왔을 때 목적을 이룰 수 있다.

18. 미래를 너무 생각하다 보면 지금을 놓치기 쉽다. 지금이 없는 미래는 없으니 지금에 충실하다 보면 어느새 미래에 와 있음을 알게 된다.

19. 지도자는 소유자가 아닌 관리자여야 한다. 진정한 내 것이란 아무것도 없다. 내게 주어진 육체, 재산을 잠시 동안 관리하다가 빈손으로 놓고 가는 것이 인생이다. 지도자는 조직의 이익을 부하에게 공정하게 나눠주어야 한다. 이익을 나눠주지 않는 지도자에게 부하는 절대 충성하지 않는다. 지도자는 목표가 있어야 한다. 지속가능하고 더불어 행복할 수 있는 비전을 보여줘야 한다. 5년 앞도 모르고 유행에 편승하는 지도자는 조직을 바르게 이끌어 나갈 수 없다. 지도자는 감정을 절제할 줄 알아야 한다. 기쁜 일과 슬픈 일이 반복될 때마다 감정에 휘둘린다면 전체 조직을 관리할 수 없다. 지도자는 열정을 갖고 무슨 일에나 100% 심혈을 기울여야 한다. 그러나 결과에 대해서는 80% 이상 기대하지 마라. 20%를 비울 수 있는 넉넉한 마음이 조직을 안정되게 한다. 무엇보다도 진정한 지도자는 개인의 안위보다 전체를 먼저 생각해야 한다.

17. Only the person who is ready can achieve his/her goal when a chance comes.

18. You are apt to lose the present if you think of the future too much. There is no future without the present. If you are faithful to the present, you will find yourself in the future while you are not aware.

19. A leader should be a manager rather than an owner. There is really nothing called mine. It is life to leave the world without taking anything after managing one's given body and property for a while. A leader should share profits fairly to his staff. Staff members will never be loyal to their boss who does not share profits. A leader should set a goal and show a sustainable vision for their team to be happy together. A leader who does not forecast the future even after five years but follows only the fashion cannot lead an organization successfully. A leader should know how to suppress his emotions. A leader cannot manage an organization well if he betrays his feelings, whenever joy and sorrow alternates. A leader should have passion and put 100 percent of his heart and soul into everything, but he should not expect more than 80 percent as a result. A generous mind capable of leaving a 20-percent margin keeps an organization stable. First of all, a real leader should care about the whole rather than an individual.

20. 대부분의 사람들이 어려운 환경 속에서 살아가고 있다. 그래서 매사에 100% 힘을 소진하다 보니 여유가 없다. 그래도 내부적으로 20% 여유는 갖고 살아야 한다. 그렇지 않으면 위급상황에 20%가 없어서 갖고 있던 80%마저 잃게 된다.

21. 삶의 지혜를 말할 때 지나치게 은유적인 표현을 하거나 뜬구름 같은 소리를 하면 지혜를 가르치는 것이 아니라, 오히려 오해와 몽상만 가르치게 된다. 그렇다고 세세히 문자에만 얽매이면 숲을 잃고 나무만 보게 되어 이 또한 지혜를 가르치는 것이 아니라 프로그램대로 움직이는 로봇 같은 맹신도만 키우게 된다. 그러므로 지혜를 말할 때는 명쾌하게 표현하되 문자에 얽매이지 않아야 한다.

22. 아들이 아버지를 닮은 것을 보고 좋아하는 것은 같은 모습의 생명이 대를 이어 지속되기를 바라는 부활을 향한 마음 때문이다. 그러나 3대를 지나다 보면 같은 모습은 점차 다른 모습으로 바뀌게 된다. 그러므로 외모가 닮은 것도 중요하지만 심성이나 정신과 같은 내면을 닮아서 대를 이어가는 것이 외모를 닮는 것보다 더 지속가능하고 뜻깊은 일이다. 그러려면 한평생을 사는 동안 적어도 한 가지 이상 지혜를 깨우쳐서 후손에게 물려줄 수 있어야 하는데 사람들은 재산을 축적해서 물려주고 물려받는 것에는 신경을 쓰면서도 정작 삶의 지혜를 물려주고 물려받는 데는 소홀하다.

20. Most people are living in harsh circumstances, so we have no allowance because we exhaust 100 percent of our energy in everything. Even so, we have to live with a 20-percent margin. If not, we lose even the existing 80 percent without the 20-percent margin for emergencies.

21. If you express too much metaphorically or unclearly, like a cloud drifting, when teaching wisdoms of life, it is not teaching wisdom but teaching a misunderstanding or a reverie. Even so, if you adhere to the letter excessively, it is not teaching wisdom but bringing up a blind believer, like a robot moving according to programming, because he cannot see the forest for the trees. Therefore, you have to express clearly and not to adhere to the letter when teaching wisdoms.

22. It is due to a mind for resurrection, looking for a life with the same features, sustainable from generation to generation, to prefer a son taking after his father, but the same feature is changed differently step by step while passing through the third generation. Therefore, it is more sustainable and meaningful to connect generations by taking after the interior, like the mind or spirit, even if the feature is important. In order to do so, people have to transfer their wisdom to their descendants after realizing them for life, but most of them are careless about wisdom. They care about properties, to be transferred after accumulating them.

23. 한 아이는 신발을 신고 그 뒤를 쫓는 아이는 신발을 벗은 채 거실을 지나 마당으로 쳇바퀴를 돌고 있다. 마당에 나서면 신발을 신고 거실에 올라서면 신발을 벗는 일반상식과 달리 새로운 행동방식이다.

24. 노동 후에 고단하면 기억이 희미해져서 아침에 했던 일이 오래전에 한 것처럼 착각을 일으킨다. 불과 몇 시간 전 일이 며칠 전 일처럼 느껴지는 것은 시간에 대한 기억이 빠르게 흐른 탓이다. 하루 24시간이라는 보편적인 시간 개념이 느끼는 사람에 따라 제각각 다르다. 인간의 기억 속에서 흐르는 감각적인 시간은 시계가 가리키는 기계적인 시간과 다르다.

25. 기업이든 종교단체이든 국가이든 기득권층이 집단을 이루는 데는 에너지가 필요하고 그 에너지는 외부로부터 세금이나 십일조나 기업이윤 형태로 끌어온다. 결국 집단을 이루지 못하고 먹이사슬의 최하위에서 살아가는 영세업자, 일용직 근로자는 가난할 수밖에 없다. 최하위 소외계층이 기대할 수 있는 것은 부자들이 헌납하는 기부금이나 종교단체의 자선사업이나 국가의 사회복지기금이지만 이것이 여의치 못할 경우 범죄를 통해 생존에 필요한 물자를 구하려 한다. 따라서 기득권층은 이들이 생산 활동에 종사할 수 있도록 배려하고 최소한의 식량과 생필품을 구하는 데 어려움이 없도록 해야 한다. 입술이 없으면 잇몸이 시린 법이다.

23. One child is turning 'round while putting on his shoes, and another child is following while taking off his shoes, from the living room to the garden. That is really a new behavioral pattern, different from common sense, to take off in the living room and to put on in the garden.

24. Sometimes a memory grows dim because of tiredness after working, so we tend to be under the illusion that work done in the morning happened a long time ago. The reason why we are under this illusion is that our memory of time flies fast. The common concept of time as twenty-four hours a day differs depending on each person's feelings. Sensible time flying in human memory is different from the mechanical time shown on the clock.

25. Vested class such as a large business, a religious body, or a government needs energy to form a group, and they get energy by means of profits, tithes, or tax from the outside. So small-scale businessmen or day workers living in the lowest level of the food chain cannot help themselves without forming a group. It is social welfare fund, charitable work, or donation from the rich that they can expect, but if it is not enough, they try to survive with criminal acts. Therefore, vested class has to help them find a job as well as get food and other necessities in life. No sharing, no well-being.

26. 눈빛 선량한 말을 밤이면 뜰에 매어 놓는데 간밤에 괴한의 습격으로 칼에 베였다. 테러 우려는 어느 때나 있으니 항상 경계할 일이다.

27. 앙골르 사원이 정글에 묻힐 것을 그 당시에 누군들 상상이나 했을까 생각하면 업적을 쌓으려는 인간의 노력이란 하룻밤의 꿈과 같다.

28. 더 높이 더 빨리 더 멀리를 슬로건으로 내세우고 벌어지는 욕망의 한계는 어디까지인가? 온갖 종류의 경기에서 열광하는 경쟁심은 어디까지인가? 작금의 세태에 대하여 역설적으로 더 낮게 더 천천히 더 가까이가 삶의 실천 방향으로 제시된다. 이러한 실천 방향은 더 많은 것을 추구하고 그러기 위하여 더 바쁘게 살아야 하는 현대인의 맹목적인 삶을 되돌아보게 한다. 대중의 선동과 유행의 흐름에 편승하여 한 방향으로 치달리는 맹목적인 삶을 되돌아보고 인간과 인간, 인간과 자연 사이에 이뤄진 본래의 모습을 회복시켜야 한다. 인간은 자연의 소리에 귀를 기울이는 가운데 자연과 하나가 될 수 있다. 자연과 하나 됨은 에고의 껍질을 벗는 것이며 잃어버린 삶을 회복하는 것이다. 끝없이 높기만 한 욕망의 기준을 더 낮게 자족하고 바쁘게 달리기만 하는 일상의 흐름을 더 천천히 되돌아보고 멀리서만 찾으려는 행복을 더 가까이에서 느끼는 것이 본래의 삶을 회복하는 길이다.

26. A horse as meek as a lamb used to be tied in the field every night, but it got a serious cut on its neck from a suspicious fellow. Since there is fear of terror anytime, precautions always ought to be taken.

27. Considering that nobody can expect the Angkor temple buried in the jungle at that time, human effort to produce achievements is just like a dream of one night.

28. How far is the limit of human desire tempted with the slogan "higher, faster, and farther"? How far is the limit of human competitive spirit excited with all kinds of game? "Lower, slower, closer" as the practical principles of life is reversely suggested regarding the current aspect. This kind of practical principle makes modern-day people look back a blind life in a rush to get some more. We have to look back, our blind life running into one direction according to mass instigation and fashion, and recover our original state—between human and human, and human and nature. Human can unite into one with nature while listening to the sound of nature. Uniting into one with nature means to break free from the ego and recover a lost life. It is a way of recovering an original life, to be satisfied with lowering the limit of endless desire, to look back at the fast flow of daily life and make it slower, and to feel happy from things that are closer and not those from afar.

29. 지역 간의 교류가 빈번해지면서 점차 조국이라는 의미는 쇠퇴하고 인종과 국가 간의 구별 없이 여러 인종들이 뒤섞여서 일하는 다국적 시대가 보편화되고 있다. 지구는 한 동네처럼 생활권이 좁아지고 경제 흐름에 따라 삶의 이동이 이뤄지고 국가의 의미는 점차 쇠퇴한다. 인류의 장래에는 이념적인 국가와 민족의 의미보다 실리적인 경제와 종교의 의미가 점차 부각된다.

30. 성공한 계층으로 분류되는 사람들은 예상과 달리 뚜렷한 목표 의식을 가지고 있었던 것이 아니고 주변 상황에 대한 대처능력과 주변 인물들에 대한 관리능력이 남달랐을 뿐이며 성공의 90%가 운이 따른 결과였음을 진술하고 있다. 이는 직선적인 목표의식보다 유연한 처세능력이 보다 현실적으로 유효한 것이며 또한 현실은 개인의 의지보다 시운의 흐름에 좌우되는 것임을 보여준다. 살아가면서 어찌 생각도 목표도 없이 살까마는 지나친 목표의식은 오히려 짐이 되어 심신을 피로하게 하고 능률을 저하시키기에 유연한 처세능력이 보다 현실에 부합되는 것임을 보여준다. 인간사에 얽힌 모든 일들은 결국 사람과의 관계에서 이뤄지는 것이니 주변 사람과 원만한 관계를 유지하는 것이 곧 성공의 길이다. 내 뜻을 세우는 것도 중요하지만 더욱 중요한 것은 주변을 잘 다스리는 것이다.

29. Since an interchange between regions is frequent, the meaning of native country has declined, and a multinational era in which several races are working together without distinguishing a race or a nation has been generalized. The zone of life becomes narrow in a global village, the movement of life progresses according to economic action, and the meaning of nation declines gradually. Practical meanings like economy and religion will be brought out more than ideological meanings, like nation and race, in the human future.

30. Unexpectedly, people classified as successful in life state that they were not conscious of their goals, but they coped effectively with the situation and managed people in their surroundings well, and 90 percent of their success is owed to good luck. This means that an ability to conduct life flexibly is actually more effective than a deep attachment to a goal, and the realities of life depend on the tide of the times rather than personal will. Even if we cannot live without a consciousness for our goals, the ability to conduct life flexibly coincides with the realities of life because excessive consciousness for a goal makes the body and the mind exhausted and lowers efficiency. Since all things are achieved according to human relationships, one way to success is maintaining good relationships with people around. It is important to set a goal, but it is more important to manage our surroundings well.

31. 기쁨과 슬픔은 상대적이어서 같은 것을 두고 느끼는 마음에 따라 기쁨이 되기도 하고 슬픔이 되기도 한다.

32. 만월은 삶의 희망이자 마음의 고향이다. 그러나 달이 차면 기울기 마련이니 희망을 지속적으로 유지하려면 달이 차지 않도록 속도를 조절하거나 목표를 변화시켜야 한다.

33. 성공과 실패는 빙산의 형국과 같으니 빙산이 수면 위로 뜨기 위해 그보다 아홉 배나 많은 얼음이 수면 아래에서 머물러야 한다. 이것이 노력이나 의지와 상관없이 전개되는 아홉수의 운명이다. 따라서 양지가 되었다고 일시적인 행운에 희희낙락할 것도 아니요 음지라 하여 핍박받는 신세를 자책할 것도 아니다. 아홉수의 음지는 평범한 위태로움에 불과하지만 아홉수의 음지를 딛고 올라선 하나의 양지는 위태로움 위의 위태로움이니 향후 전개될 운명은 예측불허다. 모든 존재가 변화하는 과정에서 수면에 폭풍을 일으키면 빙산은 뒤집히고 음지는 양지, 양지는 음지로 반전된다. 개인, 회사, 국가 등 모든 조직체는 수면 위에 떠 있는 한 조각 빙산의 형국으로 존재하다가 마침내 빙산이 광대한 대양의 수온에 녹아 없어지듯이 위태로운 존재의 게임을 마치고 우주의 품에 안겨 한 생을 마감한다. 궁극의 차원에서 볼 때 모든 존재에 특별하게 선택된 것이란 없다. 특별한 너, 특별한 신분 등 세간에 유행하는 특별함이란 선택된 품격이기 이전에 일상의 삶을 벗어나려는 착각이다.

31. Something becomes a joy or a sorrow according to the mind feeling the same things, because joy and sorrow are related.

32. A full moon is a home of mind as well as a hope of life, but you have to adjust the speed not to be full, or you have to change a goal in order to have hope continuously because a full moon eventually declines.

33. The ice that is nine times larger than an iceberg should be submerged below the surface to show only the iceberg above the surface. Success and failure are like the status of the iceberg. This is the fate of nine times happened regardless of effort or will. Therefore you should be neither joyful in fortune nor depressed in misfortune. A misfortune of nine times is risky. Furthermore, fortune standing on this misfortune of nine times is riskier. Fate cannot be forecasted. If it storms, the iceberg is overturned, while all things change. Inversely, misfortune becomes fortune, and fortune becomes misfortune. While all organisms—like persons, companies, nations, etc.—exist as the status of the iceberg above the surface, they end their lives in the universe after finishing a survival game, when the iceberg melts with the temperature of the water in the ocean. There is really nothing selected, especially in view of this ultimate aspect. A special thing followed in the vested class is a mistake to escape from daily life rather than a character selected as high birth or with a high rank.

34. 아무것도 누구도 기대하지 마라. 이것이 허망한 꼴을 당하지 않는 길이다. 아무것도 누구도 원망하지 마라. 미리 대처하지 않은 네가 잘못이다.

35. 무엇을 해야지 하면 스트레스이고, 무엇인가 할 것이 있구나 하면 즐거움이다.

36. 대부분의 사람들이 세상에 태어나서 약 20세까지는 부모의 보호를 받다가 부모 보호를 떠나게 되면 자립을 해야 한다. 부모에게서 재산을 물려받지 않는 한 직장생활을 하거나 자영업을 하게 되는데 버는 수입으로 결혼해서 아이들 교육시키고 생활하다 보면 직장생활 15년이 지나서야 겨우 집을 마련하게 된다. 그리고 60~65세 정년이 되어야 가장으로서 부양의무를 면하게 되고 정년 후 남는 여생 20~30년은 연금이나 적금으로 생활해야 하는데 중산층 이상으로 살아온 노년은 그런대로 생활유지가 되지만 서민으로 살아온 노년은 계속 생활고에 시달린다. 결국 절반 이상의 사람들이 평생 생활고에 시달리다가 세상을 떠난다. 하루를 벌어야 하루를 먹고 사는 인생살이에서 놓여나서 하루 벌이를 걱정하지 않아도 살 수 있다면 진정한 천국일 것이다. 그러나 스스로 노력 없이 얻어진 재산이나 유산으로 사는 인생이라면 천국과 거리가 멀다. 지옥을 거쳐 온 자만이 천국의 기쁨을 누릴 수 있기 때문이다.

34. Don't expect anything or anybody else; that is a way not to be betrayed. Don't blame anything or anybody else; that is your mistake not to confirm in advance.

35. If you think you ought to do something, it is stressful. However, if you think there is something new to do, it is a joy.

36. Most people have to stand on their own feet after they are independent of their parents at about twenty years old. Since they get a job or are self-employed as long as they have no inheritance from their parents, they can buy a house after working for almost fifteen years while supplying their children with food and school expenses. They can be free from the burden of supporting their family just after retiring at the age of sixty through sixty-five. The rest of their lives, for twenty through thirty years, should be covered by a pension or an installment deposit. But in old age, common people live through hardship continuously, even if the old of the vested class can live free from care. Therefore, almost half of people suffer from anxiety about money until their death. It is really a heaven on earth if one can live without suffering from anxiety about money, but it is not a heaven on earth if one depends on inheritance from one's parents because only those who suffer hell can enjoy the pleasure of heaven.

37. 생각만 하고 말로만 떠들고 있으면 아무것도 되는 것이 없다. 복잡하게 생각하고 고민하느니 우선 기본적인 것부터 하나씩 실천해가는 것이 중요하다. 그러다 보면 점차 상세한 것까지 처리할 수 있게 된다.

38. 누군가에게서 냄새가 나거든 그건 네게서 나는 냄새인 줄 알아라. 누군가에게 실망이 크거든 상대도 네게 실망하고 있는 줄 알아라. 모든 것은 네 안에서 이뤄지고 그것은 곧 너를 비추는 거울이다.

39. 화가 나는 경우가 종종 있는데 결코 화내지 마라. 상대방에 대한 경고의 메시지라면 거절의 의사 표시로 충분하다. 화를 내는 순간 감정의 중심을 잃고 다른 일까지 망치게 된다. 뿐만 아니라 감정을 정상으로 회복하는 데 몇 시간 또는 며칠이 걸릴 수도 있으니 그동안 시간을 낭비하고 마음도 상하게 된다. 상대방은 스스로 잘못을 인정했을지라도 화내는 사람을 결코 좋아할 리 없다. 또한 화가 난 와중에 나누는 대화는 부정확하고 의사전달도 잘 안 된다. 화가 나려는 순간이면 누구나 그런 실수를 할 수 있으려니 생각하고 감정을 다스리도록 하자. 돌이켜보면 누구든지 실수는 할 수 있는 것이고 경우에 따라서는 화를 낸 내가 잘못 판단하고 상대방을 오해할 수도 있는 것이다.

37. Nothing can be done if you only think and speak about something. It is more important to do something step by step from the basics rather than to think complicatedly and worry about it. If so, you can gradually perform even the details.

38. If someone smells, it may be your smell. If you are disappointed with someone, he is also disappointed with you. Everything is up to you, and that is just a mirror reflecting yourself.

39. Don't be angry even if you feel angry. An expression of refusal is enough to sound a warning to the other party. Other things are also ruined if you betray your feelings in a moment of anger. Furthermore, it will take a few hours or a few days to recover your feelings, during which time your heart breaks and you waste time. The other party does not like an angry person even if he admits his mistake by himself. A dialogue while being angry is not clear and not transmitted correctly. Considering that everybody can make such a mistake, you have to control your feelings every moment when you feel angry. If you look back, everybody can make a mistake, and you might misunderstand the other party with error in your judgment according to the circumstances.

40. 칼을 닦고 마루를 닦고 마음을 닦는다. 이 모든 것은 잠들면 할 수 없다. 깨어있어야 한다.

41. 인생이란 실패와 성공, 기쁨과 슬픔이 교차하는 기대와 실망 속에서 사는 것이다. 그러니 전부를 이루려고 안달하지 마라.

42. 찾아가서 청해야 하는 인생이라면 아직은 괴로운 인생이다. 스스로 찾아오는 인생이라야 성공한 인생이다. 하지만 찾아오는 인생일지라도 고단함이 없는 인생이라면 어찌 온전한 삶이라 하겠는가?

43. 조직을 이끌려면 계획을 세우는 머리가 필요하고 의사전달을 하는 입이 필요하다. 그러나 머리와 입만 살아있고 손발이 움직이지 않으면 운동부족에 비만으로 조직이 병든다. 조직에서 머리와 입은 합하여 다섯이면 족하고 나머지는 백이 되었든 천이 되었든 손발이 되어 실천할 수 있어야 건강한 조직이다. 인체구조를 봐도 머리와 입은 합하여 둘이지만 손발은 합하여 넷이다. 따라서 조직이 망하지 않으려면 머리와 입의 숫자가 손발의 숫자 절반을 넘지 않아야 한다.

40. Scrap the rust off the sword, scrub the floor, and improve your virtue. You cannot do all of these things while sleeping. You can do them only while awake.

41. Life is to live with expectations and disappointments, while failures and successes and joys and sorrows are alternated. So don't fret about achieving the whole thing.

42. Your life is still painful if you have to seek. It is really a successful life when someone calls for you. Even so, how can a life be perfect without fatigue?

43. We need a head to make plans and a mouth to express an intention in order to lead an organization. But the organization will suffer from obesity due to lack of exercise if only the head and the mouth are active without moving the hands and feet. Five is enough for the sum of the heads and mouths, and the remaining, even if they are hundreds or thousands, should be active as hands and feet—that is a healthy organization. In view of the structure of the human body, the sum of a head and a mouth are two, while the sum of the hands and feet are four. Therefore the sum of heads and mouths should not be more than a half of the sum of hands and feet in order for the organization not to collapse.

44. 불을 지필 때 불씨 중심이 외부에 노출되지 않도록 감싸면서 공기를 공급해야 한다. 불씨 중심이 공기에 직접 노출되면 불씨 온도가 냉각되어 불은 꺼지고 만다. 필요한 공기도 분별없이 공급해서는 안 된다.

45. 생명은 힘이 없이는 한순간도 살 수 없다. 한 호흡의 들숨과 날숨에도 힘이 필요하다. 남성적인 무력이 없으면 여성적인 매력이라도 있어야 생존할 수 있다. 이것이 현상계에서 적용되는 정글의 법칙이다. 그러나 힘만으로는 완전하지 못하다. 인간에게는 정이 필요하다. 정은 뼈대를 감싸고 있는 살과 같다. 힘이 힘으로서의 가치를 발휘할 수 있게 하는 것은 정이다. 어머니의 모정, 남녀 간의 애정, 친구 간의 우정 등 사람들은 여러 가지 정에 얽혀서 살고 있다. 그러나 정만으로 만사가 이뤄지지는 않는다. 힘이 뒷받침되지 않는 정은 뼈대 없는 살처럼 무너져 내리고 결코 이뤄지지 않는 짝사랑처럼 상처만 남긴다. 또한 힘만 있고 정이 없다면 황량한 사막에 외롭게 서 있는 스핑크스처럼 인생이 무미건조할 뿐이다. 그래서 사람 간에 미소가 필요하고 전쟁에도 도리가 있는 법이다. 세상 이치가 이러하니 가히 힘만 자랑할 것도 아니요 정에만 매달릴 것도 아니다. 힘으로 내실을 기하고 정으로 주위를 감쌀 줄 아는 것이 온전한 삶이다.

44. When you light a fire, you have to supply air while protecting the center of the fire, not to be exposed to the atmosphere. If the center of the fire is directly exposed to the atmosphere, the temperature of the fire cools down, so it is extinguished. You should not supply air imprudently even if necessary.

45. Life cannot survive without power even for a moment. Even an intake and an exhalation of breath need power. If you have no male fist, you have feminine attraction in order to survive. That is the law of the jungle applied to this phenomenal world, but it is not perfect, to survive only with power, because sentiment is necessary to human beings. Sentiment is like flesh covering bone. It is sentiment that makes power worth having. People live connected with sentiments—like maternity, affection, friendship, etc.—but all don't go well only with sentiments. A sentiment without power collapses like flesh without bone, and there is a wound left as one-sided love is not achieved. On the other hand, if there is only power without sentiment, life is dull, like a sphinx standing lonely in a desolate desert. Therefore a smile is necessary in life, and there is duty even in war. As the reason of life is like that, so you should not be proud of power only and depend on sentiment only. It is a perfect life not only to ensure substantiality with power but also to protect circumstances with sentiment.

46. (시 1)
흙에 베인 굳은 손
고단함을 껴안고

닭 울음소리마저
때 이른 꼭두새벽

어둠 사르는 선율
빈 가슴 어우르며

꿈결같이 흐르던
감미로운 환희가

아~ 그런 시가
간밤에 사라졌다.

47. 한 해가 저물고 있다. 사람들은 가족이나 친목단위로 모여 음식을 나누기도 하고 새로운 희망을 기약하며 저무는 한 해를 마무리한다. 한 해가 저무는 것은 지구가 태양을 한 바퀴 돈 것이고 사람들이 나이 한 살 더 먹는 것일 뿐 내일 아침 떠오를 태양이 오늘 아침 태양과 다를 바 없지만 사람들은 한해가 바뀌는 것에 새삼 의미를 두려 한다. 한해를 흘려보내기 아쉬워 흘러가는 세월을 마음에 새기고 싶은 것이다. 마음에 새긴들 숫자만 바뀔 뿐 달라질 것도 없지만 그래도 사람들은 한해가 바뀌는 것에 새삼 의미를 두려 한다.

46. (Poem 1)
Hugging a weary body
with hands hardened in the soil.

At the peep of day,
it is too early to crow.

While touching a void heart
with melody across darkness.

A sweet delight flowing
like a passing dream.

Oh, such a poem
disappeared last night.

47. One year is coming to an end. People finish the year while having dinner or discussing their new plans together with family or promoting mutual friendships. A lapse of one year means that the earth made one revolution according to the annual course of the sun, and people aged one year more, but people want to keep the lapse of a year in mind even if the sunrise of tomorrow morning does not differ from the sunrise of this morning. They want to keep the lapse of time in mind because they regret the passing of the year. Even if they keep that in mind, there is nothing to do but change the number of the year, but they want to keep the lapse of a year in mind.

48. 지난해는 가고 새해가 밝았다. 새해 첫 아침부터 코코넛나무들 사이로 세찬 비바람이 몰아친다. 태풍이 새해 첫날부터 들판을 지나 창밖에 몰아치고 있다. 새로울 것 없는 아침에 자연은 거친 모습으로 다가선다.

49. 더도 말고 덜도 말고 중심에 서라. 이는 경직되지도 말고 그렇다고 방만하지도 말고 항상 깨어 있어야 한다는 뜻이다.

50. 어느 조직에서나 눈에 거슬리는 자가 있게 마련이다. 그 자를 쳐내고 나면 만사 해결될 것 같지만 막상 쳐내고 나면 그와 비슷한 자가 또 생겨난다. 이는 세상사가 내 뜻대로만 되는 것이 아님을 의미한다. 그러니 더불어 공존하는 것도 삶의 지혜다.

51. 민주주의는 통제된 자유를 추구한다. 이는 타인에게도 자유를 배려하기 위한 조치다. 그러나 민주주의의 모순은 자유를 통제하는 과정에서 일어난다. 소수에 의해 다수가 희생되느니 다수에 의해 소수가 희생되는 것이 낫다는 다수주의 원칙이 첫 번째 모순이고 그러면서도 다수 의견을 소수가 대변하는 것이 두 번째 모순이다.

48. Everybody rings out the Old Year and rings in the New Year. There is a rainy wind between coconut trees in the first morning of the New Year. It storms outside the window throughout the field on New Year's Day. Nature approaches newly with harsh features, though there is nothing but a usual morning without new things.

49. No more, no less, stand just on the center. It means that you have to be awake always while being neither nervous nor careless.

50. There is always an offensive guy in any organization. A similar guy appears again after you eliminate the old one, though you expect everything will be okay after doing so. It means that everything in the world is not performed according to your intention only. Therefore coexistence is also wisdom for life.

51. Democracy pursues controlled freedom. This is a consideration to share freedom with others evenly, but a discrepancy of democracy happens in the course of controlling freedom. The first discrepancy is the principle of the majority sacrificing the minority. Nevertheless, the fact that only a minority speaks for the majority's opinion is the second discrepancy.

52. 누가 해주려니 기대하지 말고 필요하거든 스스로 해라.

53. 생존이란 무엇인가? 싸우고 사랑하는 것이다.

54. 잡아먹고 잡아먹히는 것은 선악이 아니다. 선과 악은 절대적인 것이 아니어서 주관에 따라 선할 수도 악할 수도 있는 것이다.

55. 한 세대가 교체되는 데 걸리는 기간을 30년으로 보는 것은 부모와 자식 간 평균 나이 차이에 따른 것이다. 어린 자식이 부모를 바라보는 눈높이에서 보면 30년이라는 차이가 매우 크게 느껴진다. 그러나 어린아이가 성장한 후 부모가 되어 지난 세월을 돌이켜 보면 어린아이나 어른이나 동시대를 함께 살고 있다는 데 더 큰 의미를 갖게 된다. 3세대가 동시대를 함께 사는 경우 노인과 손자가 60년이라는 세월의 차이를 넘어 같은 하늘 아래서 함께 숨 쉬며 살고 있는 것이다. 한 살 아기에게는 일 년이 인생 전부인 것처럼 느끼지만 노인에게는 일 년이란 단지 스쳐 가는 삶의 일부에 불과하다. 이와 같이 어린아이와 노인이 느끼는 시간은 다르지만 동시대에 함께 살고 있다는 것은 뜻깊은 일이다. 동시대인으로 산다는 것은 60년이라는 세월의 차이를 넘어 같은 것을 보고 느끼며 함께 살고 있다는 의미이기도 하다. 결코 60년은 과거와 미래로 구분될 만큼 머나먼 세월이 아니다. 우리 모두 동시대를 함께 살고 있는 친구들이다.

52. Don't expect anybody to help you. Do it by yourself if necessary.

53. What is to be alive? That is to fight and to love.

54. To catch or to be caught for survival is neither good nor evil. Good and evil are not absolute, so those are changeable according to subjectivity.

55. The reason why the shifting time of a generation is counted as thirty years is due to the average age difference between parents and children. The difference of thirty years is felt as a very long time in the eyes of a child looking at his parents, but he finds it more meaningful to live together in the same age if he looks back to the past after he grows and becomes a parent. In the case of living together with three generations, children and grandparents live together and breathe under the same sky regardless of their age difference of sixty years. One year is felt as a whole life in the eyes of a one-year-old baby, but one year is felt just as a moment in the eyes of an old man. Like this, time flies differently for a child and an old man, but it is meaningful to live together in the same age. Living in the same age means overcoming a difference of sixty years, to feel the same things and live together. Sixty years is not too long to be divided into the past and the future. All of us are friends living together in the same age.

56. 세상은 불필요한 욕심을 채우기에는 부족하지만 청빈낙도하기에
는 풍요롭다.

57. 삶의 축제는 이미 시작되었다. 일을 즐겨라. 그리고 가져갈 것 없
이 나눠라.

58. 지금 아니면 언제 행복하랴. 삶은 항상 가상의 꿈, 지금을 사랑하
는 것이 진정한 삶이다.

59. 대부분의 꽃들이 오엽이고 손가락 발가락이 각각 다섯 개인 것은
무슨 연유일까? 숫자 5가 갖는 특별한 의미는 무엇인가? 생명체가 오
랜 세월 진화하는 과정에서 1보다는 2가 안정되고 좌우에 각각 1개씩
있는 것보다 좌우에 2개씩 배열하여 어느 하나가 손상되어도 기능을
발휘할 수 있는 4개가 보다 실용적이며 단순한 대칭구조보다 균형을
맞출 중간자로 1을 더한 5가 유리함을 터득한 것이다. 5보다 많은 6, 7
의 경우 구조가 복잡해져서 개별 기능이 갖고 있는 장점보다 전체를
통제하기에 비효율적인 단점이 더 크다는 것도 대부분의 생명체가 5
를 선택한 이유다. 5라는 숫자는 오랜 세월 생명체가 시행착오를 거치
면서 채택한 비밀의 숫자로서 그 바탕에는 안정감, 실용성, 균형, 통제
력 등을 담고 있다.

56. The world is insufficient to meet unnecessary greed but affluent for those who live in honest poverty.

57. The festival of life has already started. Enjoy working and sharing without bringing back.

58. How in the world can you be happy without the present time? Life is always based on a virtual dream; therefore, to love at the present time is to have a real life.

59. Why do almost all flowers have five petals, and a hand and a foot consist of five fingers and five toes respectively? What is the special meaning of the number five? In the course of evolution, for a long time, life organisms know that two are better than one in order to be stable, and four consisting of two on the right and left sides respectively are more effective than two consisting of one on each side, in order for them not to lose their function even if one of them is damaged. Furthermore, they realized that five added one more as an adjustor to four, and it is more advantageous than a simple symmetric structure to keep the balance. That is why almost all life organisms choose five because the structure becomes complicated in cases of six or seven or other figures bigger than five, and it is not easy to control the system totally. Five is a secret number that life organisms choose after many trials and errors for a long time, and there is a sense of security, practicality, balance, and control in the number five.

60. 거친 광야를 헤맬지라도 미소를 잃지 마라. 미소는 지친 삶을 보듬고 마음에 여유를 준다. 미소가 있는 한 희망은 살아있다.

61. 사는 동안 먹거리에 차이가 나거든 6대 4는 허용해라. 꽃들이 저마다 다르듯이 모든 인생이 똑같을 수는 없는 법이다. 이는 종의 진화를 위해 우성을 배려하는 자연적인 이치다. 그러나 7대 3으로 격차가 벌어지면 우열의 질서를 넘어서는 변종에 의해 종의 진화는 멈추게 된다. 이는 기득권층이 알아야 할 점이다.

62. 군대에 가면 똑똑한 아이는 바보가 되고 바보는 똑똑한 아이가 된다는 말이 있다. 이는 장병들의 개성이 제한되고 군대의 규율이 우선시되어 모든 행동과 사고력이 획일화되기 때문이다. 개개인 삶의 효율성을 위하여 질서가 필요하고 질서를 유지하기 위하여 사회가 구성되지만 질서가 뜻대로 유지되는 것만은 아니다. 반군이 조직되고 테러가 일어나기도 한다. 개인과 개인, 개인과 사회 간에 합의가 이뤄지지 못하고 질서가 깨지는 것이다. 그만큼 사람마다 개성이 다양하여 모두를 만족시킬 만한 질서를 만들어내는 것이 쉽지 않다. 이 세상 어디에도 유토피아는 없는 것이다. 그래서 삶에는 항상 긴장이 내재된다.

60. Never lose your smile even if you wander over harsh wilderness. A smile refreshes your weary life and gives allowance to the mind. While you smile, there is hope.

61. Allow a ratio of 6:4 when distributing food while living. All life cannot be equal as all flowers are different. It is natural to consider dominance for the evolution of species. But evolution will be stopped by mutation overpassing the order between superiority and inferiority, if the difference is over a ratio of 7:3. The vested class should keep that in mind.

62. There is a saying that a smart guy becomes a fool and a fool becomes a smart guy when a juvenile enters military service as a soldier. It means that each personality is subjected to restriction, and all actions and thoughts are standardized because military discipline has priority over personality. This order is necessary for the efficiency of individual life, and a society is organized to keep public order, but order is not maintained as expected. Sometimes a rebel army is organized, and terror occurs. There is no mutual agreement between persons or between a person and society, so social order is upset. Like that, it is not easy to create social order in which everybody is satisfied, because personalities are diverse. There is no utopia in the world. Therefore there is always tension in life.

63. 자기주장을 할 수는 있지만, 그것이 완전한 것이 아니므로 스스로를 돌아보고 주위에 여유로움을 가져야 한다.

64. 지금 여기 꽃이 피어있는 것은 무수한 가능성 중에서 나타난 하나의 결과다. 꽃이 햇빛을 맞고 비를 머금고 바람에 흔들리는 과정에서 어느 한 가지만이라도 바뀌었다면 결과는 달라졌을 것이다. 이처럼 무수히 부딪치는 인연 속에서 그때마다 제한된 의지로 살아가는 것이 인생이다.

65. 살다 보면 주어진 수입만으로 지출을 감당할 수 없어 은행에서 돈을 빌려 쓰게 되지만 빌리는 그 순간부터 부담은 시작된다. 빚을 갚으면 그나마 다행이지만 갚지 못하면 신용불량자가 되기도 한다. 바람직한 것은 빚지지 않고 사는 것이지만 부득이 빚을 얻더라도 갚을 수 있는 범위에서 빚을 얻어 써야 한다. 그러나 무턱대고 빚을 얻어 쓰고 나중에 될 대로 되라는 막장 인생들이 의외로 많다. 돈 없으면 빈대떡이나 부쳐 먹지 요리 집이 무엇이냐 이런 단순한 이치도 실행하지 못하는 인생들이 너무 많아 고금동서를 막론하고 돈 때문에 울고 웃는다. 왜 빚을 지게 되는가? 과욕 아니면 호기가 작용하기 때문이다. 살다 보면 때로는 호기가 필요하기도 하다. 인생 자체가 일종의 모험이고 호기다. 호기가 없다면 인류역사도 없었을 것이다. 그러나 호기가 저질러 놓은 일을 감당해야 하는 것도 호기의 몫이다.

63. You can be self-assertive, but it may not be perfect. Therefore you should reflect on yourself and be generous to neighbors.

64. A flower blooming in this moment is only one thing among so many possibilities, and the result would be different if one of them has been changed while exposed to rain, wind or sunlight. It is life to live every moment with limited intention when we meet so many ties.

65. A burden starts at the moment when people borrow money, even if they borrow from the bank, due to expenses going above their income. If people can repay their loans, it is fortunate, but if not, people become bankrupt. It is desirable that people live without loans. In cases that a loan is inevitable, people have to borrow money within the limits of repayment, but there are unexpectedly so many irresponsible people who do not care about the future after borrowing money. Be thrifty if you have no money. So many people suffer all their lives from anxiety about money because they cannot execute even a simple reason like that. Why do people fall into debt? It is due to either greediness or a stout heart. Sometimes people need a stout heart while living in the world. Life is about not only adventure but also a stout heart. There would be no human history without stout hearts, but it is also the role of stout hearts to carry out their duty.

66. 가진 자를 질투하지 마라. 그것은 네가 못 가졌다고 생각하기 때문이다. 못 가진 곳에서 태어난 것은 운명이다. 그러나 질투하는 시간에 차라리 노력한다면 운명을 거부할 수는 없어도 운명을 개선할 수는 있다. 못 가진 자를 업신여기지 마라. 그것은 네가 가졌다고 생각하기 때문이다. 가진 곳에서 태어난 것은 행운이다. 그러나 너의 조상이 풍상을 겪어서 얻은 행운임을 모르고 겸손하지 않으면 행운은 곧 사라진다.

67. 인류 역사의 절반은 오해에서 이뤄진다. 국가 간의 전쟁과 종교 간의 갈등의 이면에는 서로를 이해하지 못한 오해에서 발생되는 경우가 태반이다. 일상생활 속에서 이뤄지는 개인 간의 문제도 사소한 오해에서 발생하는 경우가 많다. 사람들은 자신이 살아온 경험에서 얻은 상식과 관습 등으로 사물이나 사건을 판단하며 살아간다. 그러한 판단은 개개인의 경험에 의한 것으로 자신의 생각이 옳다는 전제하에 이뤄진다. 그러나 사람마다 살아온 경험과 가치관의 차이에 따라서 자신이 생각하고 결정한 판단이 다른 사람에게는 전혀 사실과 다를 수 있다. 따라서 오해의 늪에 빠지지 않기 위해서 자기중심적인 독단에 빠지지 말아야 하고, 주변의 입장을 두루 헤아려 볼 줄 아는 안목이 필요하다. 특히 과욕에 사로잡힐 경우 판단력이 흐려지고 오해의 소지가 높아지니 허황된 유혹에 빠지지 않도록 마음을 비우는 것이 삶의 지혜다.

66. Don't be jealous of the haves. It is because of your thoughts that you are a have-not. It is your fate to be born into a poor family, but if you make every effort instead of focusing on jealousy, you can improve your fate even if you cannot reject it. Don't look down on the have-nots. It is because of your thoughts that you are one of the haves. It is your good fortune to be born into a rich family, but if you are not modest, not knowing that your ancestors had good fortune by bearing hardships, your good fortune will soon disappear.

67. Half of human history is formed by misunderstanding. There are so many cases that wars between nations and discord between religions occurred due to misunderstandings. There are also so many cases that troubles between individuals happened in daily life due to trifling misunderstandings. People live judging things and affairs by common sense and customs learned from their experiences. Their judgments depend on individual experiences, so they are formed on the condition that a person's thoughts are correct. However, according to the differences of individual experiences and sense of values, a judgment decided by one person may be wrong to another person. Therefore people should not fall into egocentric dogmatism in order not to misunderstand, and they need to have an eye for considering the situation of their surroundings. People lose their judgment and are apt to misunderstand, particularly in cases when they're enslaved by greed, so it is a wisdom of life to have presence of mind not to yield to absurd temptations.

68. 모든 것은 이미 온전하다. 지금 이후에 모든 것이 바뀐다고 하여도 온전함은 그대로다. 과거나 미래의 일로 지금을 잃어버리지 말라. 현실은 지금이고 미래는 가상의 것이다. 과거의 기억에 사로잡힌 정신도 지금을 망각하기 쉽다. 시간이 흐르는 것은 오직 지금을 위한 것이다. 모든 것은 지금 순간에 있다. 삶도 지금에 있고 죽음도 지금에 있다. 명곡은 명연주를 통해서만 부활하듯이 삶은 오직 지금 속에서만 살아난다. 사라진 과거나 오지 않은 미래를 위하여 지금을 망각하지 말라. 삶은 과거나 미래에 있는 것이 아니라 오직 지금 속에서 살아 있다.

69. 물은 생명의 근원으로 여러 가지 덕목을 가르치고 있다. 물은 모든 것을 용해시키고 씻어 내리는 포용력이 있는가 하면 모난 바위에 부딪치면 돌아갈 줄 아는 유연성도 있다. 노도와 같이 엄청난 힘이 있는가 하면 잔잔한 호수처럼 고요함도 간직하고 있다. 물은 한없이 깊고 투명하여 계곡을 굽이굽이 돌아 흐르는 맑은 물소리는 청아하기 그지없다. 위에서 아래로 흐르는 질서 정연함은 자연의 순리를 일깨워 주고, 한번 가면 다시 돌아오지 않는 흐름은 삶의 의미를 되새겨준다. 구름은 비가 되어 강물을 이루고 강물이 흘러서 대양에 이르면 햇빛에 증발하여 구름이 되고 드넓은 하늘을 떠돌다가 숲속 골짜기로 다시 찾아와 비가 되어 흐르니 물은 끊임없이 흐르는 생명의 순환을 보여준다.

70. 천지간에 만물은 물의 흐름처럼 같으면서 다르고 다르면서 같다. 그래서 만물이자 하나인 것이다.

68. All things are already sound. Even if everything is changed forward, they are sound as they are. Don't forget the present due to things of the past or the future. The reality is at the present time, and the future is imaginary. A mind addicted to the past is also apt to forget the present. It is just for the present that time flies. All things are in the present; life as well as death is also in the present. Life is alive in the present just as a musical masterpiece is revived only by an excellent performance. Don't forget the present for the disappeared past or the future not coming yet. Life is neither in the past nor in the future, but it is alive just at the present time.

69. Water as the original source of life shows several virtues. Water possesses not only the capacity to wash all things but also the flexibility to turn around the edge of a rock. Though water holds tremendous power like raging waves, it also has calmness like a serene lake. Since water is endlessly deep and transparent, a clear sound of water is really graceful. It shows the rationality of nature, when water flows from high to low in good order, and it reminds us of the meaning of life, that water never comes back after it passes by once. Clouds become rain, then become a river, which arrives into the ocean. The ocean becomes clouds again after being evaporated by the sun, and they become rain again after wandering in the sky. Therefore water shows the cycle of life flowing endlessly.

70. Like the flow of water, all things in heaven and earth are different while being the same, and they are the same while being different, so they are one thing as well as all things.

71. (시 2)
수평선의 침묵은
무한한 도량을 헤아리게 하고

위에서 아래로 흐르는 것은
자연의 순리를 가르쳐주고

흘러가면 돌아오지 않는 것은
세월의 의미를 되새겨주고

그릇 따라 변하는 것은
천진무구함 그대로이며

낙수 한 방울 청아함에
도를 깨우칠 만하고

투명타 못해 청잣빛은
달을 건지기에 부족함이 없다.

72. 인간의 본성은 같은 경우가 많고 인간의 개성은 다른 경우가 많아서 서로 간에 같음이 많고 다름이 적으면 친구가 되는 것이고 같음이 적고 다름이 많으면 적이 되는 것이니 같음과 다름에 따라 친구와 적도 변하는 것이다. 적을 만드는 것은 미워함이 아니라 다름이요 친구를 만드는 것은 좋아함이 아니라 같음이다.

71. (Poem 2)
The silence of the horizon
shows moral sense infinitely.

Flowing from high to low
awakes the rationality of nature.

Not to come back after passing by
reminds us of the meaning of life.

To be changed according to a bowl
is innocence as is.

With the clear sound of a drop,
the truth might be awakened.

The celadon beyond transparent
is enough to reflect the moon.

72. Man's true character is almost the same, while human personality is very different. A person becomes a friend if there are many similarities and a little difference, and he becomes an enemy if there are many differences and not as much similarities. According to similarities or differences, both a friend and an enemy are changeable. An enemy is made not because of hatred but because of differences, and a friend is made not because of likes but because of similarities.

2. 즐거움

73. 원하는 것이면 무엇이든 즐겨라. 그러나 부채금지, 도박금지, 마약금지, 음주금지, 흡연금지. 이 다섯 악마에게 유혹되지 않으면 인생이 지속가능하고 어느 하나라도 유혹되면 그 인생 요절하기 쉽다.

74. 맥주의 청량함과 와인의 부드러움이 때로는 일상을 편안하게 해준다.

75. 과로하지 말고 간식은 삼가해라. 육체가 편안하지 않으면 마음이 맑을 수 없다.

76. 과잉섭취에 의한 비만은 식량 자급자족 못지않게 인류의 영원한 숙제다. 한편에서는 못 먹어 굶주리는데 과잉섭취로 비만을 자초하는 사람들은 본인 건강은 물론이고 음식으로 희생된 지구상의 모든 생물들에게 죄짓는 일이다. 야생에서 생존하는 동물들에게는 가뭄으로 굶어 죽을 일이 걱정이지 비만이란 없다. 오직 게으르고 탐식하는 인간에게만 비만이 있다. 마약, 알코올, 흡연처럼 탐식도 뿌리치기가 쉽지 않지만 적절히 먹고 절제하는 습관이 자연과 조화를 이루는 길이다.

2. Amusement

73. Enjoy whatever you want. However, no debt, no gambling, no drug, no alcohol, and no smoking. Regardless of any reasons, the less tempted you are to these five evils, the more sustainable your life becomes. Your life is apt to collapse if tempted by one of them.

74. Coolness of beer and sweetness of wine; sometimes both of them can make our lives comfortable.

75. Refrain from snacks and overworking. If a body is not comfortable, a mind cannot be clear.

76. Obesity due to excessive intake as well as self-sufficiency in food is an everlasting question of human beings. They not only lose their health but also commit a sin against all creatures on earth, sacrificed as prey so that people can bring obesity on themselves while others are starving. Animals living in the wild state only worry about starving to death due to droughts, and there is no obesity among them. There is obesity only in a lazy and voracious person. It is a way of harmonizing with nature, to be moderate in eating and drinking, and to make a temperate living even if it is not easy to restrain voracity for drugs, alcohol, and smoking.

77. 사람들은 일상의 대부분을 하지 않아도 될 일로 헛수고를 하면서 산다. 실제로 일상의 일들을 헤아려 보면 정말 필요하거나 가치 있는 것은 생각보다 그리 많지 않다. 없어도 그만 있어도 그만인 것들이 태반이다. 그런데도 사람들은 죽자 살자 티격태격하며 아무것도 아닌 일로 헛수고하며 산다. 인생에서 이것저것 빼고 나면 남을 것이 없으니 사람들은 그렇게 헛수고를 자청하며 시간을 보내는 것이다. 사람들은 시간 보내기가 무료하여 망상에 빠지지만 정작 중요한 것은 잊은 채 산다.

78. 대표적인 중독 대상으로 도박, 마약, 음주, 흡연 등을 들지만 게임, 섹스, 간식 등도 중독성이 있어서 한번 맛 들이면 쉽게 그만둘 수가 없다. 무엇인가에 빠지면 쉽게 그만둘 수 없는 것은 예술, 사업, 종교, 정치, 범죄 등도 마찬가지다. 그러고 보면 살면서 이뤄지는 모든 것들이 중독성이 아닌 것이 거의 없다. 사람들은 자신도 모르는 사이 무엇인가에 중독되어 무의식적으로 살고 있는 것이다. 문명의 발달로 여가 시간이 많아지다 보니 무엇인가에 중독되어 사는 인생들이 많아졌다. 이와 같이 살아있는 동안 무엇인가에 중독될 수밖에 없는 현실이고 보면 과연 무엇에 중독될 것인가 선택하는 것이 매우 중요하다. 한번 중독되면 그것에 집착하게 되어 쉽게 그만둘 수 없기 때문에 자신의 일상생활에 균형을 무너뜨리지 않는 것이어야 하고 타인에게 해가 되지 않는 것이어야 한다. 기왕 중독될 바에는 한 생명 다 바쳐도 좋을 대상을 찾아서 열정을 쏟는다면 그것 또한 멋진 인생일 것이다. 그러나 주변을 돌아보면 하잘것없는 것에 중독되어 스스로 시달림을 당하고 결국 인생을 탕진하는 경우가 너무나 많다. 하잘것없는 것은 버리고 소중한 것을 깨우쳐야 하는 간단한 이치를 사람들은 잊고 산다.

77. Most people live wasting labor with unnecessary things daily. If you review daily occurrences, the indispensable and valuable things are really not so many contrary to your expectation. Most daily things are as trivial as having no concern whether to be or not. Nevertheless, people live wasting labor with trivial matters while quarrelling each other desperately. As there is actually nothing except trivial matters in life, people kill time, offering themselves in wasted labor. While people fall into delusions to kill boredom and time, they live while forgetting the important things.

78. Gambling, drugs, alcohol, and smoking are mentioned as the main objects of addiction, but it is not easy to quit games, sex, and snacks because they also cause addiction. Art, business, religion, politics, and crime are also not easy to quit. Like this, almost all things in life cause nothing but addiction. People live unconsciously while addicted to something. There are so many people addicted because they have so much leisure time with the advance of civilization. In the present situation where people cannot help but be addicted to something while living, it is very important to choose a precious thing for addiction. A desirable addiction should be something that neither upsets the balance of everyday life nor harms other persons, because it is not easy to quit once people are addicted. If a person has a passion for a precious thing after looking for its worth, devoting their whole life, it will be a wonderful life. Nevertheless, if we look around, there are so many cases where whole lives are destroyed by addiction to trifles. People live while forgetting such a simple thing as discarding trifles and realizing their precious thing.

79. 인생은 경쟁으로 시작해서 즐거움으로 끝난다. 우열을 가리는 생존경쟁은 생명의 진화과정에서 필수적이며 적자생존은 엄연한 현실이다. 반면에 즐거움은 인생의 또 다른 희망이다. 경쟁이 불러오는 끝없는 긴장을 즐거움으로 극복한다. 지속적인 긴장만으로 인생은 살 수 없다. 순간순간 긴장을 이완시킬 수 있는 방편으로 사람들은 오락을 즐긴다. 오락과 경쟁은 동전의 양면과 같아서 동시적이다. 경쟁은 피를 부르고 심장을 멎게 하고 우열을 구분하고 삶과 죽음을 심판한다. 동서고금에 그칠 줄 모르고 일어나는 전쟁에서부터 각종 스포츠 경기에 이르기까지 그 배경은 경쟁에 기초를 두고 있다. 로마 시대의 검투사 경기에서 오늘날 투우 경기에 이르기까지 관중은 피를 부르는 죽음의 경기에 열광하고 스릴 속에서 스스로 살아 있음을 체험한다. 사람들은 긴장과 이완, 경쟁과 오락을 동시에 즐기는 다양한 종류의 게임을 즐긴다. 제반 스포츠 경기는 물론이고 사이버 공간을 통하여 다양한 게임을 즐기기도 한다. 인생은 게임인가? 혹자는 인생을 일장춘몽이라 하기도 하고 도박이라 하기도 하고 연극이라 하기도 한다. 꿈과 같고 도박과 같고 연극과 같은 것이 인생이라면 이러한 모든 것들은 하나의 게임과 같다. 게임 속에는 주객이 함께한다. 게임은 현실이 아니면서 동시에 현실이다. 게임 속을 넘나들며 주인공이 되고 객이 되기도 한다. 현실 속에서 상상의 세계를 보고 상상의 세계 속에서 현실을 체험한다.

79. Life starts as a competition and ends in amusement. The struggle for existence, putting superiority above inferiority, is essential in the course of evolution, and it is an undeniable fact that the fittest survives. On the other hand, amusement is another hope in life. Amusement overcomes strains rising endlessly from competition. People cannot live only in ceaseless tension, so they must enjoy amusement in order to relieve stress in every moment. Amusement is simultaneous with competition, like two sides of a coin. A competition results in bloodshed, stopping a heartbeat, putting superiority above inferiority, and judging life or death. All affairs—from wars breaking out ceaselessly across all ages and countries, to all kinds of sports and games—are based on competition. An audience is wildly exited at a game of death, spilling blood—from the contest of swordsmen during the Roman period to the bullfights of today—and they feel themselves alive with the thrill. People enjoy several kinds of games to experience tension and relaxation as well as competition and amusement simultaneously. They also enjoy not only sports contests but also several games through cyberspace. Is life a game? People say that life is a dream, gambling, or a play. If life is to be like a dream, gambling, or a play, each of them is the same as a game. There are hosts and guests together in a game. Though a game is not reality, it is a virtual reality simultaneously. While having a game, sometimes people become heroes, and sometimes they become extras. People see an imaginary world in reality, and they experience the realities of life in their imaginary world.

80. 울창한 숲에 새들이 모여들고 단비가 생명을 적셔 주듯이 사람의 심성도 그와 같이 넉넉하면 그것이 곧 즐거운 삶이다.

81. 조짐이 있을 때 주의해라. 그것은 자연이 주는 경고다. 이를 무시하고 방심하면 여지없이 탈 난다. 그러니 절제하면서 즐겨라. 절제 없이 즐기면 국가건 가정이건 인생이건 거덜 나기 십상이다.

82. 삶은 어둠 속에서 빛을 쫓는 외줄타기와 같다. 그래서 사람들은 항상 긴장된 삶 속에서 마음의 위안을 찾으려고 무엇인가 몰입하게 되는데 일반적으로 찾는 것이 돈, 섹스, 마약, 알코올 등이다. 다른 한편 창조적 또는 파괴적인 행위를 통해 삶을 추구하는 것으로 예술, 종교, 전쟁 등이 있다. 인간은 명상이나 자기성찰을 통해 잠시 집착에서 해방될 수는 있지만 일상으로 돌아오면 다시 무엇인가에 집착하고 있는 자신을 발견하게 된다. 삶이 빛을 추구하는 한 외줄타기 긴장은 계속될 것이며 숨 막히는 긴장을 극복하기 위해 그 무엇인가에 집착하려는 유혹에서 벗어날 수 없다. 유혹은 지속적인 것이어서 한번 깨우쳤다고 되는 것이 아니다. 지속적으로 매 순간 깨어있는 정신만이 집착으로부터 오는 유혹을 다스릴 수 있다.

80. Like how birds gather in the dense forest and a welcome rain wets lives, if the human mind is plentiful like that, it would be a pleasant life.

81. Be careful when there is a sign. That is an advance warning that nature gives. If you are not careful and disregard that, there is no doubt that you will land yourself in trouble. So enjoy in moderation. It is easy to collapse if you enjoy without moderation, whether as a nation, as a family, or in life.

82. Life is the same as walking along a suspended rope while following a light in the darkness. Therefore people cannot help but be addicted to things like money, sex, drugs, and alcohol to find comfort amid the tension of life. On the other hand, there is art, religion, war, etc., to pursue life through creative or destructive acts. People can be temporarily free from any attachment by means of meditation or introspection, but they find themselves addicted to something again after coming back to daily life. The tension from walking along a suspended rope will continue as long as life pursues light, so we cannot be free from temptations, being addicted to something to overcome this oppressive tension. It is also not enough to realize only once because temptations rise continuously. Only a mind awake in every moment can control a temptation caused by an attachment.

83. 삶에는 유혹이 있고 절제가 있다. 유혹은 살아 숨 쉬는 매 순간 일어나고 절제는 그런 유혹을 극복할 때마다 이뤄진다. 우리가 유혹 속에서 살고 있는지 절제 속에서 살고 있는지 구분하는 것도 쉽지 않다. 유혹과 절제는 매 순간마다 동시적으로 일어나기 때문이다. 삶은 미래에 있는가? 지금에 있는가? 아니면 과거에 있는가? 이 또한 규정하기가 쉽지 않다. 삶은 과거로부터 지금을 통해 미래로 이어지기 때문이다. 지금은 항상 유혹적으로 다가오고 그때마다 과거를 경험 삼아 미래를 기약하는 것이 절제다. 우리는 유혹 속에 살면서 절제를 추구한다. 유혹과 절제는 상반되면서 상보적이다. 유혹과 절제는 악마와 천사가 동시에 만들어내는 희로애락과 같다. 지금이 우선인가? 미래가 우선인가? 사람마다 가치관에 따라 차이가 있으나 지금을 희생할 수도 없고 미래를 포기할 수도 없는 것이 우리의 삶이다. 우리는 항상 지금 속에 살고 있기 때문에 지금은 물론이고 미래도 지금에 기초하고 있다. 우리는 시간 차이로 과거 지금 미래를 구분하고 있지만 삶은 하나로 연결되어 있다. 엄밀히 말하면 수백분의 일초도 지금이라는 것은 사실상 없다. 시간의 개념으로 보면 과거와 미래만 있을 뿐 지금은 없다. 그러나 우리는 항상 지금 속에서 살고 있다. 그러기에 우리는 시간을 넘어서 과거와 미래를 넘어서 항상 지금 속에서 영원한 지금을 살고 있는 것이다. 우리는 영원한 지금을 살면서 유혹 속에서 절제를 배우고 절제 속에서 유혹을 즐긴다. 유혹이 있기에 인생은 매혹적이고 절제가 있기에 인생은 더욱 매혹적이다.

83. There are many temptations and moderations in life. Temptations rise every second of breathing, and moderation is achieved whenever a temptation is overcome. It is not easy to distinguish whether we live in temptation or moderation because both rise every second simultaneously. Is there a life in the future, in the present, or in the past? Also it is not easy to clarify that because life is connected to the future from the past via the present. The present always approaches temptingly. Every moment, there is moderation to consider the future according to experiences in the past. We pursue moderation while living in temptation. Temptation and moderation are not only contrary but also complementary to each other. Temptation and moderation are the same as pleasure and sorrow, made by the devil and an angel simultaneously. Which one has priority, the present or the future? It depends on each person's values, but it is our life, not to sacrifice the present and not to abandon the future. The future as well as the present is based on the present because we are always living in the present. Life is connected wholly even if we distinguish the past, the present, and the future according to their time difference. In a strict sense of the word, there is no present actually, even if it is only one-tenth of a second. In view of time, there is no present, only the past and the future. Nevertheless, we are always living in the present. That is why we are living not only in the present but also in the everlasting present by transcending time, including the past and the future. We, living in the everlasting present, learn moderation among temptations and enjoy temptation among moderations. Life is attractive due to temptation, and it is more attractive due to moderation.

84. 섹스는 아이를 낳기 위한 원초적인 목적과 함께 여러 가지 부가적인 의미를 지니고 있다. 원시시대 이래 부족이 점차 발달하면서 원시인들은 아무하고나 무작위로 섹스를 하다가 서로 죽고 죽이기도 하는 다부다처보다는 일부일처가 사회질서를 유지하는 데 편리함을 깨닫게 되었다. 이에 따라 일부일처를 기반으로 혈통을 지키려는 연대의식이 가족단위로 발전하였고 성기를 외부에 노출시키지 않도록 하는 도덕과 법을 만들어서 일부일처 사회를 보다 확고히 확립하였다. 그로 인하여 성을 은밀한 것으로 강조하는 관습이 생기게 되어 섹스는 점차 과대 포장되었고 본래의 목적과 달리 은밀한 쾌락으로 발전하거나 게임으로 변질되어 거리 곳곳에 사랑 없는 섹스가 상품으로 거래되는 현상까지 생기게 되었다. 사람들은 시각 청각 후각 촉각에 미각까지 더하여 오감으로 섹스를 추구하다 보니 쾌락의 도가 지나쳐 요절하기도 한다. 그런데도 미련한 짓을 미련한 줄 알면서도 하는 것이 섹스다. 섹스의 정도는 사람마다 체력이나 취향에 따라 다르므로 이래라저래라 할 바가 아니다. 스스로 알아서 할 일이지만 은밀한 것도 과대 포장할 것도 아니므로 과도한 집착에서 벗어나 일상생활과 조화롭게 할 일이다. 두 개의 몸이 하나 되는 것이 섹스이고 두 개의 마음이 하나 되는 것이 사랑이니 섹스가 사랑과 함께 하면 이보다 더한 축복이 없을 것이다.

84. Sex has so many kinds of additional meaning together with the original purpose of getting pregnant. While a tribe developed step by step from a primitive community, primitive men knew that monogamy is more convenient to keep the social order compared to either polygamy or polyandry—which results to killing or being killed due to random sex. As a result of monogamy, a sense of solidarity developed, and a lineage succeeded from the family unit, and they firmly set up a monogamous society by establishing morals and laws against exposing genitalia. Therefore sex was excessively pulled up, developed as a secret pleasure, or deteriorated as a game, different from the original purpose, step by step, because a custom emphasizing sex to be a secret arose. So the phenomenon of transacting loveless sex like commodities on the streets occurred. Sometimes people meet a premature death from excessive pleasure while they have sex—with such five senses as vision, hearing, smell, touch, plus taste. Nevertheless, it is stupid of them to have sex like that though they know the consequences. There is no standard for sex because the degree of sex is dependent on individual stamina or taste. Sex should be done with individual intention, but it should harmonize with daily life without too much attachment, because it is neither a secret nor a thing pulled up excessively. Since it is through sex that two bodies become one, and it is love that makes two hearts become one, it will be more blessed if sex can be together with love.

85. 아비 잘 만난 자는 돈 걱정 없어 여유 있게 즐기고 아비 잘못 만난 자는 쌈짓돈 절약해야 즐길 수 있는데 그 와중에도 아무것이나 즐기며 사는 자가 있는가 하면 한 가지도 못 즐기고 일찍 세상 하직하는 자도 있다. 그런데 더 이상한 것은 즐기지도 못하고 세상 하직하지도 못하고 그렇고 그렇게 사는 자들이 너무 많다는 것이다.

86. 특별한 재능이 없는 평범한 사람들이 살아생전에 할 수 있는 것은 아이를 낳아 키우는 것과 나무를 심어 가꾸는 것이다. 나무는 공기를 맑게 하고 시원한 그늘을 제공하고 맛있는 과일과 아름다운 꽃을 선사하니 이보다 더 귀한 것이 이 세상에 무엇이 있겠는가?

87. 서 있으면 앉고 싶고 앉으면 눕고 싶어지는 것이 육체의 나태함이다. 게으르기 시작하면 한없이 게을러진다. 자기조절하기가 쉽지 않은 것이다. 식욕을 자제하고 운동을 꾸준히 해야 몸의 균형을 유지할 수 있는데 작심삼일 만에 포기하니 비만을 탈출하기도 쉽지 않다. 이 모든 것은 삶의 문제이며 극기의 문제다. 살아있다는 자체가 긴장이며 극기를 필요로 한다. 나태하고 게을러서는 생존할 수 없다. 나뭇가지에 앉은 새를 보아라. 한시라도 가만히 있지 않고 바삐 움직인다. 적으로부터 자신을 보호하고 먹이를 찾아 끊임없이 두리번거린다. 작은 새도 이러하거늘 하물며 인간으로 생존하려면 우선 스스로를 다스리는 의지가 필요하다. 자기 자신조차 다스리지 못하는 자가 어찌 주위와의 경쟁에서 살아남을 수 있겠는가?

85. A wellborn guy lives in affluent circumstances, while a lowborn guy lives from hand to mouth, and among them, there are not only guys enjoying anything but also guys dying early without enjoying even one thing, and what is more surprising, there are so many guys living as so-and-so without enjoying anything or dying early.

86. What common people without talent can do while alive is to bring up children and to plant trees. Since trees make air fresh, provide cool shade, and present delicious fruits and beautiful flowers, what in the world is more precious than trees?

87. It is laziness of the body to want to sit down when you stand and to want to lie down when you sit. You become lazy once you begin to be lazy. It is really not easy to control yourself. You can keep in shape through exercising daily and restraining your appetite continuously, but it is also not easy for you to overcome obesity because you cannot keep your resolutions longer than a week. All of these things are not only a survival problem but also a self-control problem. Life itself is filled with tension and needs self-control. You cannot survive with negligence and laziness. Look at a bird sitting on the branch of a tree. It is never at a standstill and moves busily to protect itself from hazard and to find a prey. Since even a tiny bird is like that, you as a human being needs the will to control yourself at first. If you cannot control even yourself, how can you survive in competition with your surroundings?

88. 사람들은 태어나서 나이가 들어감에 따라 자신도 모르는 사이에 행복한 모습을 잃어간다. 사람들은 살아가면서 점차 욕심이 많아지고 반복된 하루가 지루하고 사는 것이 우울해지고 점차 웃음마저 잃어간다. 이런 것들은 행복을 잃어가는 불행의 시작이자 늙음의 상징이다. 이를 극복하기 위하여 사람들은 여러 가지 방법을 동원한다. 마약, 음주, 도박, 섹스, 모험 등과 같은 환락에 빠져 행복을 추구하기도 하고, 주의, 신념, 종교 등과 같은 정신활동으로 행복을 추구하기도 한다. 그러나 환락은 일시적인 감각활동으로 그 순간이 지나면 사라져버린다. 주의, 신념, 종교 등은 의지로 얻을 수 있지만 인위적인 것으로 어느 시기에 의지가 바뀌면 변화될 수 있는 것들이다. 지속적이고 자연스러운 행복은 아니다. 그렇다면 진정한 행복은 어디에 있는가? 행복은 평상심에 있다. 행복은 천진무구한 웃음에서 찾을 수 있다. 아이들은 많은 것을 요구하지 않고 단순하다. 아이에게는 매일매일의 삶이 신비스럽고 새롭다. 아이는 주위의 모든 것을 있는 그대로 받아들인다. 아이의 생각은 자유롭다. 아이에게는 사는 것이 곧 즐거움이다. 아이의 웃음에는 행복이 깃들어 있다. 행복은 아이의 참모습에 있다. 아이의 참모습은 나이에 상관하지 않는다. 나이가 행복의 기준이 되지 않는다. 아이 같은 노인이 있는가 하면 노인 같은 아이가 있기 때문이다. 진정으로 행복한 사람은 웃음을 잃지 않고 언제나 가슴속에 평상심을 가꾸며 산다.

88. People are losing a happy mind unconsciously while becoming old. They are greedy for life and feel boredom for a routine day, so they sink into melancholy and lose a smile step by step. These are the start of unhappiness and the symbol of old age. They mobilize so many methods to overcome these. One person pursues happiness by indulging in pleasures, like drugs, alcohol, gambling, sex, or adventure. Another pursues happiness by indulging in mental activities, like a principle, a belief, a religion, etc. But the pleasure disappears as soon as the memory of the activity gradually fades away. A principle, belief, or religion can be gotten by willpower, but someday these can be changed according to a changeable mind because these are artificial. These kinds of happiness are neither sustainable nor natural. If so, where is happiness truly? Happiness is in the composed mind. Happiness can be found in a simple and innocent smile. A child does not require much, and he is simple. Life in every day is new and mysterious to children. They accept everything from their surroundings as is. Children's thoughts are free. Life is a pleasure to children. There is happiness in children's smiles. Happiness is a real feature of children. The real feature of child is not related to age. Age is not the standard of happiness because there is not only an old man like a child but also a child like an old man. A really happy person does not forget to smile and always lives with presence of mind.

89. 인생은 노력인가 즐거움인가? 생존하려면 노력해야 하고 음미하려면 즐겨야 하지만 그렇다고 어느 하나만을 선택해야 하는 것도 아니다. 때로는 노력도 하고 즐기기도 하는 것이 인생이다. 그러다가 늙고 병들면 돌아가는 것이 인생이지만 지금 건강하게 살아있다는 것만으로도 행복한 것이니 마음이 행복하면 그것이 곧 즐거움이다.

90. 남태평양에 인접한 이곳, 해안가는 오천 년이 넘는 세월을 지나는 동안 지각변동에 의해 바다였던 곳이 융기되어 평야를 이루고 있다. 그런 까닭에 이 지역 농가에서 밭을 갈거나 건물을 지으려고 땅을 파다 보면 석회암이 출토되기도 하는데 그중에 조개화석이 함께 발굴되기도 한다. 큰 것은 100킬로가 넘는 조개화석도 있는데 오랜 세월 지각변동에 의해 조개가 진주로 변한 것들이다. 진주가 된 조개화석은 자연이 이곳 주민들에게 베풀어준 천혜다. 저마다 다양한 모습으로 빚어진 조개화석의 물결무늬 형상을 물끄러미 바라보고 있으면 수천 년 세월의 풍랑과 함께 일렁이는 남태평양 파도의 신선한 바다 냄새를 머금은 듯이 우윳빛 도는 반투명한 빛깔이 매혹적이다. 지금은 화석이 되었지만 오랜 세월 지나온 생명의 흔적을 고스란히 그대로 간직하고 있다.

89. Is life an endeavor or a pleasure? People have to endeavor to survive and pleasure in something to appreciate, but it is not mandatory to choose one of them. Life is not only to endeavor but also to pleasure from time to time, then to pass away if one is old or ill, but it is pleasurable if a mind feels happiness, because it is already happy to be alive and healthy now.

90. Since this area changed from being underwater by uplifting strata for more than five thousand years, plains have been formed along the seaside adjoining the South Pacific. Therefore limestone is excavated while farmers cultivate the field or workers dig the ground to put up a building, during which time fossil seashells are often excavated together with limestone in this area. There is a big fossil seashell weighing more than one hundred kilograms among them, and it consists of a pearl changed from shells by crustal movements for a long time. The fossil seashell becoming a pearl is a gift of nature given to the residents in this area. While gazing at the corrugated pattern of fossil seashells formed with various features, their milky, translucent color shows great charm, as if they have the fresh smell of sea rising from the wind and waves in the South Pacific for a few thousand years. Though they now have become fossils, they keep a trace of life just as they were.

91. 저녁 식사가 끝난 후 모두들 만족하며 즐거워한다. 그런데 뒤늦게 나온 아이스크림 때문에 아이들끼리 다툼이 벌어졌다. 덤 때문에 다투는 모습을 보니 인간의 삶을 보는 듯하다.

92. 무미건조한 삶을 새롭게 변화시킬 수 있는 인생의 불은 무엇인가? 창조를 위해서는 정열이 필요하고 정열은 일상의 즐거움에서 시작된다. 어차피 인생에서 가져갈 것이라곤 아무것도 없다. 그러니 무엇을 주저하고 무엇을 애달파할 것인가? 근심걱정은 골수를 상하게 할 뿐 인생에 도움이 안 된다. 즐겁게 사는 것이 현명한 인생이요 즐겁게 죽는 것이 성숙한 인생이다. 흙이 불을 통해서 도자기로 새롭게 태어나듯이 인생도 즐거움을 통하여 새롭게 태어난다. 마음이 비어야 자유롭고 자유로움이 있어야 신선함이 있으며 신선함 속에 즐거움이 있다. 인생이 달궈지려면 시련이 따르게 마련이고 시련을 즐길 수 있는 정열이 필요하다. 지칠 줄 모르고 타오르는 정열은 어떤 시련 속에서도 삶을 북돋아 준다. 외모로 허세를 부리는 폼생폼사(FORM生FORM死)가 아니라 즐겁게 살고 즐겁게 죽을 줄 아는 펀생펀사(FUN生FUN死)가 멋진 삶이다.

91. Everybody is satisfied and pleasured after having dinner, but a quarrel occurs between children due to ice cream served late. It looks like our life, how they quarrel for addition.

92. What is the passion of life, to renew a tasteless life? Passion is necessary for creation, and passion starts with fun in everyday life. There is really nothing to take from life after all. Therefore what makes you hesitate, and what will you feel sorry for? To worry is not useful to your life. It only hurts your marrow. To live pleasantly is to have a wise life, and to die pleasantly is to have a mature life. As clay is newborn as pottery by fire, life is newborn by fun. There is freedom with a pure mind, there is freshness with this freedom, and there is fun with such freshness. There are trials while heating up life, and passion is necessary to enjoy such trials. Tireless passion stimulates life among so many trials. It is really a lovely life, not to bluff with external features, but to live and die pleasantly.

93. 형상을 지닌 것 중에서 가장 소중한 것은 무엇인가? 육체는 바위나 쇠보다 연약하고 수명도 짧지만 형상을 가진 것 중에 으뜸이다. 건강한 육체 없이는 세상 어떠한 만물과도 조우할 수 없다. 사람은 건강한 육체와 함께 그 모습을 형상화한다. 형상을 지닌 것 중에서 건강한 육체에 버금가는 것은 무엇인가? 수많은 인연 가운데 좋은 친구를 만나기란 쉽지 않지만 좋은 친구는 건강한 육체만큼이나 소중하다. 천만금 재화가 있다 하여도 건강한 육체와 좋은 친구가 없다면 일상은 활기차지 못하다. 사람들이 부를 추구하는 목적은 건강한 육체와 좋은 친구를 얻고자 함에 있다. 그러나 재화가 곧 건강한 육체와 좋은 친구 그 자체는 아니다. 이미 건강한 육체가 있다면 세상 부의 반절을 얻은 것이요, 좋은 친구까지 얻었다면 세상 부의 전부를 얻은 것이다. 호화로운 저택에 병든 노인이 홀로 살고 있다고 상상해보라. 얼마나 쓸쓸하고 외로운가. 호화로운 저택이나 금은보화도 건강한 육체와 좋은 친구가 없다면 아무런 쓸모가 없다. 동서고금을 막론하고 사람들이 부를 추구하고 있지만 부의 근본적인 가치는 그 자체에 있는 것이 아니다. 건강한 육체와 좋은 친구가 한데 어우러져 춤사위를 펼친다면 이미 만물 가운데 으뜸을 이룬 것이다.

93. Which is most precious among all creations having shape? Though a body is milder and has a shorter life than rock and steel, this body is at the top of all creations having shape. It is impossible without a healthy body to encounter any creation in the world. A human being takes shape together with a healthy body. What is most precious, next to a healthy body, among all creations having shape? It is not easy to become acquainted with a good friend in numerous fate, but a good friend is as precious as a healthy body. Even if there is a tremendous amount of fortune, daily life is not full of vigor without a healthy body and good friends. The reason why people pursue fortune is to get a healthy body as well as good friends. However, fortune itself is not a healthy body and good friends. If you have a healthy body, it means that you already have half a fortune in the world, and if you have good friends, it means that you already get all fortune in the world. Imagine that a sick old man lives alone in a lordly mansion. How lonely and helpless he is! Even a lordly mansion and treasures are useless without a healthy body and good friends. Though most people across the ages and in all countries of the world lust for fortune, the fundamental value of fortune is not in itself. If people dance, harmonizing with a healthy body and good friends, that is already at the top of all things in the universe.

3. 삶의 현장

94. 지구상에는 아시아 같은 대륙이 있는가 하면 겨우 등대 하나 서 있는 작은 섬들도 있다. 그중에서 이곳은 남태평양에 위치하는 중간 크기의 섬이다. 16세기 중엽 스페인이 점령한 후 장기간에 걸쳐 통치하다가 19세기 말 미국이 점령하여 통치하였고 2차 세계대전 때 일본이 잠시 점령하여 외세의 영향을 많이 받은 곳이다. 혈통은 스페인 혼혈이 많고 사회 정치구조는 미국식으로 되어 있다. 이곳은 미스 유니버스를 배출한 곳으로 혼혈 덕택에 미인도 많고 반면에 뚱보도 많다. 개발도상국이 대부분 그렇듯이 이곳도 빈부격차가 심하여 서민들의 월급이 1만 5천페소(미화 300불)수준에 불과한 데 반하여 고급 레스토랑 고급 외제차가 즐비하다. 가톨릭 국가라 낙태하지 않고 아이를 낳아 가족 수가 많고 성이 개방되어 미혼모도 많다. 가족 중심으로 생활하며 4대가 한집에 사는 경우도 있다. 여성의 사회진출도가 높은 편으로 남아선호사상도 없다. 데릴사위를 하여 딸과 한집에서 사는 경우가 많다. 오랜 식민지로 지내온 탓인지 새로운 변화를 추구하기보다는 현재의 불편을 그대로 안고 산다.

그래서 국회의원이든 시장이든 3선 당선되는 것이 보통이고 대물림하여 당선되는 경우도 많다. 대다수의 시민들은 정치인이나 공무원들이 청렴하지 않다고 생각하면서도 그게 그거라는 생각에 별다른 변화를 기대하지도 않는다. 지리적으로 남서쪽에 이슬람 국가인 말레이시아, 인도네시아가 위치하고 있어서 무슬림 인구가 전체 인구의 10~20% 정도 된다. 무슬림 자치구역이 따로 구분되어 있고 기독교도와 이슬람교도가 공존한다. 경제 상권은 중국과 일본 자본이 대부분을 차지하고 한국기업도 일부 진출하고 있다. 도로는 해안선을 따라 순환도로

3. The Scene of Life

94. There is not only the continent of Asia but also an islet where only a lighthouse stands on the earth. Among them, this area is a medium-sized island located in the South Pacific. In the middle of the sixteenth century, this territory was occupied by the Spanish. Then it was colonized for a long time until the United States took over this territory at the end of the nineteenth century. The Japanese also occupied this territory during World War II. Therefore, there is a lot of lineage mixed with Spanish, and the structure of their society and politics is American style. Miss Universe was produced in this district, and there are so many fatties as well as beautiful women due to their mixed blood. There is a big difference between the wealthy and those in poverty, like in all developing countries. There are so many high-class restaurants and foreign cars while a common person's salary is only PhP 15,000 (USD 300) per month. There is a lot of large families because induced abortion is not allowed by the Catholic religion. Also there are so many unmarried mothers because of open sexual relations. Their living style is family-oriented, and sometimes four generations live together in the same house. The ratio of women joining society is high, and there is no preference for sons. There are a lot of cases where parents live together with their married daughter by adopting the son-in-law into their family. They live in inconvenience as is, without pursuing social changes due to the influence of colonizers for a long time.

So politicians like congressmen or mayors are normally elected three times, and sometimes these positions are passed on from parent to child. Most citizens think that politicians and government officials are not cleanhanded, but they don't expect them to be

가 있고 내륙을 횡단하는 도로가 있는데 고속도로라고 하지만 2차선 도로로 평균시속 60km 수준에 불과하다. 현재 도로 확장공사를 곳곳에서 추진하고 있어 향후에는 도로사정이 개선될 전망이다. 중산층 이상 되어야 자가용을 보유할 형편이 되고 서민들은 소형 트럭을 개조해서 만든 짚니를 시내버스처럼 이용한다. 대중교통으로 택시도 있지만 대부분 짚니를 이용한다. 이곳 일용직 노동자의 평균일당이 400페소(미화 8불)임을 감안하면 택시를 타고 다니기가 쉽지 않다. 그래도 서민들이 살아갈 수 있는 것은 먹음직한 빵을 5페소에 살 수 있기 때문이다. 빵 가게에 따라서 모양만 다른데 50페소 하는 빵도 있으니 돈의 가치란 사는 방식에 따라 천차만별이다.

changed fairly because there is little to choose from. There are Islamic countries like Malaysia and Indonesia in the west-southern part geographically, so about 10 to 20 percent of their total population is Muslim. There is a Muslim autonomous region set up separately, and Christians and Muslims coexist. The commercial power in this area consists of Chinese and Japanese capitals, and some Korean capital is also invested here. Highways pass along the coast, and inland, but the average speed in the highway is about sixty kilometers per hour due to heavy traffic and having only a two-lane road. The situation of their highway will be improved in the near future because a lot of highways are under construction to expand lanes. A family richer than middle class is able to own a car privately, while common people use jeepneys remodeled from small trucks as public transportation. There are taxis, but most people use the jeepneys. Considering that the real wage of a laborer is only PhP 400 (USD 8) per day, it is not easy for common people to use taxis. Nevertheless, it is possible for them to live even with low wages because they can buy delicious bread for only PhP 5. The value of money is really different according to lifestyles, because a similar size of bread is sold at PhP 50 in the different bakery.

95. 한낮 온도가 평균 35℃를 오르내리는 날씨에 조금만 움직여도 땀이 난다. 그래서인지 사람들이 느리게 움직인다. 에너지 소비량이 많은 성장기 아이들이나 건설현장의 육체노동자들을 제외하면 대부분 사람들의 활동량이 작고 비만도가 높은 편이다. 국민소득이 적지만 상대적으로 식비가 저렴하고 아열대지방이라 먹거리가 많아서 거리를 배회하는 극빈층을 제외하고 굶주리는 사람들은 없다. 더운 지방이라 땀도 많이 나고 국민소득이 낮아서 사람들이 마른 체격일 거라는 예상과 달리 서양 사람들의 비만지수와 비슷할 정도로 이곳 사람들의 비만도가 높다. 기후나 국민소득과 상관없이 비만은 세계가 직면하고 있는 문젯거리다. 현재 세계인구가 80억을 넘었는데도 불구하고 비만 인구가 많다는 것은 지구용량이 아직은 넉넉하다는 것인데 언젠가는 세계인구가 100억을 넘어 지구용량이 한계에 다다를 것이다. 비만은 인류의 적이자 자연의 순리에 반하는 것이다. 탐식하지 말고 적절히 먹을 것이며 부지런한 생활습관으로 하루 활동량을 건강하게 유지해야 한다.

96. 인허가 서류를 신청하는데 관공서의 행정이 턱없이 느리다. 책임자는 자리를 비우고 언제 올지 모른단다. 그런데 더욱 이상한 것은 대기 중인 사람들이 불평 한마디 없이 마냥 기다린다는 것이다. 불평해봤자 오히려 손해라는 것을 알고 있는 이들은 관습에 젖어 깊은 불감증 속에서 살고 있다.

95. There is really horrible sweat even with little action because the weather is so hot, hovering around 35°C. Therefore people are active but in a slow manner. Almost all people, except growing children and laborers in the construction field, are obese due to little activity. Even if their income is low, they are not starving, except for the indigenous people wandering the streets, because food expenses are relatively cheap, and there are so many kinds of food due to their subtropical region. Contrary to expectations that they will have slim figures because of profuse sweating due to the hot weather in subtropical regions and their incomes are low, the obesity index of this region is so high as to be comparable to that of western countries. Regardless of climate and income, obesity is a critical problem with which the world is confronted. There are so many obese people in the world though the population of the world is already over eight billion. It means that the global capacity is still enough to feed them, but the global capacity will reach its limit when the population of the world is over ten billion. Obesity is an enemy of mankind as well as an activity against the rationality of nature. People should not eat voraciously and keep a healthy activity, and be in the habit of exercising daily.

96. The conduct of government offices is too slow to handle office work, like permissions. A petty official says that she doesn't know when a director in charge will come back into the office after he went out, and what is stranger, people stand by endlessly without any complaint. People live insensitively while immersed deeply in the customs of society because they know that a complaint brings loss rather than gain.

97. 이곳은 계절의 변화 없이 연중 내내 무더운 탓에 매사가 느리다. 국내선 비행기를 수십 차례 타보지만 정시에 출발한 적은 거의 없고 30분 늦는 것은 기본이다. 비즈니스맨들과 약속시간을 정해 놓고 제 시간에 만난 적도 드물다. 차량수리를 의뢰하거나 물건을 주문하면 며칠 늦는 것은 보통이고 심지어 몇 달 늦는 경우도 있다. 비자를 신청하거나 등기이전을 하려면 거의 3개월 이상 일 년 가까이 걸린다. 사람들의 시간 개념은 시계에서 극명하게 나타난다. 학생들이 차고 다니는 손목시계건 이발소 벽시계건 간에 제대로 맞지 않고 보통 5~10분 정도는 틀린다. 시간을 꼭 맞춰야 한다는 개념이 매우 희박하다. 이런 생활습관으로 볼 때 꼭 필요한 경우를 제외하고는 결코 서두르지 않는 것이 열대지방의 생존방식이다. 불필요하게 서둘렀다가는 더위에 열 받아 제풀에 지친다. 마냥 기다릴 줄 알아야 살아남는다.

98. 온대지방 사람들은 사계절이 분명하여 여름에 부지런히 곡식을 키워서 겨울을 대비하지만 아열대지방에서는 계절에 대한 준비가 따로 필요 없다. 그래서인지 사람들은 무슨 일이든 닥쳐서야 그제야 움직이지 사전에 대비하는 준비성이 부족하다. 기후의 영향이 문화습관의 차이마저 가져온다.

97. Every affair is late due to the hot weather throughout the year, without a change of season. Domestic airlines are always delayed, and they depart more than thirty minutes late—not departing just on time ever. Meeting on time is seldom achieved after making an appointment for business. It normally takes a few days, or sometimes a few months, if a car repair or something is ordered. It takes more than three months or almost one year to extend a visa or register a lot. Their concept of time is clearly shown on their watches. Almost all students' watches and barbers' clocks are not on time. They differ more than five up to ten minutes. They don't care about keeping time. Considering this kind of habit, it is the lifestyle of subtropical regions not to hurry except in imperative cases. People would be exhausted from overheating under the hot weather if they rush their job unnecessarily. People can survive by waiting patiently.

98. People in temperate regions prepare for the winter by growing agricultural products during the summer because the four seasons are clear, but people in subtropical regions don't make preparations for the seasonal change separately. That's why people don't go into action until something happens, and they lack preparations in advance. An influence of climate brings a difference in cultural habits.

99. 트럭이 진흙탕 도로에서 미끄러지자 지나가던 짚차가 자발적으로 나서서 견인해주어 곤경을 면한 적이 있는데 이는 개인마다 타고난 심성이 착함을 보여주는 예다. 그러나 관공서나 대형 상점과 같은 조직체에서 만나는 대부분의 공무원이나 점원은 이미 짚차의 주인 같은 너그러운 마음을 가진 개인이 아니다. 자기 생존에 열중하여 다른 사람의 불편을 생각할 여유가 없다. 개인과 기관이 모두 건재하려면 시민들에 의한 공동체 모임과 사회감시망이 활발히 가동되어야 한다.

100. 소화기관과 호흡기관이 부실하면 먹고 숨쉬기가 여의치 않으니 건강할 수 없다. 달고 짜고 매운 자극적인 음식은 위장에 손상을 주니 삼가할 일이다. 나태한 것도 문제지만 과로하는 것도 금물이다. 더위에 과로하여 땀을 많이 흘리면 체온조절이 어려워지고 기침을 동반하게 된다.

101. 이곳에는 계절의 변화가 없는 반면 날씨가 변화무쌍하다. 한낮의 뜨거운 태양인가 하면 어느덧 먹구름이 몰려오고 비를 뿌린다. 세찬 바람이 몰아치면 무더위는 서늘한 날씨로 바뀌고 더위에 지친 심신을 추스르게 한다. 계절의 변화는 없지만 수시로 바뀌는 날씨 덕택에 사람들은 지루한 삶에 신선한 활력을 얻고 나무들은 태양과 비바람의 리듬 속에서 싱싱하게 성장한다. 이곳 날씨는 청명한 날은 35℃, 구름 낀 날은 32℃인데 밤새 비바람이라도 몰아치면 25℃까지 내려가서 서늘하다 못해 춥기까지하다. 온대지방에서는 25℃면 쾌적한 느낌인데 온대지방과 아열대지방 간에 느끼는 체감온도가 분명 다르다.

99. When a truck was stranded in a muddy road, a passerby towed the truck by his jeep free of charge; that serves as an example of a good personality individually. However, most officials or clerks in organizations, like a public office or a big store, are already not individuals with big hearts like the owner of the jeep. They are so absorbed in their survival that they cannot afford to care about the inconveniences of other people. Community groups and surveillance networks of society should be activated by citizens in order that both individuals and organizations are well.

100. You cannot be healthy if your digestive and respiratory organs are weak, because eating and breathing become difficult. You should refrain from stimulating food—like those that are sweet, salty, and hot—because they are harmful to the digestive organs. Overworking as well as being lazy should be forbidden. If you sweat heavily from overwork in hot weather, you suffer from cough because it is not easy to regulate body temperature.

101. There is no changing between the four seasons in this region, but the weather is unstable, so a sunny sky is suddenly covered with dark clouds. Then it rains heavily after while none is aware of it. The hot weather becomes cool after rainy winds blow hard, so mental and physical exhaustion due to the heat is overcome. A boring life gets fresh energy, and all trees grow well with the rhythm of the sun and windy rains, owing to the unstable weather, even though there is no change in the season. The temperature on a sunny day is 35°C, and a cloudy weather is at 32°C, but it is chilly rather than cool when the temperature suddenly falls to 25°C due to heavy rains all through the night. A weather of 25°C is agreeable in temperate regions, but feeling temperature in body between temperate and subtropical regions is certainly different.

102. 이곳은 3월부터 5월까지 강수량이 줄어드는 건기가 되어 무더운 날씨가 지속되다 보니 땀이 많이 나고 체온 조절에 이상이 생겨 기침환자가 많아진다. 사계절이 뚜렷한 온대지방에서는 환절기에 기침환자가 많아지는데 아열대지방은 환절기는 없지만 땀이 많이 나는 날씨에는 각별히 체온조절에 유의해야 한다. 아열대지방이라고 방심했다간 예상과 달리 기침으로 고생하게 된다. 아열대지방은 일교차가 심하여 새벽녘에는 춥기까지하다. 일교차가 심할 때는 특히 감기를 조심해야 한다. 열악한 환경에서 스트레스를 받거나 과로하게 되면 면역체계가 저하되어 병에 걸리기 십상이다. 아열대지방이라 추위 걱정은 안할 것으로 생각하지만 기침은 어디에나 있다. 생존하는 데 며칠 굶어도 살 수 있지만 몇 분간 숨을 못 쉬면 죽는다. 노환으로 죽는 경우 대부분 폐렴증세가 사인의 직접원인이니 사는 동안 호흡기를 건강하게 해야 한다.

102. The dry season starts in March, and hot weather without rain continues until May. A lot of people suffer from cough because regulation of body temperature is unusual due to heavy sweating. There are so many afflicted with cough at the turn of seasons in temperate regions, but people should be careful about the regulation of their body temperature when they sweat heavily even though there is no turning of seasons in subtropical regions. If people are careless in subtropical regions, they will suffer from cough unexpectedly. It is even chilly at dawn because the diurnal range is severe in subtropical regions. Especially, people should be careful about a cold when the diurnal range is severe. If people get stressed or overworked in poor surroundings, they will be ill because their immune systems become weak. Though people think that they don't need to worry about cold in subtropical regions, they should be careful about cough. People can survive even if they don't eat for a few days, but they cannot survive if they don't breathe for a few minutes. It is essential to keep respiratory organs healthy because pneumonia is a common direct cause of death in old age.

103. 며칠간 무더위가 계속되더니 남태평양에서 끓어오른 열기가 남쪽 하늘에 먹구름을 몰고 오기 시작한다. 해 질 녘이 가까워지자 먹구름 사이로 천둥번개가 여러 차례 울부짖더니 마침내 장대비가 쏟아진다. 거센 바람을 동반한 폭우가 지붕 창문 가릴 것 없이 휘몰아친다. 그 바람에 한낮에 끓어오르던 더위는 서늘해지고 지친 나무들의 잎이 다시 무성해진다. 건기가 끝나가는 무렵이라 가뭄에 시달리던 수목들에겐 단비와도 같다. 폭우가 쏟아진 지 한 시간 만에 기온이 떨어지고 더위가 한풀 꺾였다. 오늘 저녁은 주위에 풀벌레소리 대신 개구리 울음소리가 우렁차게 들려온다. 비는 태양이 만들어내는 지구 자정활동 중에서 으뜸가는 진객이다. 태양과 비가 만들어내는 자연의 조화 속에서 모든 생명들이 위대함과 축복을 동시에 체험한다.

103. Since the hot weather continues for days, the heat rising up from the South Pacific Ocean starts to bring dark clouds in the southern sky. At last, it rains heavily with the approach of sunset. After then there is thunder together with a flash of lightning between dark clouds. A storm together with a torrential rain rages upon roofs and windows, so the heat rising up all day cools down, and wilted trees leaf out again. It is really a long-awaited rain for trees suffering from prolonged drought at the end of dry seasons. The temperature falls down, and the heat cools down within one hour after it rains heavily. Sonorous cries of frog instead of the chirping of crickets come into hearing from all around tonight. A rain is really a welcome guest that is the greatest one among the self-cleansing activities of the globe formed by the sun. All lives experience the greatness and the blessing simultaneously in harmony with nature, formed by the sun and the rain.

104. (시 3)

모두 다 지쳤구나.
한 템포 쉬어가자.
쉴 틈 없이 왔지만
아직 갈 길은 멀다.

죽기 전에
다다를 수 없을지도 모를
먼 곳을 향해
가고 있는지도 모른다.

내일이면
다다를 수 있는 것처럼
꿈을 꾸며
하루하루를 걷고 있다.

그러나 갈 길은 아직 멀다.
지나온 세월이
아득하듯이,

그러니 한 템포 쉬어가자.
어쩌면 쉬는 것이
걷고 있는 것인지도 몰라.

바쁜 사람들아
한 템포 쉬어가자.
쉬는 것이
걷고 있는 것인지도 몰라.

104. (Poem 3)
All of us are tired out.
Let's rest for a tempo.
Even if we went on without rest,
the way to go is still so far.

Before dying,
we might be going on
toward the place
where is too far to arrive.

By tomorrow,
while dreaming as we could arrive,
we are walking on day by day.

But the way to go is still so far.
As the passed time and tide
were so far away.

So, let's rest for a tempo.
Probably to rest;
that might be walking on.

Though it is a busy life,
let's rest for a tempo.
To rest;
that might be walking on.

105. 모닥불에 코코넛 껍질이 타고 있다. 코코넛 껍질 위로 뭔가 움직인다. 작은 벌레가 불길을 피해 앞뒤로 바삐 움직이지만 금방 사방이 불길에 휩싸여 퇴로가 없다. 위급한 순간 살아나갈 길은 오직 날아가는 길뿐이다. 그러나 불행히도 이 벌레에게는 날개가 없다.

106. 덤불 속에 잘못 들어갔다가 불개미에 쏘였다. 불과 두세 걸음 사이에 수십 마리가 발등에 기어 올라 사정없이 독침을 꽂은 것이다. 모기는 물리는 순간 따끔하다가 서서히 가렵기 시작하는데 불개미는 독침을 꽂는 순간 즉시 통증이 심하고 시간이 지나면서 통증이 사라진다. 불개미는 자신들의 영역방어에 반사적으로 작용하여 죽음을 무릅쓰고 침입자에게 혼신을 다해 독침을 꽂는다. 작은 미물이지만 군집된 다수의 힘은 인류보다 더 오랜 세월 동안 생존할 수 있게 한 원동력이다. 다수의 생존을 위해서라면 한 개체의 죽음에는 별다른 의미를 두지 않고 즉각적으로 반응하는 완벽한 연대의식이야말로 무적의 힘이다. 작아도 작은 것이 아니다. 사자무리보다 인간보다 더 강한 종족이라 할 만하다.

105. Coconut husk is burning on a bonfire. There is something moving on the coconut husk. There is no way to escape from the fire even though a little insect hurries forward and backward because its surroundings are enveloped in flames at once. A way to survive at the emergent moment is to flit, but the insect has no alae unfortunately.

106. People got stung by red ants as they approached bushes by mistake. A lot of ants stung people's feet ruthlessly while people took two or three steps forward. It has an itch, little by little, like a mosquito bites, but people feel a severe pain just when a red ant stings. After that, the pain is relieved step by step. Red ants act instinctively to protect their territory, so they sting invaders at the risk of their death. Even though they are minute forms of life, the power of a congregate group is the motive for surviving longer than the advent of human beings. They don't care about an individual's death for the congregate group, so their perfect sense of solidarity to react at once is indeed an invincible power. They are not such minute things as they seem. They deserve to be stronger than lions and humans.

107. 인근 코코넛 나무들 사이로 낮은 구릉을 이루며 초지가 조성되어 있는데 여러 종류의 동물들이 함께 산다. 말, 물소, 소, 돼지, 염소, 닭, 개, 고양이를 키우고 두꺼비, 뱀, 도마뱀, 새들이 자생한다. 이들의 생존방식은 단순하다. 생물 종에 상관없이 우호적이면 가깝게 지내고 적대적이면 경계하고 이해관계가 없으면 에너지를 절약하기 위해 무관심하다. 같은 종족이라 해도 적대적이면 경계하고 다른 종이라 해도 우호적이라 생각되면 가깝게 지낸다. 동양인, 서양인, 아프리카인, 아랍인, 동남아인이라는 민족이나 국적이 중요한 것이 아니고 나와 친구가 될 만한 사람인가 아닌가가 중요한 것이다. 지구상의 모든 생물들은 서로 도움이 될 수 있는 상대를 필요로 한다. 혼자의 경험보다 상대의 경험을 공유하는 것이 생존하고 진화하는 데 효율적이기 때문이다. 태초의 생물은 암수가 한 몸이었지만 진화과정에서 암수를 분리하여 서로 돕고 사는 것이 효율적임을 터득한 것이다.

108. 새가 나뭇가지에 앉아서 쉬지 않고 두리번거리는 것은 첫째, 적의 공격을 피하고 둘째, 먹이를 찾고 셋째, 짝을 찾기 위함이다.

109. 수고양이들끼리 싸운다. 고양이들끼리 치열하게 싸울 때 한집에서 살고 있는 개는 구경만 하고 아무 관심도 없다. 싸움은 끼리끼리 하는 것이지 격이 안 맞으면 싸울 일도 없다.

107. Several kinds of animals live together in a meadow consisting of a hill planted with coconut trees. People breed horses, buffalos, cows, pigs, goats, fowls, dogs, and cats. Toads, snakes, lizards, and birds grow wild in this area. Their strategy for survival is simple. Regardless of species, they become intimate if they are friendly with each other, they are on watch if they are hostile, and they are unconcerned about saving energy if they have no interest. Even though they are the same species, they are on watch for hostility. They become intimate if they feel friendly even though they are different species. A race or nationality—like Oriental, Occidental, African, Arab, Southeast Asian—is not important, but it is important whether he becomes friendly to them or not. All lives on earth need companions, able to help each other, because common experiences are more efficient than a solitary experience in surviving and evolving. Lives in the beginning of the world had both sexes by themselves, but they understood that it was more efficient to help each other by separating male and female in the course of evolution.

108. The reason why a bird looks around restlessly while on a tree is, first, to protect itself from a natural enemy; second, to catch a worm; and third, to find a fit mate.

109. Male cats fight each other. A dog living together with cats in the same house doesn't care about their fight and only looks on. Like attracts like; there is no fight on a different level.

110. 비가 오는 와중에 어미 잃은 새끼 고양이가 건물 밖에서 떨고 있다. 보름 전에는 2년가량 함께 지내던 고양이가 갑자기 사라졌는데 스스로 집을 나갔는지 어디서 사고를 당해 죽었는지 알 수 없던 터라, 태어난 지 2주 정도 되어 보이는 새끼 고양이를 집에 데려와 키우기로 했다. 우선 빈 종이박스로 집을 만들어 주고 밥하고 생선부스러기를 주었더니 배가 고팠던지 허겁지겁 먹는다. 그러고는 박스 안에 가만히 있지 않고 사람 곁으로 다가와서 온몸을 비벼댄다. 따뜻한 체온이 새끼 고양이에게 어미 품처럼 느껴지는 것 같다. 있던 고양이는 없어지고 없던 고양이가 새로 함께하였으니 있다가 없고 없다가 있는 것이 우연인가, 인연인가?

111. 이곳 사람들은 집집마다 부업 삼아 싸움닭을 기르는데 동트기 전 이른 새벽이면 온 동네가 닭 울부짖는 소리로 가득하다. 한 마리가 울기 시작하면 온 동네 닭들이 울기 시작하는데 그 소리가 마치 밤을 설친 영혼들의 울부짖음 같다. 새벽하늘을 찢기라도 하듯이 울어대는 닭 울음소리도 동트기 시작할 무렵이면 잠잠해지는데 그 뒤를 이어서 고목나무 가지 사이로 지저귀는 새소리는 정말 아름답고 청명하다. 아침 5시 깨어나면 아직 동트기 전이라 창밖은 어둠으로 깔려있다. 이른 닭 울음소리가 벌써 시작되었지만 아름다운 새소리는 이제 막 시작이다. 그중에서 뛰어나게 매혹적인 새소리가 있는데 그 감미로움은 천국의 노랫소리처럼 달콤하다. 그렇게 비몽사몽 30분쯤 지나노라면 동이 터 오르기 시작하고 주위가 밝아지면서 천국의 노랫소리도 함께 사라진다. 그리고 하루가 성큼 다가선다. 짜인 계획 없이 스스로 생각하고 행동하며 하루를 맞이한다. 아침마다 집 앞에 똥 싸놓고 도망가는 동네 개들과 마루 구석에 제멋대로 새끼를 낳고 들랑거리는 암고양

110. A kitten lost a mother cat and is shivering from cold outside a building in the rain. A cat living there for two years suddenly disappeared two weeks ago, and nobody knows whether it left home by itself or it was killed in an accident, so the kitten, about two weeks old, was picked up for breeding in a home. First of all, a kennel was made of carton for the kitten. The kitten ate a sliced fish hurriedly as soon as it was fed. Then the kitten rubbed itself against a human hand restlessly. The kitten seemed to feel warm by nestling in its mother cat. Since an existing cat disappeared, and a kitten that used to be nonexistent appeared, is it a coincidence or fate to be from not to be, and not to be from to be?

111. People in this district breed fighting cocks as a side job, so the whole village is full of cries early in the morning before dawn. If an old cock starts crying, all starts crying, so their cries seem to be the shout of a soul tossed and turned all night. They cry loudly as if their shouts tear the sky, but they calm down in the gray dawn. Then the birdcall warbling between old trees is really beautiful and clear. It is still dark in the gray dawn when the alarm goes off at five. The cries of cocks already start, but the birdcalls start just now. Especially, there is an attractive sound among them, so its sound is really sweet, like a song of heaven. While it takes about thirty minutes being half asleep and half awake like that, the day breaks, and the song of heaven also disappears. A day starts without any schedule. The sun is already high, and the heat of a hot wind approaches between coconut trees, while people are in a psychological warfare with so many dogs in the vicinity taking shits at their entryway and running away every morning. Then there's the psychological warfare between a half-tailed kitten raised since it was deserted and an ownerless cat having kittens in the corner of a hall as it pleases. Since noon already passed, the

이와 주워서 기르는 꼬리 잘린 어린 고양이 간의 신경전에 끼어들다 보면 아침은 벌써 지나고 태양의 열기가 코코넛 나무들 사이로 무더운 바람을 몰고 온다. 어느새 정오가 지나고 태양의 그림자가 나무 그늘 사이로 점점 길게 드리운다. 그렇게 하루는 기대하지 않는 사이 왔다가 기대하는 사이 가버리곤 한다.

112. 갈 곳 없는 동물들은 맘에 드는 인가 주변을 맴돌다가 집주인이 묵인하면 제집인 양 눌러앉아 터전을 잡고 집주인이 쫓아내면 도망갔다가 다시 돌아와 주변을 맴돌면서 기생한다. 기존에 이미 다른 동물들이 터 잡고 있는 경우에는 치열한 몸싸움을 벌이고 승자는 집주인의 승낙과 상관없이 터전을 장악한다. 집주인이 동물들에게 배려하는 것이라곤 아침, 저녁에 남은 밥찌꺼기를 모아다 주는 것뿐이다. 그러면 서열 순서에 따라 덩치가 큰 개가 먼저 먹고 고양이가 먹은 후 마지막으로 갈 곳 없는 병든 개들이 남은 밥통을 기웃거린다. 주민들이 동물들을 묵인하고 키우는 이유는 잔 밥을 처치할 수 있고 개 짖는 소리에 누가 왔음을 알고 쥐가 설치는 것을 고양이가 방지하기 때문이다.

113. 점박이 염소가 비 개인 오후에 코코넛 나무 사이 풀밭에서 두 마리 새끼를 낳았다. 일 년 전에도 삼쌍둥이를 낳았는데 다시 쌍둥이를 낳았으니 경사스러운 일이다. 이제 삼쌍둥이는 거의 어미만큼 자랐는데 그중에 막둥이는 겁이 많아 지금도 도망치기 일쑤다. 이제 갓 태어난 새끼를 바라보니 귀여워 애완용으로 키워도 될 것 같다. 염소를 물끄러미 바라보고 있노라면 노란색 눈동자가 특이하게도 초점이 있는지 없는지 무엇을 향하는지 알 수가 없어서 현재가 아닌 먼 과거나 미래를 내다보는 듯하다.

shadow of the sun becomes longer and longer between trees. Like that, a day used to come while nobody expects, then goes away while something is expected.

112. While homeless animals wander around a house and the vicinity, they fix their residence as if it was theirs, if a house owner permits tacitly. If the house owner drives them out, they are parasitic while wandering in the vicinity. In case other animals already fixed their residence there, they have to fight for their lives, and the victor secures the grounds regardless of the consent of the house owner. All the house owner has to do is to feed leftover food to the animals. If so, a big dog eats first, and the cats eat next. Then ill dogs put their heads in the residue basin according to rank. The reason why residents in this area breed animals tacitly is that they can dispose of food leftovers by feeding animals, dogs send out signals by barking at strangers, and cats prevent rats from running wild.

113. A spotted goat bred two kids on the grass between coconut trees one afternoon after raining. The goat bred three kids one year ago, and it is a joyful event that the goat bred two kids again. The three older kids already grew as tall as their mother, but one of them used to run away because it is a coward. The two newborn kids are so cute that it seems possible to breed them like pets. While staring at the two newborn kids in the face, nobody can figure out whether the eyes of the kids converge into a focus or not because their yellow-colored eyes are peculiar, so they seem to foresee not the present but the days long past or the future.

114. 갈색 수말이 초지에서 자라는 잡초로 식욕을 채우는 데 부족함이 없는 듯 농장에서 데려온 지 일 년이 지났는데 살이 토실하고 건강하다. 그래도 온종일 매여 있으니 답답할 것이다. 한번은 물을 먹이기 위해 자리를 옮기는 동안 고삐를 놓아주었더니 쏜살같이 달리기 시작하더니 도로 밖으로 나가버렸다. 그 후로는 도로를 지나다니는 행인이나 차량들과 충돌할 우려가 있어 자리를 옮길 때마다 각별히 신경이 쓰인다. 말은 달려야 말인데 초지에 온종일 매여 있는 것이 안쓰럽다. 말이 잔디깎이 역할을 할 뿐만 아니라 말똥이 거름 역할을 하는 덕택에 잔디가 잘 자라기는 하지만 달리지 못 하는 말을 보니 행복하지 않을 듯하다. 준마는 달리고 싶다. 온종일 풀만 뜯어 먹고서는 살 수 없다.

115. 별다른 재능 없는 사람들이 평범하게 할 수 있는 것은 후손을 남기는 것과 나무를 심어 가꾸는 일이다. 후손을 낳아 기르는 것은 일생을 통해 일정 기간만 가능하지만 나무를 심어 가꾸는 것은 죽을 때까지 평생을 두고 가능하다. 인류는 후손을 통해 생명을 이어나갈 수 있는 한편 나무를 통해 삶의 터전을 풍요롭게 가꿔나갈 수 있다. 나무는 사람들에게 그늘을 만들어 휴식공간을 제공할 뿐만 아니라, 나뭇가지에 맺힌 꽃은 기쁨과 향기를 선사하고 과일 열매는 맛있는 먹거리가 되고 목재로도 활용되고 홍수 시 침수를 예방하고 대기를 정화시켜 주기도 하니 나무는 지상의 보배 중의 보배요, 평생을 심고 가꾸어도 후회하지 않을 살아있는 예술품이다. 나무야말로 인류의 영원한 친구이자 동반자다.

114. A brown horse has been plump since he was brought from a farm a year ago. The grass growing in the meadow may be enough to feed the horse, but he will get bored because he is tethered to a stake all day. At one time, the horse rushed to the road as soon as he got free rein while being moved to drink water. Whenever the horse is moved, it is necessary to keep a tight rein on him so he would not crash into cars and passersby. As it is, a horse should run. It is sad to tether a horse all day. Even though the horse plays the role of grass clippers and the grass grows well due to horse dung, the horse seems unhappy as he cannot run in the meadow freely. The noble horse wants to run, so he cannot be satisfied only with feeding on grass.

115. One thing to be done by a normal person having no talent is to bring up his children, and the other thing is to plant trees and grow them. It is possible only for a short part of a lifetime to deliver babies and bring them up. However, for a long part of a lifetime, it is possible to plant trees and grow them. Human beings can transfer genes continuously by means of descendants, and they can make ecology abundant for their descendants by means of trees. Trees provide not only a cozy place with their shadow but also pleasure and scents with their flowers, and their fruits and stems become healthy food as well as industrial products—such as furniture, pulp, and biomass. Furthermore they can prevent floods and protect the globe from climate change. We will never regret planting trees and growing them our whole lifetime because trees are treasures of the world and work alive. Trees are really everlasting companions as well as friends of human beings.

116. 삼 년 전 울타리 한구석에 심어 놓은 가시꽃나무 묘목들이 이제 무성히 자라서 울타리 전체에 돌아가며 한 그루씩 옮겨 심는 작업을 하고 있다. 백여 그루 나무를 한 달 넘게 심다 보니 어느덧 내일이면 마무리되는 날이 다가왔다. 곡괭이로 구덩이를 파다 보면 어떤 때는 코코넛나무 뿌리와 부딪히기도 하고 어떤 때는 석회암에 부딪히기도 하여 어깨에 통증이 심해져서 밤잠을 설친 날이 여러 날이고 손가락마다 가시에 찔려 성한 곳이 없다. 가시인가 꽃인가 가축들이 뜯어 먹지 못하도록 잎줄기 사이사이로 가시를 돋게 했는데 그것이 미안했던지 잎줄기를 변화 시켜 붉은 꽃 흰 꽃을 피워 올린 것이 가시꽃나무다. 철조망이야 몇 년 지나면 녹슬어 버리지만 가시꽃나무는 세월이 가면 갈수록 더욱 튼튼히 자라서 몇십 년도 거든히 울타리 역할을 할 것이다. 콘크리트 벽보다 삭막하지 않고 친환경적이어서 더욱 좋다. 예전에는 동네 애, 어른 할 것 없이 오토바이를 몰고 나와 낮은 구릉 위로 조성된 코코넛 나무들 사이를 내달리곤 하여 잔디가 남아나질 않았는데 가시꽃나무로 울타리를 만들면서 잔디들이 파릇하게 예전 모습을 되찾아가고 있다. 아마 옮겨 심은 나무들의 뿌리가 안착되는 내년쯤에는 전체 울타리는 붉은 꽃, 흰 꽃으로 만발하리라.

116. Seedlings of a thorny flower tree, which were planted in the corner of a fence three years ago, were already growing well, so people transferred them along the fence. Since tree planting continued for a month, it will be finished by tomorrow, the transfer of about one hundred trees. While people dig in the ground with pickaxes, sometimes they butt against the roots of coconut trees or limestone, so they suffer a pain in the shoulder all night, and all hands and arms are pricked by thorns. Is it a thorn or a flower? The thorny flower tree might be sorry for putting forth thorns so as not to be grazed by cattle, so it blooms into red and white flowers by transforming its stem. Wire entanglements will rust away within a few years, but the thorny flower trees will grow well as time passes by, so they will serve as a fence for a long time. Furthermore, it is less desolate than a concrete wall, and it is environmentally sound. In former days, everybody—not only boys but also men—drove motorcycles and passed through between coconut trees in a hill, so the grass became withered by the tracks of motorcycles, but the grass comes out and becomes fresh and green as it was after a fence of thorny flower trees was made. All fences will be in full bloom of red and white flowers about this time next year when all trees take root.

117. 몇 날을 두고 구멍을 파도 뿌리 끝이 드러나지 않는다. 나무 둥치에 비하면 정말 뿌리 깊은 나무다. 파고 또 팠다. 눈물은 아무 의미도 없었다. 오로지 땀만이 눈앞을 가렸다. 뿌리 끝은 보이지 않았지만 고래 등에 창을 꽂듯이 뿌리 끝을 향해 힘차게 괭이를 꽂고 또 내리꽂았다. 석양에 붉게 타는 하늘이 어둠에 스러지는 광경을 보고서야 하루가 지나가고 있음을 알았다. 그렇게 옮겨 심은 나무들이 죽기도 하였지만 살아남은 대부분 나무들이 어느덧 집 주변 울타리를 이루고 있었다. 한낮의 불볕더위도 밤이 되면 서늘해지고 손마디가 저려오는 고단함에 잠을 뒤척이다 보면 어느새 창밖에는 아침 해가 떠오르고 고목나무 사이로는 갓 태어난 새들이 지저귀며 가늠할 수 없는 생명의 기쁨을 연주하고 있었다.

118. 양기를 받고 사는 모든 생명은 햇빛에 고마워해야 한다. 그런 다음 생명체의 대부분을 구성하고 있는 물에 대하여 고마워해야 한다. 그리고 그늘과 휴식을 안겨주는 나무들에게 더욱 고마워해야 한다. 사람들은 햇빛과 물과 나무들로 이뤄진 자연에 대하여 감사하는 마음으로 시작해서 감사하는 마음으로 끝을 내야 한다.

117. The end of a root is not exposed even though people dig in the ground with pickaxes for a few days. Contrary to the trunk, the tree really roots deep. People dig in the ground continuously. Tears have no meaning, and they only sweat buckets all over their body. Even though the end of a root is not exposed, people dig and dig in the ground with pickaxes, like how a spear is hurled toward a whale. No sooner had the western sky been aglow with the setting sun than it was realized that a day had passed into dusk. Some trees that were transferred like that died, but most of the trees formed a fence around a house while none was aware of it. The sweltering heat of the midday sun became cool at night, the sun rose out of a window while tossed and turned with fatigue all night, and newborn birds on an old tree began to ad-lib their joy for life, unable to figure it out.

118. All life getting sunshine should thank the sun. Then they should thank the water, which their major portions consist of. Furthermore they should thank the trees for providing them with a resting spot as well as a shade. People should live and die with a thankful mind for nature, consisting of sunshine, water, and trees.

4. 이런 인생

119. (시 4)
초콜릿보다 진한
가슴 저미는 향수

고단한 그리움이
파도처럼 밀려와

지평 너머 그윽이
펼쳐진 저녁노을

붉은 입김 물드는
하늘과 땅 사이로

빛과 어둠 껴안고
하루 꿈이 저문다.

120. 도로 맞은편에 사십 대 외국인이 사는데 비만 오면 난리다. 그 사람 집은 도로보다 지대가 낮아서 빗물이 집 마당으로 유입되기 때문인데 그 화풀이로 앞집 담벼락에다 흙탕물을 집어 던진다. 앞집 담벼락 빗물 구멍에서 물이 흘러나와 자기 집 마당으로 유입된다는 것인데 주위 사람들은 집 지을 때 지대를 높이지 않은 것이 잘못이라고 한다. 그래도 그 사람은 자신의 잘못은 생각하지 않고 비만 오면 앞집 담벼락에다 화풀이를 한다. 정신질환이 있거나 지적 수준이 낮아서 그런 것이려니. 좋은 이웃을 두는 것은 좋은 친구 못지않게 중요하다.

4. These Kinds of Lives

119. (Poem 4)
Sweeter than chocolate,
nostalgia stirs in my heart.

With a calm fatigue,
a yearning surges like waves.

Beyond the horizon deeply,
the glow of sunset spreads.

Between heaven and earth,
a breath is tinged with red.

Hugging light and darkness,
a dream of a day falls away.

120. A foreigner about forty living across the road is in uproar whenever it rains. Rainwater flows into his house because the ground level of his house is lower than the road level. That is why he flings mud at the wall of the opposite house in a fit of anger. He thinks that rainwater flows into his house because of a hole located on the wall of the opposite house, but neighbors say that he didn't level up the ground by mistake when he built the house. Nevertheless, he doesn't care about his mistake and flings mud in a fit of anger whenever it rains. He seems mentally ill or lacking intellectual faculties. A good neighbor is no less important than a good friend.

121. 인근에 육십 대 외국인이 산다. 집도 가족도 없이 혼자 산다. 가진 것이라곤 자전거와 한쪽 유리가 깨진 안경이 전부다. 거지신세가 분명한데 거지행색을 하고 다니지는 않는다. 물어보니 10년 전에 이곳에 와서 현지 여자와 함께 살았는데 여자가 전 재산을 가지고 도망가는 바람에 지금과 같은 신세가 되었다는 것이다. 다시 본국으로 돌아가지 않느냐고 물으니 돌아간들 만나볼 가족도 없고 별 볼 일이 없어서 그냥 그대로 산단다. 저녁 식사를 함께 해보니 3인분을 거든히 먹어 치운다. 평소 굶주리고 사는 것이 분명한데 누구에게 구걸하지도 않는다. 주면 먹고 안 주면 그만이다. 그래도 건강관리를 잘하는지 외모는 멀쩡하다. "왜 혼자 삽니까?"라고 물으니, "돈 없으니 여자가 없지요?"라고 대답한다. 인근 농장에서 숙식하도록 안내했더니 반나절 만에 나와 버렸다. 어디에 구속되어 지내는 것이 싫은 게다. 그는 자전거를 타고 하루 종일 시내 곳곳을 돌아다니다가 저녁 무렵 그의 쉼터로 돌아가곤 하는데 언제 봐도 그의 표정은 편안하다. 가진 것 없이 자유롭게 사는 인생이다.

121. A foreigner about sixty lives in the vicinity. He is homeless and lives alone. All he has is a bicycle and broken glasses. He is wretchedly poor but doesn't go begging. He came here ten years ago and lived together with a native woman, but she ran away after gathering all his properties, so he was reduced to beggary like this. There is no family who will receive him with great joy even if he goes back to his country, so he has no choice but to live as pitiful as he does now. He eats three times as much as the others when he is invited to dinner. It is obvious that he is usually hungry, but he doesn't go about begging. He tries to get food if possible, but he doesn't fret about food if it's impossible. Even so, he seems to keep his health well, so he is always neat in appearance. Somebody asked him, "Why are you living alone?"

"No money, no girl," he replied.

He got out of a farm within half a day after being introduced to board and lodge there. He doesn't want to be bound to stay anywhere. He used to go by bicycle from place to place. Then he comes back to his temporary shelter at dusk. He always looks tranquil. He has nothing, but nevertheless he lives freely.

122. 시내 중심가에서 어젯밤 3인조 강도가 여대생이 혼자 사는 아파트에 침입하여 강간한 후 살해하고 도주한 사건이 발생했다. 대통령은 범인들을 사형 시켜 강력한 법질서를 보여주겠다는 것이고, 종교단체에서는 사형은 면해야 한다고 주장하고 있는데 대부분 시민들의 여론은 사형을 지지하는 듯하다. 유사한 사건들을 보면 대부분 약한 자를 대상으로 범행이 이뤄진다는 것과 범인들도 역시 사회적으로 약자 신분에 있는 사람들이 대부분이다. 약자들은 항상 피해의식이 잠재하고 있어서 피해를 당하기 전에 먼저 공격해야 피해를 면할 수 있다는 묘한 심리를 안고 있다. 그러다 보니 스스로 자신의 범죄행위를 합리화하여 범행을 시도하게 되고 범행대상도 공격하기 어려운 강한 상대보다도 공격하기 쉬운 약자를 선택한다. 따라서 범죄를 줄이려면 기득권층은 사회적 약자에게 함께 살 수 있도록 실제적인 지원을 해야 하고 일반시민들은 자기방어를 할 수 있도록 항상 깨어있어야 한다. 살아있다는 것은 외줄타기와 같은 긴장의 연속이고 생명의 진화과정에서 적자생존은 엄연한 현실이며 결코 정글의 법칙만은 아니다. 죄악은 약자의 마음에서 일어났다가 약자와 함께 사라진다.

122. There was a trio of burglars who broke into a downtown apartment where a college woman lived alone, and they ran away after violating and killing her last night. The president announced that he will strictly impose law and order by condemning the murderers to death, while a religious organization insists that the murderers should escape the chair. The citizens' public opinion seems to support capital punishment. In similar cases, criminal accidents occur for the weak, and most criminals are also weak in social standing. The weak always feels subconscious damage, so he has delicate shades of psychology to escape damage by attacking in advance before being damaged himself. That is why criminals enact their crimes by rationalizing their criminal behavior, and they choose the weak rather than the strong since they are easy targets. The vested class should support the weak to reduce criminal incidents, and citizens should always be awake to protect themselves. To be alive is a continuous tension, like walking along a suspended rope, and the survival of the fittest in the course of evolution is not only the law of the jungle but also a grave reality. Vices rise from weak minds, then disappear with the weak.

123. 90세 할머니가 15년 전 우연히 막내딸과 헤어진 후 생사를 모르고 지내다가 인터넷을 통하여 다시 연락이 되었다. 그동안 막내딸은 마닐라에서 고등학교 선생으로 직장생활하며 결혼해서 중산층 가정을 이루고 있었다. 작년 10월 인터넷을 통하여 모녀간에 서로의 거취를 알게 된 후 하루가 멀다 하고 전화를 걸어서 감격적인 대화를 나누곤 하였다. 처음에는 막내딸이 민다나오에 당장 찾아가서 뵙겠다고 하다가 며칠 지나면서 막내딸은 12월에 할머니가 마닐라에 와서 함께 사는 것이 어떤지 제안하여 현재 살고 있는 손녀딸 집보다는 막내딸과 함께 여생을 보내는 것이 낫겠다는 꿈에 한껏 부풀었다. 그러나 시간이 지나면서 매일 통화하던 횟수가 점점 줄더니 12월이 지났는데도 할머니를 모셔갈 기미가 없다. 새해 들어 벌써 4월이 되었는데 이제는 연락조차 없다. 90세 할머니를 마다하지 않고 7년째 함께 살고 있는 손녀딸이 기특하기도 하여 이런 상황을 알고 주위에서 할머니에게 물었다. "막내딸이 좋아요? 손녀딸이 좋아요?"

그러자 할머니는 서슴없이 대답한다. "둘 다 좋아요."

막내딸을 원망하는 기색이 전혀 없다. 이것이 90세가 되어도 변하지 않는 어머니의 마음이다.

123. A ninety-year-old woman was reunited with her youngest daughter through an internet café after they were separated accidentally fifteen years ago, during which time this youngest daughter had married and lived a middle-class life as a high school teacher in Manila. They used to call every day and share emotional conversations after knowing each other last October. For the first time, the youngest daughter planned to visit Mindanao to meet the ninety-year-old woman. Then she suggested that the ninety-year-old woman move to Manila in December so they can live together. The ninety-year-old woman was delighted to live together with her youngest daughter because it would be better for her to do so than to live with her granddaughter, like she was doing now. However, as more time passed, the youngest daughter was calling less often, and there was no longer any intention to invite the ninety-year-old woman even when December had passed. It already had become April since the New Year started, and there is no more calling from the youngest daughter now. Somebody asked the ninety-year-old woman, after knowing that her granddaughter is praiseworthy for having lived together with her for seven years, "Which one do you prefer? Your youngest daughter or your granddaughter?"

The ninety-year-old woman replied without hesitation, "I love both of them."

She never voiced any complaint about her youngest daughter. It is maternity not to be changed even if she became ninety years old.

124. 초등학교조차 졸업하지 못했다. 집안 형편이 어렵기도 하고 공부하는 것이 싫었다. 그러다 보니 또래들은 벌써 고등학교를 졸업하는 나이가 되었다. 힘든 노동은 싫고 무학력에 쓸 만한 일자리를 얻기란 쉽지 않다. 어미는 오래전에 도망가고 없고 아비는 새장가 들어 따로 나가 살고 있으니 달리 방도 없이 할아버지 집에서 함께 사는데 할일 없이 놀고먹자니 요즘은 할머니 성화도 만만치 않다. 이래저래 스트레스가 쌓이면 음악을 크게 틀어놓고 흥얼거리거나 오토바이 타고 머플러가 터질 듯이 집밖으로 달려 나가는 것이 전부다. 이웃에서 소리를 낮추라는 항의를 할아버지, 아비를 통해서 해보지만 잠시 그때뿐 들을 생각도 없다. 장래가 구만리 같은 인생이 이렇게 주변머리가 없으니 어찌하랴. 그곳에 직업훈련원이라도 있었다면 좋으련만.

125. 인근 무료 가설 숙소에 홀아비 목수가 산다. 일당 400페소(미화 8불)로 중학교 다니는 아들과 장애 딸아이를 먹여 살려야 하는데 일이 없는 토요일과 일요일을 제외하면 수입은 열악하다. 그뿐만이 아니다 일을 마치고 주급을 받는 금요일 저녁부터 술로 괴로움을 풀기 시작하여 일요일까지 술을 마시다 보니 월요일에는 꼼짝 못 하고 드러눕는 신세가 되어 화요일부터 일을 한다. 결국 4일 날품 팔아 일주일 먹고사는 셈인데 그의 동생들도 거의 비슷한 생활을 한다. 고단한 노동에 알코올 중독으로 찌든 인생들에게 내일은 어디 있는가?

124. A juvenile didn't graduate even from elementary school because he was of low birth and didn't like to study, during which time juveniles about his age are already overage for high school. It is not easy for him to get a job without a diploma because he doesn't like physical labor. Since his mother ran away a long time ago, and his father lives separately after marrying another woman, he has no choice but to live with his grandparent. Recently his grandmother often blames him for playing away his time without a job. Whenever he feels stress with this and that, all he does is play loud music or go out by motorcycle as fast as he can, with the muffler busting. Neighbors protest, asking his father and grandfather to lower the noise, but he doesn't like to follow orders. Since the juvenile who still has a long way to go is already broken like that, what can be done for him in the future? It would be good for him if a vocational training center was there.

125. A carpenter lives in widowhood at a temporary lodge in the vicinity. He has to take care of a high school son and a disabled daughter, but his daily wages of eight dollars is not enough because he has no job on Saturday and Sunday. Furthermore, he drinks sorrow down from the evening of Friday, when he gets weekly wages, and then is overcome with liquor until Sunday. He is laid up with exhaustion on Monday, so he can start work on Tuesday. After all, he is supposed to survive for a week with four daily wages. His brothers also live similarly. Where is the future of lives exhausted with labor and alcohol?

126. 함께 거주하는 건물에는 노래방이 있는데 점심이 지날 무렵이면 가게를 돌보는 점원의 멋들어진 팝송을 시작으로 해서 밤 10시 미성년 통금 때까지 취객들의 질러대는 가지각색 노래들이 건물 주변에 울려 퍼진다. 처음에는 웬 소음인가 싶더니 6개월이 지나고 난 지금은 주변에 사는 인생들의 삶을 듣는 듯하다. 노래방 단골손님으로 나이 든 목수는 주말만 되면 왜소한 외모와는 달리 떠나버린 여인을 그리워하는 팝송을 구성지게 부른다. 젊었을 적 밤무대에서 활동했다는 뚱보 여자는 가끔씩 찾아오는데 적어도 10곡 이상은 불러야 직성이 풀린다. 알아들을 수 없는 기이한 노래도 있는데 나이 든 목수를 버리고 떠난 여자가 남기고 간 장애 아이의 노래다. 기이한 목소리지만 가난한 목수는 장애 딸아이의 기를 살려 주고 싶어서 가끔 노래를 부르게 한다. 노래는 고금동서 모든 사람들이 교감을 나누는 축복의 선율이다. 조각난 상념들이 리듬에 실려 바람을 타노라면 맺힌 한의 깊이에 따라 풀어내는 음색도 천차만별이다. 한 많은 인생들의 한풀이가 그렇게 흐른다.

127. 여기서 보면 천국이고 저기서 보면 지옥이요, 이 편에서 보면 천사이고 저편에서 보면 악마이니, 기쁨과 슬픔이 교차하는 세상에 수많은 인생들이 그렇게 쉴 없이 오고간다.

126. There is a karaoke bar in a new building, and various kinds of songs—starting from pop music that a shopgirl sings along, to the broken music that drunkards sing out—sound in the vicinity of the building until the minority curfew hour of ten in the evening. At first, it sounded like noise, but it sounds like lives in the surroundings nowadays after six months passed. Contrary to his lean appearance, a carpenter frequents the karaoke bar and sings pop music, yearning for his ex in a soft voice every weekend. A fat woman who was active at night clubs in the time of her youth visits the karaoke bar once in a while, and she is not satisfied unless she sings along to more than ten pieces of music at least. There is also a strange song that is hard to understand; it is a song of a disabled girl whom the ex of the carpenter left. Even though her voice is strange, the poor carpenter lets his daughter sing a song to encourage her once in a while. A song is the melody of blessing, to share each other's feelings in all ages and countries. While so many pieces of thought fly away in the rhythm of the wind, their expressed tone of song is multifarious according to the depth of their regrets. Regretful lives fulfill their desires like that.

127. If you look from this side, there is heaven, and in that side, there is hell. If you look from here, there is an angel, and in there, there is a demon. Like that, a lot of lives come and go ceaselessly in the world, where joys and sorrows alternate.

128. 신체장애 딸아이가 운다. 가게에 진열된 옷이 맘에 드는데 홀아비는 사줄 형편이 안 된다. 그래도 아비는 졸라대는 딸을 더 이상 실망시킬 수 없어 주말 품삯을 받으면 갚기로 하고 옷을 사준다. 아이는 장애인이지만 여느 여자아이와 같이 예쁜 옷을 갖고 싶은 게다. 아비는 가난한 목수지만 여느 아비처럼 딸아이를 실망시키고 싶지 않은 게다. 아이가 집안 형편도 모르고 졸라대는 것도 어느 철부지 아이와 똑같다. 아이는 장애아이가 아니고 아비는 가난한 아비가 아닌 게다. 오늘만큼은 아이와 아비에게 부족함이 없다.

129. 가난한 목수가 끝내 저세상으로 갔다. 나이보다 십 년은 더 늙어 보이는데 왜소한 체구에 주말이면 으레 술에 취해 있고 일할 때도 항상 줄담배를 태웠으니 건강이 좋았을 리 없다. 평소에 여러 지병이 있는 데다가 아내마저 장애 아이를 낳고 도망가 버렸으니 심신이 모두 온전했을 리 없다. 그래도 손재주와 기술이 좋고 일할 때는 열심히 일하곤 했다. 콘크리트 작업이 끝나갈 무렵 쓰러져 병원에 실려 간 후 2차례 수술을 받고 나흘 만에 숨졌는데 무료병원이라 진통제가 없어 고통을 못 이기고 숨진 것이다. 그는 이제 가고 없다. 바람에 꽃이 소리 없이 지는 것은 이승과 저승 사이가 너무나도 가까워서일까? 아홉 살 난 장애 딸아이가 하염없이 운다.

128. A disabled daughter cries. A widower cannot afford to buy a dress for her, but he buys a dress on credit on the condition that he pays money after receiving his wages next weekend. He doesn't want to disappoint his daughter asking for a dress anymore. Though the girl is disabled, she wants to have a pretty dress like other girls. Even though the widower is a poor carpenter, he doesn't want to disappoint his daughter like other parents. The girl is the same as a mere child asking regardless of the circumstances of her family. The child should not be disabled, and the father should not be poor. There is no shortage to the child and the father at this moment.

129. A poor carpenter closed his day at last. He looked ten years older than his age and couldn't be healthy because he chain-smoked while working hard, and he used to get drunk with his lean build every weekend. He was exhausted both in mind and body because he suffered from his chronic disease and his wife ran away after giving birth to a disabled girl. However, he was skillful and used to work hard. He fainted and fell down while concreting on the first floor and was sent to the hospital run by the city, free of charge. Then he died within four days after being operated on two times, having mortal agony without pain-killing drugs. He is no more. Is it because the distance between this world and the other world is too close that a flower fades silently with the wind? A disabled daughter about nine gives vent to her tears.

130. (시 5)
노래 불러라.
산 자만이 할 수 있는
목청 돋우고
노래 불러라.

풀어헤친 저녁놀
동무 삼아
잃어버린 꿈을
노래 불러라.

그리움도
고단함도
살아있는 자유로움을
노래 불러라.

별빛 흐르는
밤물결 타고
아직 살아 있음을
노래 부르다,

함께 스러져도 좋을
산 자만이 할 수 있는
노래 불러라.

130. (Poem 5)
Sing a song.
At the pitch of your voice,
sing such a song
as only the living can do.

While making a friend
with the glow of the sunset,
sing such a song
as to revive a lost dream,

With a yearning
as well as fatigues,
sing such a song
as to evoke freedom in life.

While flying with the wave
in the starry night,
sing such a song
as to be still alive.

Though all of us die together,
sing such a song
as only the living can do.

131. 내란으로 난민이 발생하여 그 여파가 주변지역으로 전파되자 전면전에 취약한 측은 테러조직으로 저항한다. 테러조직은 지역주민의 비호가 필요하므로 현 체제에 불만을 품은 자들의 거주지를 거점으로 활동한다. 테러에 가담했다가 죽은 자의 아내는 자살폭탄으로 남편의 죽음을 복수하기도 한다. 죽음이 두렵지 않은 것은 죽으면 바로 천국으로 간다는 종교적인 세뇌작용이나 마약중독 때문이다. 불행한 이들은 이 세상을 지옥이라 느끼고 차라리 죽어 천국을 선택하려고 한다.

모든 분쟁은 불공정한 사회에 대한 반발에서 시작된다. 모든 사람들의 삶이 똑같을 수는 없지만 차이가 과도하면 불행한 측은 자살폭탄으로 천국을 대신하려 한다. 불행하게 사느니 함께 죽는 것이 덜 억울하다는 생각이다. 국제적인 분쟁은 선진국과 후진국 간의 대립에서 시작되어 이제는 국가 간의 대립보다 기득권층과 소외계층 간의 갈등으로 나타나고 있다. 기득권층과 정면대결이 불리한 소외계층은 테러조직에 가담하고 테러조직의 주동자는 이들의 조직을 강화하는데 종교나 민족주의를 내세운다. 모든 분쟁은 겉으로는 민족이나 종교를 내세우지만 실상은 기득권층과 소외계층 간의 삶의 질의 차이가 원인이다. 차이가 크면 분쟁이 일고 차이가 작으면 평화가 유지된다. 개개인의 능력과 출생지와 주변 환경 등의 요인으로 모든 사람들의 삶의 질이 같을 수는 없다. 그러한 차이를 인정하되 차이가 커지면 분쟁을 가져오고 차이가 작아지면 평화가 유지된다는 사실을 기득권층이나 소외계층은 함께 이해하고 배려해야 한다.

131. The aftereffects of refugees fleeing due to the rebellion spread in the surroundings, so the weak side in an all-out war is resisting by means of terrorists. The terrorists operate at a place of residence, not satisfied with the existing system because they need protection and shelter absolutely. Women whose husbands died as terrorists try to avenge their husbands by suicide bombing. They are not afraid to die because they are either brainwashed into going to heaven just after death or drug addicted. The unfortunates presume the world as hell, so they prefer going to heaven by suicide bombing. All conflicts are due to backlash against an unfair society. All life cannot be equal, but the unfortunates try to replace heaven with suicide bombing in case the difference in the quality of life is severe. They think it is better to die together than to live unfortunately. Conflicts have occurred between advanced countries and less developed countries before, but now the discord spreads between the vested and the alienated classes rather than between countries. The alienated classes, which are at a disadvantage in a frontal confrontation with the vested classes, participate in terrorism, and the leader of the terrorists takes advantage of racism or religion to strengthen their structure. Actually all conflicts are based on the difference in the quality of life between the vested and alienated classes, even if either racism or religion is put up apparently. Conflicts occur if the difference is big, and peace is maintained if it's small. All life cannot be equal according to causes such as individual ability, native place, and surroundings. The vested and alienated classes should not only accept the difference but also understand together the fact that conflicts occur if the difference is big and peace is maintained if it's small.

132. 어느 날 갑자기 진귀한 새들이 노니는 푸른 정원과 향수 뿌린 욕조에서 재벌노인과 살게 된 모델은 신데렐라가 된 것처럼 행복하다고 말한다. 이것이 여자와 돈과 행복의 관계다. 같은 시간에 아프리카 대륙의 가뭄은 가난을 대물림하고 있다. 흑인 농부와 아녀자와 검은 피부에 하얀 눈동자만 껌벅이는 아이들. 그들이 살고 있는 황량한 벌판과 열사의 태양. 텅 빈 사막의 지평을 무덤 삼아 죽은 낙타의 사체에서 체액은 이미 증발해버리고 뼈는 모래가 되어 바람에 흩날린다. 검은 대륙의 가난과 박토에서 태어난 자들의 숙명이다. 같은 시간에 예루살렘의 성벽에 머리를 기대고 기도하는 사람들. "왜 그러느냐?"라고 물으면 그들은 주저 없이 말한다. "이곳이 세계의 중심이기 때문에."

그들이 열망하는 평화의 기도에도 불구하고 전쟁과 무고한 테러 행위는 세계 도처에서 일어나고 있다. 그들은 서로 자신들이 중심이라고 하는 상반된 생각 속에 자신들의 정당성을 주장하고 있지만 그 대가는 항상 죽음을 동반한다. 서로가 정당하다고 주장하는 치열한 삶의 현장을 침묵에 묻고 유구한 세월을 흘러온 지구는 오늘도 팔십억에 이르는 제각각 인생들을 품어 안고 무한한 우주 속을 돌며 길고 긴 항해를 계속하고 있다. 바람꽃은 오늘도 어둠 속 수많은 별들의 무리 한 자락 끝에서 피고 지고 있으니 호사스러움에 행복해진 모델과 사막에서 바람이 되어버린 낙타와 성벽에 기대어 기도하는 사람들과 전쟁과 테러로 죽어가는 수많은 영혼들 모두가 서로 중심이라고 말하기 전에 그들의 좌표가 끊임없이 변하고 있음을 헤아려야 한다.

132. A model who suddenly lives with a rich old man in a lordly mansion, having a perfumed bathtub and a green garden where rare birds hover, says that she is happy, like Cinderella. This is the relationship between a woman, money, and happiness. At the same time, a long drought transmits extreme poverty from generation to generation in Africa. A black peasant, his wife, and their children blink their white eyes, surrounded by dark skin. In the vast wildness where they are living, the sun of the burning desert shines. Body fluids have already evaporated from the carcass of a camel that died on the horizon of the empty desert, and the skeleton is blown off together with sand by the wind. Those are the fate of people born in poverty and the infertile land of the black continent. At the same time, people pray with their heads leaned against the ramparts in Jerusalem. "Why like that?"

If asked, they say without hesitation, "Because this place is the center of the world."

In spite of their prayer of peace, which they are longing for, war and terrors on innocent people occur all over the world. They mutually insist on their justice with the contrary thought that they deserve to be at the center, but the cost of this insistence is always accompanied by death. The earth passed an infinite time while putting the scene of fierce life, insisting on justice to the silent, sails continuously rounding the infinite universe while holding each life of eight billion even today. As a windflower blooms and fades on the edge of the galaxy even today, the model living in great splendor, the camel becoming the wind in the desert, the people praying with their heads leaned against the ramparts, and the numerous souls that died in wars and terrors—all of them should think over their coordinates moving continuously before saying that they are in the center.

제2편

바람은 꽃이 되어

〈여름밤 해변에 핀 바람꽃, 수묵담채화〉

Chapter 2

As the Wind Becomes a Flower

5. 빛과 어둠

133. 생명은 빛으로부터 오고 빛은 어둠으로부터 온다. 빛 속에서 펼쳐지는 모든 현상계의 모순은 어둠으로 극복된다. 빛이 반짝였다가 사라지기까지, 생명이 탄생하여 죽음에 이르기까지 어둠은 만물의 어머니와도 같이 모든 것을 하나로 품어 안는다. 빛이 연출하는 모든 현상계는 우주의 모태인 어둠의 춤사위에 따라 일어났다 사라지는 한편의 춤이다. 어둠이 베풀어준 한 자락 춤사위에 바람꽃이 피고 진다.

5. Light and Darkness

133. Life comes from light, and light comes from darkness. Discrepancies of all phenomena displayed with light are overcome by darkness. While light disappears after flashes and life dies after birth, darkness holds all in one like a mother of all things. All phenomena performed by light are a dance that disappears after rising according to the trail of darkness as the matrix of the universe. A windflower blooms and fades away, having a dance with the trail spread by darkness.

134. 바람과 바람이 빛 속에서 조우하며 순간처럼 왔다가 순간처럼 사라진다. 모든 것은 빛과 같이 왔다가 빛과 같이 사라진다. 빛은 실체이며 창조의 표현이다. 빛은 소유하지도 않고 소유되지도 않는다. 오직 스스로를 보여줄 뿐이다. 어둠을 가르고 허공에 오색을 흩뿌린다. 푸른 하늘과 타오르는 노을, 쪽빛 바다 모두가 빛의 노래다. 빛은 존재의 열정이며 아무것도 필요로 하지 않는 침묵이다. 빛의 강렬함은 사막을 태우고 빛의 부드러움은 풀잎과 친구 되어 속삭인다. 빛은 손에 만져지지 않으면서 모든 것을 보여주고 없는 듯이 있으면서 모든 것을 나타낸다. 빛은 존재의 표현이다.

135. 빛은 존재의 근원이며 빛으로부터 태어난 것이 생명이다. 빛은 잠깐 보였다 사라지는 찰나적인 것이지만 빛으로부터 태어난 생명은 자식이 어미의 품을 그리듯 빛을 그리워한다. 여기에서 생명체의 운명은 시작된다. 생명체는 회귀와 진화라는 모순 속에서 항상 고독하다. 왜 고독한가? 그것은 빛에 대한 그리움 때문이다. 그리움은 아직 이뤄지지 않는 꿈이며 이뤄진 것은 이미 그리움이 아니다. 빛은 찰나적이고 위태롭고 불완전하지만 한편으로 존재를 표현하고 꿈을 실현하는 오색의 마법을 지닌다. 생명체는 빛의 마법에 걸려 있다. 마법에서 풀려날 수 있는 길은 빛으로부터의 해방뿐이다. 그러나 빛은 놓아주지 않는다. 빛의 현란한 마법 속에서 피보라치는 심장과 꿈틀거리는 성기, 괴성과 주술, 정글의 변태와 오색의 살육, 미칠 듯한 고통과 반전되는 희열, 가진 것의 허망함과 텅 빈 웃음, 창백한 사상과 종교, 도취된 예술과 오감, 뇌리를 파고드는 치열한 삶의 파편들이 운명의 끝자락 어둠의 홀에 빨려 빛을 떠나게 될 때 비로소 고요한 침묵이 영원을 맞이한다. 빛이 사라진 어둠에는 순수 무구한 허공 즉 고요한 침묵만이 거한다. 침묵은 찰나의 빛도 존재의 모든 모순도 품어 안은 채 우주의 무한한 배경이 되어 어둠 속에 여울진다.

134. The wind meets wind in the light, then comes in a moment and disappears in a moment. Everything comes with the light and disappears with the light. Light is a reality and the expression of creation. Light neither possesses nor is possessed. It shows only itself. It breaks darkness and emits colorful brightness into the void. All of the blue sky, the burning sunset, and the navy-blue sea are a song of the light. Light is the passion of existence, a silence to need nothing. Its intensity is strong enough to burn the desert, while its softness whispers to a leaf of grass amicably. Light could not be caught, but it exists as if not to be and shows everything. Light is the expression of existence.

135. Light is the origin of existence, and it is life to be born from light. Even if light is an instant thing, disappearing in a moment after showing for a while, life born from light longs for it like a baby longs for his mother. The fate of life starts at this point. Life is always lonely in the discrepancy between evolution and revolution. Why is life lonely? The reason is that it longs for light. The longing is a dream, not to be achieved yet. To achieve it is to stop the longing. Light has magic powers to express existence, and it can achieve a dream even if it is instant, dangerous, and defective. Life is put under the magic of light. The only way to overcome this magic is to be released from the light, but light does not allow life to be released. When so many fractions of life—such as a bloody heart, a wriggling genitalia, a strange scream, magic words, an abnormality in a jungle, a slaughter in the light, a suffering pain, reversed ecstasy, the emptiness of possession, a false smile, faded thoughts and religion, intoxicated art and feelings—leave the light by being sucked into the hole of darkness on the edge of fate, a calm silence greets eternity. There is nothing but this calm silence—that is, the pure void in the darkness after light disappears. Silence is waving inside the darkness as the eternal background while holding the instant light and all discrepancies of existence.

136. (시 6)

살아도 살았다 하지 말고
죽어도 죽었다 하지 마라

세월이 흘러가도
생사는 언제나 한결같으니

있어도 있다 하지 말고
없어도 없다 하지 마라

허공이 텅 비어도
꽃은 언제나 피고 지나니

137. (시 7)

세월이 오겠느냐 마음이 오는 게지
오는 바 없는 하늘과 땅

세월이 가겠느냐 마음이 가는 게지
가는 바 없는 바람 소리 물소리

오가는 마음에 해 뜨고 달 져도
지평선 너머에 침묵은 그대로

136. (Poem 6)
Don't say it is alive even though it is alive,
and don't say it is dead even though it is dead.

As life and death are always constant,
even though time flies.

Don't say it is even though it is,
and don't say it isn't even though it isn't.

As a flower always blooms and fades,
even though the void is empty.

137. (Poem 7)
To come is only a mind-set, as if time and tide never come,
so heaven and earth never come.

To go is only a mind-set, as if time and tide never go,
so the sound of the wind and the wave never go.

Even though the sun rises and the moon sets,
in the mind coming and going,
a silence remains beyond the horizon as it is.

138. (시 8)

티끌 속에 도시는 혼돈하고
하늘은 그대로 높기만 하다.

뒤엉킨 영혼들이
분별없는 붓으로 화폭을 이루고

함부로 쏟아놓은 언어가
순간을 영원처럼 담고 있다.

타오르는 번민으로
세상이 하얗게 재가 되어도

임은 아무 말 없이
있는 그대로 보여주고 있다.

139. (시 9)

배고픔과
거짓 배고픔과
헛된 배고픔이
삶을 휩쓸어도

기다림도 없이
구할 것도 없이
침묵은 언제나
그대로였다.

138. (Poem 8)
A crowded city is in chaos,
and heaven is too high to reach.

Entangled souls paint
a picture with an imprudent brush,

and a reckless language pretends
to be an eternity in a moment.

Even though the world is burned
as white as ash in anguish,

while keeping silent,
thou void show all things as is.

139. (Poem 9)
Even though a hunger,
a false hunger
and a vain hunger,
swept over life,

without awaiting,
or pursuing anything,
silence, as is,
always remains.

140. 검은 눈동자 동굴 속으로 물결 따라 흐르는 어둠이여! 적막을 헤치고 솟아나는 여명이여! 천지간에 산 자를 죽었다 하지 말라. 외로움이 태곳적 전설이 되어 가슴에서 산산이 부서질지라도. 동굴 속으로 빈 배는 물결 따라 흐르고 바람꽃의 울음소리 여명의 불기운이 되었나니. 이제 적막은 불타오르고 하늘은 비로소 열렸다. 어둠의 물결을 밀어내고 바람꽃의 춤사위는 천지가 되었다. 밀어의 속삭임이 동굴 속에서 동굴 속으로 해를 잉태하고 산고의 날은 밝아 바람꽃의 울음소리 여명을 깨웠나니. 외로움은 어둠의 장막을 헤치고 이제 태양은 밝아온다. 태양은 자비로운 빛을 온 누리에 뿌리며 생명을 주도한다. 태양은 아무것도 구하지 않고 베풀 뿐이다. 베푸는 손길은 넓고 풍요롭다. 태양은 둥근 모습처럼 항상 부드러운 미소를 머금고 있다. 그 미소는 소리 없는 가운데 찬란하게 빛난다. 변함없는 모습으로 찾아와서 이른 새벽을 깨우고 찬란한 빛으로 온 누리를 감싸 안다가 석양 녘에 조용히 물러서서 어둠 속에 휴식한다. 태양은 새벽을 가르는 나룻배에 금빛 물결을 인도하고 이름 모를 산사에 핀 꽃에게 다가가 부드러운 입김으로 꽃잎을 흔들며 속삭인다. 태양은 영롱한 이슬 속에 온 세계를 무지갯빛으로 담아내고 드높은 창공에 투명함을 보여주며 바다에 잠기는 금빛 물결로 가슴을 한없이 어루만져 준다. 태양은 무한한 정열로 모든 생명에 기운을 불어넣고 끊임없는 사랑의 빛을 베풀어준다. 태양은 지상의 절대자이면서 동시에 밤하늘에 빛나는 수많은 별들 중에 하나의 작은 별이 되어 무한한 영광이 한낮 허공 속의 티끌임을 보여준다.

140. Darkness flows with a wave toward the black pupil of a cave! Dawn breaks through silence! Don't say that one alive between heaven and earth died even though loneliness breaks to fragments in your heart, becoming a legend in ancient times. As a wave flows with an empty boat into a cave, and the cry of a windflower breaks dawn full of glory, the world is open at last while the sun rises brightly in silence. The dancing trail of a windflower becomes heaven and earth by pushing out the wave of darkness. The birth of the sun is conceived from cave to cave in whispers, and the cry of a windflower breaks dawn while enduring birth pangs. Once loneliness breaks through the veil of darkness, the sun rises at last. The sun leads all creatures, shining on earth mercifully. The sun has mercy without pursuing anything, and its warm helping hand is extensive and plentiful. The sun always smiles as tenderly as a round shape, and its smile is bright soundlessly. The sun awakes the early morning, rising with a constant feature, and brilliantly hugs all things in the world. Then it takes a rest in darkness, setting beyond the horizon silently. The sun guides a boat passing at dawn with a golden wave, and it whispers to a flower blooming at an unknown temple by shaking petals with a soft breath. The sun makes a rainbow-tinted world in the clear dew, shows the transparent sky deeply, and touches everybody endlessly with a golden wave sunk in the sea. The sun encourages all creatures with infinite passion and gives an endless shine of love. As the sun is not only the absolute being on earth but also a tiny star among a great number of stars twinkling at night, it shows that infinite glory is only a dust in the void.

141. (시 10)
물살 도는 계곡
산허리 감싸 안아 휘돌고

이끼 먹은 물소리
어우르는 청잣빛이 시리다.

꿈꾸는 달빛
구름에 젖가슴 풀어 헤치고

고개 넘어 숲 사이
흐르는 바람 소리 적막하다.

142. (시 11)
여름이 익어가는 오후
물오른 해바라기 꿈을 꾸고

잠자리 하늘 눈 빙그르르
쇠스랑 발가락 얼굴 비비다

까치발 아이 그림자에
부러진 가지 끝 날개가 쫑긋

투명한 거미줄에 잡힐세라
텅 빈 하늘 날쌔게 차오른다.

141. (Poem 10)
Valley swept by the current
turns around a hillside.

The murmur of a mossy creek
is as chilly as celadon.

Moonlight having a dream
leaves a bosom open in the clouds.

Between woods beyond the hill,
the sound of the wind is lonely.

142. (Poem 11)
In the afternoon of summer ripening,
a mature sunflower dreams,

while a dragonfly turns its eyes toward the sky
and rubs its face with a rake of toes.

By the shadow of a child stretching on his toes,
its alae are pricked up at the end of a broken branch.

Then it flits fast into the sky,
not to be captured by transparent cobwebs.

143. (시 12)

산촌에 햇살이 살고 있다.

수목 첩첩한 계곡에 바람이 살고
항아리 물속에 한 조각 구름이 산다.

토담집 옛 주인 소식은 없고
단지마다 하늘 담아 놓고서
한없는 기다림에 가슴 저민다.

도리깨 물레 다듬잇돌 절구
빛바랜 도구마다 길고 긴 숨결 배어나고
군불 짓는 장작더미 제 몸 살라 너울대면
타오르는 꿈들이 스러질 듯 피어난다.

길섶에 핀 꽃들은
파란 하늘 온몸에 적시고도 모자라서
사라진 시간 꺾어다가
얼굴 붉게 물들이고
하늘 한번 보고 향기 토하고
햇살 한번 품고 춤을 춘다.

어제도 오늘도 항상 거기에
모두 다 떠났어도
햇살을 품고 하늘을 본다.

143. (Poem 12)
Sunshine lives in a mountain village.

Wind lives in a woody valley,
and a piece of cloud lives in a water pot.

There is no word from an old host of an adobe hut,
and it gets weary to wait endlessly
while each pot is filled with the sky.

Flail, spinning wheel, fulling block and mortar,
each worn-out implement is soaked with deep breath,
and yearning dreams come again as if disappeared
while firewood burns itself with wavy flames.

As flowers blooming on the wayside are not satisfied
even though their bodies are all wet with the blue sky,
they dye their faces red
by cutting the time gone away,
giving off a fragrance after facing the sky once
and dancing after hugging the sunshine once.

They are always there today as well as yesterday,
even though everybody left,
and look at the sky while holding the sunshine.

144. (시 13)
해는 언제나 시작이다.

봉봉이 불을 먹고
광야가 열려오면

어둠을 가르는 여명으로
바다를 풀어헤친 가슴에
불기운이 솟는다.

천지를 향해 차오르다
허공으로 꺼꾸러져
추락하는 영겁

천년을 부르던 침묵이
임의 넋인 양
한 마리 불새가
하늘 속 심연을 날아간다.

144. (Poem 13)
The sun is always a start.

When the wide field opens
from peak to peak, full of fire,

at dawn parting the darkness,
the heat of fire rises
from the bosom spread over the sea.

While it rises in heaven and earth,
into the void,
an eternity is falling.

As if the millennium-old silence is
the spirit of lost love,
into the abyss of the firmament,
a phoenix is flying.

145. 노력과 능력과 기회와 환경에 따라 사람마다 주어지는 처지가 제각기 다르다. 그러므로 가진 자는 있음이 없음을 낳고 없음이 있음을 낳는 유무상생의 이치를 깨우쳐야 한다. 바람 불어 꽃이 피니 바람인가? 꽃인가?

146. 예전에 명절 때면 이웃 간에 주고받는 선물이 설탕 한 봉지였던 것을 안다면 지금의 빈곤은 절대적인 빈곤이라기보다는 상대적인 빈곤의 의미가 크다. 빈곤으로부터의 해방은 불필요한 물질적 욕구를 줄이는 것이다. 정신적인 자족이 진정한 의미에서 풍요로움의 기초가 된다. 누구나 마음의 궁핍으로부터 자유롭고 행복할 권리가 있다. 빛과 어둠은 차별이지만 낮과 밤은 교차하는 것이니 행복의 기회는 누구에게나 평등하게 주어지는 것이다.

147. (시 14)
우리의 만남은
바람과 꽃이 되고

우리의 헤어짐은
침묵과 하나 되니

빛은 오고 가도
어둠은 그대로다.

145. The situation given to each person is different according to their endeavor, abilities, opportunities, and circumstances; therefore the haves should realize that to be comes from not to be and not to be comes from to be. As a flower blooms with the wind, is it the wind or a flower?

146. If you know that only a small sack of sugar was exchanged between neighbors as a festive present in the old days, the poverty of nowadays has the meaning of relative poverty rather than absolute poverty. Freedom from poverty is to reduce our desire for unnecessary wealth. Spiritual satisfaction is the basis of richness in a real sense. Everyone has the right to be happy and to be free from poverty of the mind. Light and darkness are distinct, but the opportunity for happiness is given to everyone evenly because the day and the night always rotate.

147. (Poem 14)
As our meeting becomes
the wind and a flower,

and our farewell is
together with silence,

though light comes and goes,
darkness remains as it is.

148. (시 15)

떠나온 길은 멀지 않건만
태중의 상처 부여안고
화살을 주우며 불러본 "오빠"

산딸기 잃어버린 젖가슴
브래지어로 동여매고
핏빛 창가에 어릿한 그림자

무너지던 밤마다
몸이 날개인 양
먼 하늘 사이로 별을 헤인다.

148. (Poem 15)
Though it's not too far from the left way,
by enduring the wound of the womb,
"Big brother!" one calls, picking up arrows.

Bosoms lost wild berries,
hiding those behind a brassiere,
a shadow looming on a bloodred window.

Every night breaking to pieces,
as if a body is a wing,
one counts stars far up into the air.

149. (시 16)
밤은 깊어 영시인데
홍등 아래 졸고 있는 그림자
술 취한 몸이 시인 양
쪽방에 이끌려 껍질을 벗는다.

가냘픈 어깨 위로 바람 스치고
공테이프 돌아가는 유행가에
가슴은 아직도 순결인 듯
찰랑이는 입술에 미소가 맴돈다.

태중의 찢어진 지폐가
사랑을 잉태할 리 없건마는
오늘 밤도 꿈을 꾸는 눈동자에
도시의 별빛이 흔들린다.

149. (Poem 16)
As midnight deepened,
a shadow falls asleep under the red light.
As if a drunk body is a poem,
it is stripped off after being led into a side room.

A wind brushes a lean shoulder,
with popular songs played on an endless tape.
As bosoms are still innocent,
a smile plays around lapping lips.

Though the torn bill of the womb
cannot get pregnant with love,
on pupils dreaming of even tonight,
urban starlight twinkles.

150. 사람들이 편의상 이천 년 전 과거를 기준해서 서력기원으로 햇수를 헤아리고 있는데 이는 과거의 사건이나 미래의 일들이 정해져 있고 지금의 좌표가 한해씩 증가하고 있다고 보는 것이다. 그러나 지금은 원년으로서 좌표상에서 항상 원점에 위치하는 것이며 과거의 사건이 -선을 따라 지금으로부터 점점 멀어지고 미래의 일들이 +선을 따라 지금을 향하여 점점 가까워지고 있는 것이다. 지금이란 시간의 흐름을 보여주는 기준점이지 시간 따라서 흐르는 것이 아니다. 깨어있는 모든 사람들에게 지금은 항상 시간의 원점이자 시작이다. 그래서 영원한 지금인 것이다.

151. 늙고 병든 사자가 무리로부터 이탈되어 하이에나에게 포위되었다. 사자 덩치가 하이에나보다 다섯 배나 크지만 열 마리가량 되는 하이에나의 전후방공격을 방어하기가 버겁다. 그래도 쉽게 무너지지 않고 사투를 벌이자 이를 멀리서 관망하고 있던 동료 사자가 다가오면서 상황은 반전되고 하이에나 무리가 물러선다. 다행히 목숨이 연장되기는 하였지만 결국 병든 사자는 죽어서 하이에나의 밥이 되었던지 열사의 태양 아래 증발하였으리라. 지고함도 쇠퇴하면 초라한 것이고 다수가 모이면 작아도 강한 것이고 투지가 있으면 도움이 따르는 것이고 바람처럼 왔으면 바람처럼 돌아가는 것이다.

150. People count the number of years according to AD, based on the past, two millenniums ago, for convenience's sake; it means that the present coordinates are increasing every year, while a past event and a future affair are fixed. However, the present as the first year always stays on the origin of coordinates, while a past event becomes far off from the present on the minus line and a future affair comes close to the present on the plus line. The present as a datum point is not to fly together with time but to show the passage of time. The present is always the origin of time as well as the starting point for all awaking people, so it is called the everlasting present.

151. An old, ill lion is isolated from its group and surrounded by a pack of hyenas. The lion is five times bigger than a hyena, but it is not easy for the lion to defend itself against the attack of about ten hyenas from all directions. Nevertheless the lion fights desperately not to collapse, so the situation is reversed, and the pack of hyenas step back immediately after another lion observing the developments from afar approaches. Fortunately the lion escaped death for a while, but the lion would die in the end and would either become a prey for hyenas or be evaporated by the scorching heat of the desert. Even supremacy is pitiful in decline, and even the small is strong when together. There is help if there is a fighting spirit, and all is gone with the wind if it comes with the wind.

152. 욕망에 들끓으면 정신 이상을 초래하거나 정신이상까지는 아니더라도 늘 불만스럽거나 불만까지는 아니더라도 항상 만족이 없으니 그런 욕망, 그런 인생에서 무슨 행복이 있겠는가?

153. 욕망이 마음에 일면 마음은 욕망의 그릇에 갇히게 되고 욕망이 미치는 거기까지가 마음의 한계가 되어 거기에서 마음이 닫히게 된다. 무엇에 집착하면 곧 그것이 욕망이다. 욕망의 불길은 한번 타오르면 재가 되어야 끝이 나는 것이니 욕망은 한낱 불나비의 꿈이다. 한번 돌이켜 허공 속으로 마음이 열리면 막힘 없이 흐르는 바람처럼 욕망도 사라진다. 욕망이 사라져 버린 마음은 초연하니 걸어도 춤추는 듯하고 일을 하여도 구애됨이 없으니 매사가 즐겁다. 어떠한 욕망의 그물에도 걸림이 없으니 바람꽃은 가히 초인의 모습이다. 막힘이 없으니 시종을 묻지 않고 있는 그대로 온전하다. 있으면서 없으니 무한한 도량을 헤아릴 길이 없다. 욕망의 덫으로부터 놓여나 바람처럼 사는 삶이라면 이미 그 자체가 행복이다. 바람의 꽃이여! 욕망의 바다에 닻을 내리려고 수고하지 마라. 불어오는 바람에 돛을 세우고 순간의 자유를 즐겨라.

152. It brings a mental disorder if consumed with desire. It is dissatisfied even if it doesn't bring a mental disorder. There is always no satisfaction even if it isn't dissatisfied. How can you expect happiness in such a desire and such a life?

153. If desire rises in the mind, this mind is put in a prison named desire, and it is closed there as desire becomes its limit. If you are attached to something, it is just a desire. If the flame of desire starts burning, it burns continuously until it becomes ash, so a desire is nothing but a dream of a moth. Once a mind is changed and it is open toward the void, desire also disappears like a wind blowing without blocking. As the mind without a desire is aloof from the world, every affair is happy, as if walking is like dancing, and there is no adherence even to every work. A windflower might well be a transcendent figure because it is free from the net of any kind of desire. As there is no barrier, it is sound as it is, without asking the beginning and the end. As it is not to be while it is to be, there is no way to count infinite liberality. It is already happiness itself, if it is a life like the wind, free from the trap of desire. A wind of flower! Don't let pain anchor in the ocean of desire. Enjoy freedom every moment while spreading a sail before the wind.

154. 모든 것이 선이다. 나 없이 있는 그대로가 선이다. 있는가 하면 없고 없는가 하면 있으니 천지만물 그대로 허공이다. 도심의 혼잡을 벗어나 도착하니 경내는 조용하기만 하다. 흩날리는 눈발이 가득히 밤하늘을 수놓는다. 밤 아홉 시에 시작해서 새벽 세 시에 끝나는 참선을 위하여 선원의 불빛이 고요히 어둠을 밝히고 있다. 선방에 들어서니 외국인 스님을 포함해서 사람들이 모여 있다. 죽비소리에 참선은 시작되고 벽을 향한 공간 속으로 침묵이 흘러간다. 만법귀일 일귀하처 시간이 흐르면서 화두는 점점 벽 속으로 사라지고 일상의 문제가 화두를 대신한다. 지금 하는 일을 계속해야 할 것인지, 그만둔다면 무엇을 해야 하는지 입안에 고이는 옥침을 나눠 삼키며 심신을 가늠하지만 마음은 허공을 헤매고 하얀 벽이 몸과 맘 사이를 오르락내리락 할 때쯤에야 죽비소리와 함께 침묵에서 깨어난다. 모두 긴 숨을 몰아쉬고 얼굴을 부비고 다리를 주무른다. 그리고 십 분가량 선방을 배회하듯 줄지어 걷는다. 다시 죽비소리가 울리고 각자 제자리에 돌아가 참선에 들어간다. 밤 열 시를 가리키는 괘종시계가 속절없이 울린다. 침묵과 혼돈, 죽비소리와 함께 다시 한 시간이 지났음을 알린다. 그리고 또다시 죽비소리. 그렇게 침묵과 숨소리와 텅 빔 속에서 자정 열두 시가 넘어서고 있다. 참선의 중반이 지나고 있는 것이다. 새벽 세 시 참선을 마치고 선방 내리막길을 돌아서니 벌써 새벽 예불을 드리러 사람들이 경내로 올라온다. 오가는 마음에서 무엇을 보았는가? 꼭두새벽 허공에 하얀 바람꽃이 흩날린다.

154. Everything is in meditation. It is meditation to be without myself. As it is not if it is, and it is if not, all creatures is the void as is. There is only calm inside the temple where people arrive, getting out of urban congestion. Large flakes of snow flutter in the night sky. The temple is lit up with a light in the darkness of the night for meditation from 9:00 p.m. to 3:00 a.m. There are followers, including a foreign monk, in the meditation room. People begin meditation with the sound of a bamboo stick sitting down in front of a wall, and a deep silence continues in the space between the walls. Since all creatures return to one, where does one return to? Longer time flies, further the fundamental subject disappears into the wall, and daily questions take the place of the fundamental subject. Is the present job worth continuing? If not, what kind of a new job is available? A mind wanders in the void while trying to control itself by swallowing saliva, and it is not until the white wall goes up and down before the eyes that a mind is awakened from silence with the sound of a bamboo stick. Everybody takes a long breath, rubbing their faces and massaging their legs, then walks along the wall for about ten minutes. With the sound of a bamboo stick, everybody returns to their seat and is lost in meditation again. A wall clock rings hollow to show 10:00 p.m. It rings again to let another hour pass with silence, then chaos and the sound of a bamboo stick. Then the sound of a bamboo stick is heard again. Like that, it is past midnight in the silence, breath, and emptiness. It already passed through the midterm. Other people already come inside the temple for worship when people walk down a descending path after ending meditation at 3:00 a.m. What is awakened in the coming and going mind? The white petals of a windflower flutter quite early in the morning.

6. 바람은 꽃이 되어

155. 바람꽃은 감추어져 있지 않다. 바람꽃은 도처에 피어있는 것이다. 말로부터 자유로운 것이 바람꽃이다. 행하는 모든 것이 바람꽃이다. 천지간에 바람꽃 아닌 것이 없으니 바람꽃을 세삼 구할 바 없다. 바람꽃을 구했다 하면 이미 그것은 바람꽃이 아니니 바람꽃은 없는 듯이 있는 것이다. 바람꽃은 자연의 흐름 속에서 피어난다. 흐르는 물, 흐르는 바람 속에서 바람꽃이 피어난다. 물은 흐르는 것이요 흐름이 곧 생명이다. 생명에는 흐름이 있다. 흐름은 삶과 죽음을 이어주고 생명을 살아있게 해준다. 바람꽃에는 자유가 있고 생명이 있고 흐름이 있다.

6. As the Wind Becomes a Flower

155. A windflower is not hidden. A windflower blooms everywhere. A windflower is to be free from language. Everything to act is a windflower. It is not necessary to look for a windflower because there is nothing but windflowers all over the world. If you get a windflower, it is already not a windflower. A windflower is to be as if not to be. A windflower is blooming in the stream of nature. It is blooming in the flowing water and the blowing wind. Water is to flow, and the flow is just life. There is a flow in life. The flow connects life with death, and it stimulates our life. There is freedom, life, and flow in the windflower.

156. (시 17)
바람은 꿈을 꾸네.
꽃이 되는 꿈을 꾸네.

바람은 꽃이 되고
꽃은 바람이 되어

꽃은 꿈을 꾸네.
바람이 되는 꿈을 꾸네.

허공에 바람 일고
바람에 꽃이 피네.

156. (Poem 17)
The wind is dreaming.
It is dreaming to become a flower.

As the wind becomes a flower
and a flower becomes the wind,

a flower is dreaming.
It is dreaming to become the wind.

The wind rises in the void,
and a flower blooms with the wind.

157. (시 18)

너는 바람꽃이어라
오가는 계절 속에
말없이 피어나는 바람꽃이어라

텅 빈 울림 속에
햇살을 보듬고
숨결이 되어버린 바람꽃이어라

너는 바람꽃이어라
하늘 향해 얼굴을 묻고
그리움이 되어버린 바람꽃이어라

침묵의 기도 속에
생명을 꿈꾸다가
신비가 되어버린 바람꽃이어라

157. (Poem 18)
You might be a windflower.
In the seasons coming and going,
you might be a windflower blooming silently.

While hugging the sunshine
in the sonority of the void,
you might be a windflower becoming a breath.

You might be a windflower.
While putting your face into the sky,
you might be a windflower filled with nostalgia.

While dreaming of life
with the prayer of silence,
you might be a windflower becoming the mystery.

158. (시 19)
서리 얼은 가지마다 백화라
투명한 돌기 사이로
맴도는 청자 물빛
찬바람이 시리다.

한 자락 휘감긴 하늘에
쩡그렁 울고 간 가슴
태곳적 숨결이 허공에 배이고
고목으로 껍질 벗은 아릿함이
어름을 쪼갠다.

휘늘어진 진주알 송이마다
인고의 마디 손가락을 헤이고
복받친 환희가 서러워 엉킨 자국
어찌 매화만이 꽃이랴!

순백의 세월이 천년을 머금고
살풀이하던 먼 산자락에
시절을 잊어버린 설화의 꿈이
바람결에 스친다.

158. (Poem 19)
White flowers bloom on each frosted branch.
The water color of celadon is reflected
between transparent protrusions;
it is chilled with cold wind.

In the sky wound around,
a heart pounded with sorrow.
Eons-old breath soaks in the void,
and the pain of an old tree stripped off
breaks ice.

In the drooping clusters of pearl,
patient endurance of time is counted.
As it is a tear-stained look with joy,
how can an apricot be the only flower!

While the pure time of millennium is detained,
beyond the exorcised hill,
the dream of a snow flower forgetting a season
passes on the wind.

159. (시 20)
계곡에는 나무와 침묵과
이따금 부서지는 바람 소리가 있다.

산등성이에 어둠이 찾아와
뉘엿뉘엿 햇살이 능 마루에 기울고

골짜기 넘어 이어지는 길섶에
마른 가지 드높은 둥지가 외롭다.

풀잎 사이로 드러난 황톳빛에
나그네 숨결이 차마 배이고

여울지는 적막이
한 많은 나무들의 울음인가?

스쳐가는 구름이 인연인 양
청록빛 하늘이 깊기만 하다.

160. 어느 날 갑자기 허공 속에 바람꽃이 피어나서 한바탕 춤사위를
펼치다가 홀연히 사라졌다. 생명의 오고감이 흐르는 바람꽃과 같다.

159. (Poem 20)
In the valley there are trees, silence,
and a blowing wind sometimes.

As dusk deepens in the mountain,
the sun sinks step by step beyond the ridge.

Along the road behind the valley
is a lone net on a high branch.

Ocher exposed between grass leaves
is soaked with the breath of a traveler.

Echoes resound desolately.
Is that the cry of regrettable trees?

As if a floating cloud is predestined,
a bluish green sky is really deep.

160. One day a windflower bloomed suddenly in the void, then disappeared after dancing for a while. The coming and going of life is like that of a windflower.

161. 진화의 끝자리에서 외줄 타듯이 위태로운 긴장을 배경으로 피어난 것이 바람꽃이다. 모든 생명체는 허공 속에 기적과 같이 피어난 바람꽃이라 할 것이니 생존의 위태로움은 가히 아침 이슬과 같다. 바람꽃은 긴장 속에 숨을 쉬며 허공과 연을 이어가다가 호흡이 멈추면 생명을 풀어 헤치고 허공 속으로 회귀한다. 그 과정은 태어남과 죽음에 이르기까지 기적과 같이 이뤄지지만 바람꽃은 언제나 일상처럼 피고 진다. 긴장 속에서 피어나는 바람꽃은 무엇을 말해 주는 것인가? 위태로움과 수고로움과 고뇌가 바람꽃의 전부는 아니다. 바람꽃이 위태롭기만 하다면 밤하늘에 허공을 가르고 사라지는 한줄기 혜성과 다를 바 없을 것이다. 바람꽃에 부여할 가치는 기적이라기보다 평범함이다. 평범함은 모든 존재의 중심에 위치한다. 중심에서는 찰나적인 선동이나 유행도 사라지고 삶과 죽음과 그로 인한 수고로움과 긴장마저 사라진다. 모든 것이 사라진 순수 속에서 바람꽃은 오롯이 피어난다. 태양 아래 흔들리는 바람꽃은 시간을 초월한다. 어느 순간 존재의 정점에서 태양과 바람을 맞이하고 스스로 살아있음에 새삼 수고로움을 묻지 않고 있는 그대로 찬란한 빛과 매혹의 향기를 발산한다.

161. A windflower blooms in the background of a dangerous tension, like walking along a suspended rope at the end of evolution. The danger of all life is really like dew in the morning, because all lives are the same as a windflower blooming in the void by a miracle. A windflower returns to the void after ending its days if it ceases to breathe while breathing in strain and forming ties with the void. Even if the course from womb to tomb is performed by miracle, a windflower always blooms and fades like daily life. What is the meaning of a windflower blooming in strain? Dangers, efforts, and pains are not the whole figure of a windflower. If a windflower is only dangerous, it will not be different from a comet disappearing in the night sky. A windflower's worth is in its commonness rather than a miracle. Commonness is situated in the center of all things. An instant instigation or fashion disappears in the center, and life and death as well as efforts and tension due to life and death disappear. A windflower blooms perfectly in the pureness where all things disappear. A windflower swaying in the sun transcends time. It meets the sun and the wind at the zenith of existence in a moment, and it shows a glorious color and gives off a fascinating perfume without mentioning efforts anew for living by itself.

162. 몸은 세포로 구성되고 세포는 분자들로 구성되고 분자들은 원자들로 구성되고 원자들은 원자핵과 전자들로 구성된다. 원자핵보다 원자가 십만 배나 크고 원자보다 세포가 이십만 배나 크고 세포보다 사람이 팔만 배나 크니 원자핵이나 전자의 크기에 비한다면 인간의 육체는 가히 헤아릴 수조차 없는 천문학적인 크기가 아닐 수 없다. 그러나 백오십억 광년을 헤아리는 우주에 비하면 인간의 육체는 어떠한가? 빛의 속도가 초속 삼십만 킬로미터이니 빛이 일초 동안 달려가는 거리는 사람보다 일억 구천만 배나 크고 일 광년 거리는 빛이 일초 동안 달려가는 거리의 삼천만 배나 크고 관측 가능한 우주 경계는 이보다 백오십억 배나 크지 않은가! 우주 속을 떠도는 수많은 은하계 중의 어느 한 은하에 속해서 그 속을 돌고 있는 수천억 개의 별들 가운데 작은 별에 불과한 태양을 생명의 빛으로 삼고 태양계를 돌고 있는 행성 중의 하나인 지구상에서 팔십억의 인간이 살고 있으니 광활한 우주에 비하면 태양마저 티끌일 뿐인데 하물며 인간의 육체를 비교하여 무엇하리오. 공간뿐 아니라 시간의 크고 작음은 어떠한가? 하루살이에 비해서 인간의 수명은 삼만 배나 긴 생을 살고 있지만 백오십억 년을 지나온 우주에 비하면 인간의 수명은 이억 배나 짧은 찰나를 살고 있다. 인간의 육체를 놓고 볼 때 보는 시각에 따라서 크고 작음이 이와 같이 다르니 무엇을 크다 하고 무엇을 작다 하리오. 바람꽃은 있는 그대로 피고 질뿐이다.

162. The human body consists of cells, a cell consists of molecules, a molecule consists of atoms, and atoms consist of an atomic nucleus and electrons. An atom is one hundred thousand times as large as an atomic nucleus, a cell is two hundred thousand times as large as an atom, and the human body is eighty thousand times as large as a cell. Therefore it is certain that the human body is large astronomically as compared with an atomic nucleus and electrons. However, compared with the universe as large as fifteen billion light-years, how is the human body? As the speed of light is three hundred thousand kilometers a second, the distance that light covers for a second is 190 million times as large as the human body. The distance of a light-year is thirty million times as large as the distance that light travels for a second. How wonderful is it that the boundary of the universe that we are able to observe is fifteen billion times as large as the distance of a light-year! Eight billion people live on earth, which is one of the planets belonging to the solar system, revolving around the sun—which is nothing but a small star among the tremendous number of stars belonging to one of the galaxies among a lot of galactic systems flying in the universe. The sun is only a dust compared with the vast universe. So it is ridiculous for the human body to be compared with the universe. What is time as well as space? Compared with a mayfly, a human being lives thirty thousand times longer, but he lives only for a moment—five billionths—as compared with the universe of fifteen billion years. As time and space are variable according to a viewpoint, like the human body, what can be said to be big or small? A windflower as is only blooms and fades.

163. 인류의 조상은 이백만 년 전에 지구상에 출현한 이래 지금까지 지진, 해일은 물론이고 화산 폭발이나 대홍수, 기후변화에 따른 빙하기 등 가혹한 자연의 재앙에 대항하여 끈질긴 생명력으로 살아왔다. 뿐만 아니라 자연이 평화로울 때에는 인간들 간에 전쟁으로 스스로 재앙을 자초하기도 하였다. 이처럼 인류의 역사는 도전의 역사다. 끝없는 시련 속에서 생존을 향한 도전 정신은 에베레스트 등정이나 극지방 탐사 등을 통하여 인위적으로 표출되기도 한다. 산이 있기에 오른다는 끝없는 도전정신이 생존이유가 되고 있다. 도전이 없다면 생존의 의미가 없다. 때문에 열정을 불태우는 도전이 동서고금에서 끝없이 이뤄지고 있다. 도전의 역사는 삶의 과정이며 흐르는 세월 속에서 도전은 또 다른 도전을 부른다. 자연의 재앙이나 종족 간의 투쟁 속에서 벌어지는 시련이 바람꽃을 진화시키기도 하고 때로는 퇴화시키기도 한다. 진화를 통하여 바람꽃은 새롭게 피어나고 바람꽃이 지는 것은 또 다른 생명을 예고한다. 시련에 대한 도전은 생존의 무대 위에 펼쳐지는 격정의 춤사위다. 휘몰아치는 시련을 즐길 수 있는 바람꽃이기에 그 자체만으로도 아름답다.

163. Since the progenitor of the human race appeared on earth two million years ago, they have persistently lived with a life force against natural disasters, such as earthquakes, tsunamis, volcano explosions, deluges, as well as the ice age, according to climate change. In addition, while nature was peaceful, they brought disaster on themselves by raising a war between them. Like that, human history is a history of challenges. Sometimes a challenging spirit for survival in endless trials is artificially expressed through the ascent of Mount Everest or a polar expedition. The endless challenge to climb it since there is a mountain becomes a survival reason. There is no meaning of survival without a challenge. Therefore a lot of challenges with fiery passion are endlessly offered across the ages and in all countries of the world. The history of challenge is the process of life, and a challenge evokes another challenge in time and tide. Sometimes natural disasters or the trials of fierce battle between tribes make a windflower evolve or sometimes retrograde. A windflower blooms anew through evolution, and another life is predicted when a windflower fades away. A challenge to trials is a dance of passion spread in the stage of survival. As it is, a windflower enjoys the raging trials. A windflower itself is enough to be beautiful.

164. 저녁마다 야자수 나뭇잎에 물을 뿌려주는데 지난 주말 스프레이 물병이 고장 나서 살펴보니 연결된 스프링이 끊어져 있다. 철물상에 가보니 스프링만 팔지 않는다. 다른 데는 멀쩡한데 이천 원도 넘게 주고 새 물병을 사려니 왠지 아깝다. 다시 할인점을 찾아보니 마침 이천 원 미만짜리 스프레이 물병이 남아있다. 스프레이 물병에 생수 한 병까지 사고도 이천 원이 안 된다. 멀리까지 온 보람이 있어 돌아오는 발걸음이 가볍다. 가로등 불빛이 희미한 도로변에 중학생들로 보이는 아이들이 물건을 팔고 있다. 그러나 행인들 발걸음은 바쁘기만 할 뿐 아무도 관심이 없다. 둘러보니 샤프연필이 눈에 띈다.

"이거 얼마니?"

"천 원이요!"

지갑을 열어보니 만 원짜리 뿐이다. 만원을 건네주니 아이가 잔돈을 거슬러 주려 한다.

"거스름돈은 필요 없으니 그냥 만 원 다해라!"

"와!"

아이들이 동시에 환호한다. 초 여름밤 하늘에 갑자기 바람꽃이 피어난다. 한꺼번에 열 명의 손님이 물건을 팔아준 꼴이니 아이들이 감동할 만도 하다. 조금 전까지 이천 원도 아까웠는데 이제 만 원을 주어도 아깝지 않으니 숫자놀음이란 바람 따라 변하는 것이다.

164. It was found that a spring inside was broken after checking why a bottle of daily spraying water for a decorative plant was out of order. They don't sell only the springs at the hardware. One is unwilling to buy a whole new spraying bottle for more than two dollars because the broken bottle is still faultless except for the small spring. As it happened, a spraying bottle worth less than two dollars is at another grocery store. Both spraying bottle and a bottle of drinking water are less than two dollars. The coming back step is light. Teenagers like junior high school students are selling something beside a road under a dim streetlight. However, passengers have no concern except walking busily. Immediately upon looking around, one sees sharp pencils come in sight.

"How much is it?"

"One dollar"

There is only ten-dollar bills inside a wallet. A boy tries to return the change as soon as he receives a ten-dollar bill.

"You don't need to return change. Have ten dollars all."

"Wow!"

All of them cheer at the same time. A windflower suddenly blooms in the summer night sky. As it is, just like that ten customers buy things at once. It is quite natural for them to cheer. Paying two dollars was begrudged until a few minutes ago, but now giving ten dollars is not begrudged. The concept of amount is changeable according to the wind.

165. 나이를 먹게 되면 육체가 늙는 것보다도 마음이 늙어서 더 문제다. 대부분의 사람들은 나이를 먹을수록 생각이 고집스럽고 편협하고 자기중심적이고 가슴이 메마르고 언행마저 거칠어지기 쉽다. 그렇지 않아도 나이 들면 이빨이 빠지고 머리털이 빠지고 피부마저 주름져 볼품없는 모습으로 변하는데 거기에 생각마저 메마르고 마음마저 거칠어진다면 어느 누가 말 한마디라도 따뜻이 건네며 노인을 상대하고 싶겠는가? 마음이 늙으면 패기가 사라지고 추억만 남게 되고 주위를 배려하는 마음보다 자신의 안위가 우선하고 아집과 편견 습도락에 빠지기 쉽고 보수적인 입장만을 추구하고 허세로 늙음을 위장하다가 이도 저도 아니 되면 체면 몰수하고 추한 언행마저도 서슴지 않으니 세간에 철들자 망령 난다는 말이 바로 이런 노인을 두고 하는 말이다. 이와 같이 추한 늙은이로 생을 마감해서야 어찌 아름다운 바람꽃이라 하겠는가? 세월이 흐른 만큼 나이에 걸맞게 철이 들고 망령됨이 없이 죽기 전까지 청정한 모습으로 젊은이의 귀감이 된다면 설령 외모가 늙었다 해도 멋진 노인이라 할 것이다. 이것이 시간의 장벽을 넘어 막힘 없이 사는 바람꽃의 초연한 모습이다. 비록 육신은 늙었을지라도 풍상을 살아온 덕스러운 마음으로 주위를 배려하며 산다면 늙어도 늙은 것이 아니요 항상 젊게 사는 삶이리라.

165. If a person becomes old, it is a serious problem that the mind becomes older than the body. Most people are apt to be obstinate, intolerant, selfish, hard-hearted, and rudely behaved with age. Though they are unlike that, they change and have poor features— toothless, hairless, and wrinkled with age. Therefore, if they are hard-hearted and rudely behaved, who would want to become warmly acquainted with them? If a person becomes old in mind, he loses his vigor and remains only in reminiscence, and he prefers his safety to having consideration for his neighbors, indulges in egotism, becomes prejudiced as well as dissipated, pursues only a conservative position, and behaves rudely in no measured terms, if it is not effective to disguise oldness as a bluff. As the proverb says, he becomes senile as soon as he reaches the age of discretion. Like that, if one's life ends as an ugly old person, how can a windflower be beautiful? If a person has discretion with age as much as time flies and exemplifies himself to young people with right conduct until he dies without getting senile, he deserves to be respectable in spite of his age. This is a serene appearance of a windflower living freely over the barrier of time. Though a body becomes old in years, it is not an old life as is but a youthful life if he has consideration for his neighbors, with a virtuous mind enduring the hardships of life.

166. 인생의 멋은 갈필에 있다. 바람 한 점 들지 않는 비좁은 틈 사이로 말달리듯 차오르는 하얀 지평에 머뭇거리지 않는 한 줄기 화두가 던져진다. 눈을 감아도 갈필은 허공을 달리고 어둠이 앞을 가려도 묵향은 허공을 휘감는다. 예리한 칼처럼 붓은 허공을 베고 낙점으로 회귀하던 운필은 마냥 아득하다. 힘이 있어도 무례하지 않고 유연한 흐름에 막힘이 없으니 순간의 울림이 가히 영원하다. 한 바퀴 원을 휘돌아 멈추는 듯 이어지는 바람은 해가 구름을 가르는 듯 다시 이어지는 곡선으로 여인의 가슴을 넘는다. 검은 머리칼 나부끼며 달리던 산야에 심장의 고동소리 울린다. 불과 찰나에 살다간 자취를 갈필에 묻고 떠나버린 한 호흡은 이제 소식이 없다. 이 밤이 지나 새벽이 되면 피가 배인 자리에 한 자락 검은 짐승이 백지에 몸을 풀고 침묵하리라. 선을 넘어 바라보는 눈동자마다 바람꽃을 몰고 오는 뇌우의 골짜기 속으로 해골이 되어 달리리라. 하잘것없는 얼굴에 분 바르고 묵향에 흩날리는 갈필이 되리라. 이미 살아있음은 멋이다. 백과 흑이 짜리를 틀고 마주하는 텅 빈 진실이다. 하나 되려고 선을 찾다가 있는 그대로 되어버린 아름다움이다. 둘은 멋이 아니다. 하나이기에 멋이다. 인생을 어찌 복제할 수 있는가? 겁 없는 아이처럼 살다간 노인의 미소는 바람과 함께 사라진 허공의 노래다. 있는 그대로 바람꽃의 춤사위는 한 점 갈필이면 족하리라.

166. The flavor of life is in a wild brushstroke. A ready streak of topic is thrown into the white rising horizon as if a horse runs between openings that's so narrow that even a breath of wind cannot pass through. Though eyes shut, one sees a wild brushstroke run into the void, and a scent of India ink spreads in the void even if it is dark. A brush like a sharp sword cuts the void, and a brushstroke returning to the starting point is still far away. Though it is powerful, it is not rude, and there is no obstruction in the flexible flow, so a moment of echo might well be eternal. The wind blowing without stopping at the turning point gets over the bosom of a woman, with a curved line connected again as if sunshine passes through clouds. The beating of a heart echoes in the fields and mountains where someone runs with dark hair waving. There are no more tidings from a breath gone, leaving a trace lived only for a moment in the wild stroke of a brush. A dark beast will fall into silence while exposing itself on the white drawing paper soaked with blood in the coming dawn after tonight passes. It will run as a skeleton in the valley of a thunderstorm, driving a windflower into each pupil looking over a line. It will make a wild stroke of brush with a scent of ink stick, powdering a humble face. To be alive is already a flavor. It is a vacant true, facing black and white. It is the Beautiful to become itself as is in the course of looking for the Good in order to become one thing. Two things are not a flavor. It is a flavor because it is one thing. How can a life be duplicated? The smile of an old person that passed living like a child, not cowered, is a song of the void disappearing with the wind. A wild brushstroke is enough to become a windflower's dancing as is.

167. 바람꽃의 춤사위가 펼쳐지면 밤하늘에 별자리가 뿌려지고 달빛은 구름에 휘감긴다. 삼라만상은 바람꽃의 춤사위에 따라 오색 빛을 뿌리며 모습을 드러낸다. 바람꽃의 춤사위가 깊어지면 안개가 서리고 산은 운무에 가려지다가 빠른 리듬과 함께 폭풍우를 몰아친다. 바람꽃이 무아지경에 이르면 휘몰아치는 춤사위는 파도가 되고 화산이 되어 변화무쌍한 장관을 연출한다. 바람꽃은 자연의 리듬에 따라 수천 수만 가지로 분화되어 현상계에 출현한다. 자연의 리듬을 타고 춤이 휘돌아갈 때마다 삼라만상은 모습을 드러냈다가 춤이 멈춰서는 순간 삼라만상은 허공으로 사라진다. 바람꽃은 한 자락 한 자락마다 춤사위를 이끌어가니 삼라만상 어느 것 하나 소홀한 것이 없다. 선과 악, 귀한 것과 천한 것이 한데 어우러져 장대한 바람꽃의 춤사위를 연출한다. 바람꽃과 춤 사이에는 주객이 없다. 춤추지 않는 바람꽃이 없고 바람꽃 없는 춤이 없으니 춤사위가 곧 바람이자 꽃이다.

168. 바람꽃은 영원을 추구하지도 완전을 추구하지도 않는다. 전체와 하나 되는 소박함 속에서 순간의 자유를 사랑할 뿐이다.

167. While the dance of a windflower spreads, a lot of stars constellate in the night sky, and the moonlight is reflected between the clouds. All creations expose their features, shining brilliantly in various colors according to the dance of a windflower. As the dance of a windflower becomes intense, it is misty, and a mountain is veiled in cloud and mist. Then it storms in quick rhythms. When a windflower attains a spiritual state of selflessness, a swirling dance presents a grand spectacle, varied like waves and volcanoes. Windflowers appear with so many thousand features in the world according to the rhythms of nature. All creations show their features whenever they dance with the rhythm of nature, and they disappear into the void at the moment when they stop dancing. There is nothing but the precious things in the world because windflowers lead each step of the dance. The magnificent dance of windflowers is performed by harmonizing everything—from the good and the bad to the precious and the trivial. There is no host and no guest in the relationship between windflowers and dance. The dance is just the wind as well as the flower because there is no windflower without dancing, and there is no dance without windflowers.

168. A windflower does not pursue either eternity or entirety. It only loves freedom in the moment, with the simplicity of becoming one together with the whole.

169. 태양이 황도를 따라 하늘에 포물선을 그으며 지나가듯이 인생도 허공에 포물선을 그으며 지나간다. 물이 흐르고 바람이 불고 계절이 바뀐다. 시절 속에서 꽃은 피고 지고 아이의 웃음소리도 언젠가는 노인의 추억이 된다. 흘러오는 구름을 품어 안고 흘러가는 바람을 떠나보내며 순간은 침묵한다. 수천 년을 지나온 문명도 풍상에 부서지는 모래가 되고 티끌이 되어 사라진다. 이렇듯 바람꽃은 순간 속에 피고 지고 순간은 영원한 지금이다.

170. 길섶에 꽃이 피었다. 석양 녘에 하늘을 향해 바라보는 꽃잎이 하늘빛에 함박 물들어 작은 얼굴마다 한 조각 한 조각 하늘을 담고 있다. 꽃잎이 어쩌나 작은지 오엽으로 구성된 한 송이 꽃의 크기가 좁쌀만 하다. 그러나 자태는 너무나 뚜렷하고 당당하여 있는 그대로 살아 있음을 보여준다. 삶의 정수가 무엇인가 묻지 않아도 꽃은 아무도 찾지 않는 길섶에서 삶의 정수를 누리고 있다. 무심결에 손끝을 스치자마자 꽃송이가 순식간에 떨어진다. 아무런 저항도 없이 아무런 비명도 없이 한 세계가 소리 없이 지고 만다. 순간 그대로가 전부다. 스스로를 내세우려는 에고의 목소리도 없이 모든 순간을 침묵으로 받아들인다. 꽃은 주저하거나 망설임이 없이 흘러오는 자연에 스스로를 내맡긴다. 꽃 속에 하늘이 있고 하늘 속에 꽃이 있으니 꽃의 하늘이요 하늘의 꽃이다. 온 세계가 한 송이 바람꽃이다.

169. As if the sun passes while describing a parabola in the sky according to the ecliptic, life passes while describing a parabola in the void. Water flows, the wind blows, and the seasons change. Flowers bloom and fade in season, and someday the laughter of a child will become a memory of an old man. A moment falls into silence while holding the coming clouds and letting the leaving wind go away. Even civilizations that had passed for thousands of years disappear by becoming the sand and dust crushed with wind and frost. Thus, a windflower blooms and fades in a moment, and a moment is the everlasting present.

170. There are flowers on the side of a road. Each little face of these flowers mirrors the sky while dyed a rose color by the sunset. A flower consisting of five petals is very small, like millet, but it shows itself to be alive as it is because its figure is very clear and stately. The flowers enjoy the very essence of life on the side of the road without question about said essence of life. A blossom falls down as soon as it's touched unintentionally. A world is scattered soundlessly without any resistance or any scream. A moment as is consists of the whole. It accepts every moment in silence, without the sound of the ego standing for itself. It leaves itself to the rhythm of nature without any hesitation. It is the heaven of a flower and it is a flower of heaven because there is heaven in a flower and there is a flower in heaven. All over the world is a blossom of windflower.

171. 아침 태양이 뜨고 석양이 진다고 똑같은 하루가 지난 것은 아니다. 사람마다 시간은 다르게 흐른다. 허둥지둥 서두른다고 일을 많이 하는 것도 아니다. 서두르면 서두를수록 부족해지는 것이 시간이다. 바람꽃은 시간 속에 피어있는 것이 아니다. 시간에 쫓기는 것도 아니고 시간을 쫓아가는 것도 아니다. 허공에서 순간순간 피어나는 것이 바람꽃이다. 시계 속의 시간은 숫자로 정한 가상의 약속일 뿐 삶을 살아가는 기준이 아니다. 서두를수록 부족해지는 시간보다 스스로 기울이는 주의력에 따라서 전개되는 시간이야말로 진정한 의미를 갖는다. 절대적인 시간이란 없다. 누구에게나 적용되는 시계 속의 시간은 가상의 시간일 뿐이다. 사람마다 시간은 다르게 흐르고 너와 나의 상대적인 관계 속에서 시간이 존재한다. 단순한 삶일수록 시간은 여유 있게 흐르고 복잡한 삶일수록 시간은 부족하게 느껴진다. 부족한 시간에 허둥대는 것은 바람꽃의 진정한 모습이 아니다. 임의대로 흘러가는 시간이 바람꽃에게 무슨 의미가 있는가? 시간은 지극한 주의력 속에서 바람꽃과 함께 피고 질 때에 진정한 의미를 갖는다. 다가오는 시간을 여유롭게 바라보는 것도 달아나는 시간을 허둥대며 쫓아가는 것도 각자의 마음에 달려있다. 시간은 결코 주어지는 것이 아니라 스스로 만들어나가는 것이다. 사람마다 느끼는 시간이 각기 다르고 각자의 주관에 따라서 상대적으로 흐르는 것이 시간이다. 스스로 시간을 다스려 가는 풍요로움 속에서 진정한 삶의 자유를 누려야 한다.

171. Though the sun rises at dawn and sets at dusk, it is not the same day that passed. Time flies differently according to each person. It is also not good to work very hard if you are in a hurry. The more hurry-scurry you are, the shorter time is. A windflower is not to bloom in time, and it is not to pursue time or not to be pursued by time. A windflower is to bloom every moment in the void. Time shown on a watch is only a virtual promise to be determined by numbers, not a standard for living life. Time spread according to attention paid by people rather than time shortening because of being in a hurry is really meaningful. There is no absolute time. Time shown on a watch, applied to everybody, is only virtual time. Time flies differently according for each person, and time exists relatively between you and me. Time flies slowly in a simple life, and time is felt to be insufficient in a complicated life. To be in a hurry is not a true figure of a windflower. What does it mean for a windflower that time flies arbitrarily? Time has a true meaning only when it blooms and fades together with a windflower while paying attention to the surroundings. It's up to each person's mind whether to look at the approaching time affluently or to follow time as it runs away in a hurry. Time is never to be given but to be spared by each person. Time is to be felt differently by each person, and time flies relatively according to each person's subjectivity. People should be blessed with the freedom of true life in affluence of time managed by themselves.

172. 바야흐로 봄은 무르익어 도로변에 봄기운이 화창하다. 상춘객을 따라 길목을 돌아 나서니 홍백매가 파란 하늘 아래 만개하였다. 꽃잎 여문 채로 가지 끝에 매달린 봉오리도 있지만 대부분 꽃들이 만개하였다. 이미 춘풍에 지는 꽃잎도 있다. 가까이 다가서니 흐드러지게 핀 매화의 암향이 바람결에 그윽하다. 이끼 문은 고목의 자태는 오백 년 역사를 간직한 듯 의연하다. 고목의 둥지에서 뻗어난 가지가 세월의 무게로 휘어져 내리다가 다시 새로운 생명력으로 하늘을 향해 뻗쳐 오르니 가지마다 순백의 오엽이 춘광에 눈부시다. 소리 없이 웃는 모습이 미인의 자태인 양 고혹적이다. 한설을 이겨낸 까칠한 가지의 무성한 휘늘어짐은 화선지에 거침없이 써내려 간 갈필처럼 유연하고 힘이 있다. 잉잉거리는 벌도 아직 제철이 아닌데 작은 꽃잎마다 무수히 피워 올린 향기는 무엇을 향한 그리움인가? 묻는 이도 답하는 이도 없이 오늘도 매화는 오백 년 세월을 간직한 채 우아한 미소로 맑은 하늘을 우러른다. 가히 암향 천 리 그대로다. 산문을 나서는 내리막길 길섶에는 봄볕 아래 쑥잎이 흙 내음과 어우러져 파릇하다. 돌아오는 길에 경내 초입 찻집에서 시름을 잊고 벗과 함께 햇차를 즐기노라니 시구가 절로 난다.

173. (시 21)
한오백년 긴 세월 휘늘어진 가지마다
홍백매 오엽송이 춘광에 눈부시고
합장하듯 여문 꽃잎 눈발같이 흩날리니
고혹적인 자태가 꿈결속의 여인인 양
머나먼 암향 천 리 바람결에 그윽하다.

172. As the spring is really ripe, there is a lovely feel beside a road. No sooner had picnickers turned the corner than white and red apricot blossoms were in full bloom in the blue sky. There are some buds hanging on a branch, but most blossoms are in full bloom. There are blossoms already falling with the spring wind. When I come closer to the apricot trees, the fragrance of the blossoms in full glory is sweet on the wind. An old apricot tree covered with lichen is stately as if it's keeping a history of five hundred years. Petals on each branch are brilliant in the spring sunshine because the branches from the trunk of an old tree spread out again in the sky with their life force as if they bend with the weight of years gone by. This soundlessly smiling feature is fascinating like a beautiful woman. The luxuriance of haggard branches standing in the cold of winter is flexible and powerful like a wild brushstroke written on a white drawing paper. While buzzing bees are still out of season, what is the fragrance of blossoms longing for? Nobody asks, and without answer, does apricot blossoms keeping time and tide for five hundred years look up with elegant smiles toward the clear sky. It may well be a faraway diffused fragrance as is. Mugwort is fresh and green, combined together with an earthy smell beside a downhill road from a temple gate. While I enjoy a cup of green tea for relaxation with an old friend at a teahouse on the way, a poem occurs by itself.

173. (Poem 21)
On each branch luxuriating with time for five hundred years,
white and red apricot blossoms are brilliant in the spring sunshine.
While petals as if in prayer are blown off like snowflakes,
as a fascinating feature seems to be a woman in a passing dream,
a faraway diffused fragrance is sweet on the wind.

174. 바람은 천지간에 만물이 자유롭게 존재함을 상징하고 꽃은 개체로 태어난 삶들이 자기완성에 이름을 상징하니 전체와 개체가 화합하듯 바람과 꽃이 하나 되어 피어난 것이 바람꽃이라. 바람과 꽃이 함께하니 하나가 둘이 되고 둘은 하나가 되어 스스로 친구가 되고 친구는 바로 자신이더라. 그렇게 오고감이 천지에 퍼지고 만물은 하나같이 친구가 되더라. 하나 속에서 무한함을 보고 무한함 속에서 하나를 보니 만물에 생기가 일어 생명이 잉태하고 육체는 영혼을 맞고 영혼은 육체를 맞이하더라. 모든 사상과 종교가 다스려지고 강변에 반짝이는 둥근 자갈처럼 자연 그대로 돌아가니 원만한 순환의 이치가 무릇 천지에 퍼져 시간은 항상 지금에 있고 항상 새롭게 다가와 신선한 바람과 꽃이 화목하여 외롭지 않더라. 이것이 영육이 함께하는 천지고 믿음과 신이 함께하는 축복이요, 행복이고 온전함이더라. 하나를 두고 바람이라 하기도 하고 꽃이라 하기도 하니 이는 서로가 서로를 있게 하는 하나 됨이라. 그러하니 하나를 둘이라 하지 않고 둘을 하나라 하지 않고 그대로 온전하여 삶과 죽음이 함께 어우르고 너와 내가 함께 어우러져 바람과 꽃이 되니 바람인들 꽃인들 거기에 어인 분별이 있으랴! 자유로움이 곧 창조요 존재의 근본이며 지고함이니 과거로 지금을 소홀히 하지 않고 미래로 지금을 속박하지 않고 영원한 지금이더라.

174. As the wind symbolizes that all things in the heavens and the earth exist freely, and a flower symbolizes that individual lives accomplish perfection of self, so it is a windflower that blooms by uniting the wind with a flower as if the whole and an individual are in harmony. As the wind and a flower are together, so they form a friendship, and a friend is just the self, since one becomes two and two becomes one. Like this, the coming and going spreads into the heavens and the earth, and all things form a friendship without exception. As there is infinity in one thing, and there is one thing in infinity, so all things are full of vigor and pregnant with life, and a body meets a soul, and a soul meets a body. As all thoughts and religions are put in order, and we go back to nature itself like the round gravels by the riverside, so time is always in the present and is always new, and a fresh wind and a flower are not lonely in harmony because the reason of the cycle spreads into the heavens and earth broadly. It is in the heavens and the earth where a body and a soul are together, and it is a blessing, happiness, and soundness, where faith and God are together. As one thing is called the wind or a flower, they help each other to become one thing. Therefore one is not called two, and two is not called one, and everything is sound as it is. As life unites with death, and you unite with me, so those become the wind and a flower. What a distinction there is regardless of the wind or a flower! Since freedom is just creation, the origin of existence, as well as supremacy, there is the everlasting present—while not neglecting the present due to the past and not restraining the present due to the future.

175. (시 22)

미혹함이 끝이 없구나.

어둠 속에 악마를 보는 것은

네 마음의 환상이리니

이 모든 환상은 미혹하기 때문이다.

시작도 끝도 없는 마음속에

어느 날 네가 찾아와

부평초 같은 마음 되어

고독에 지친 네가

너이고 싶은 집착으로

어둠 속에서 악마를 만드나니

네 진정 모든 것을 놓는다면

무구한 자유로움에

미혹함이 없는 바람이 되고

어둠과 빛을 구별하지 않고

악마와 천사를 차별하지 않고

오로지 순수 무구한 바람이 되어

어느 곳에나 있고

어느 곳에도 머물지 않는

바람이 되리라.

175. (Poem 22)
How endless a delusion is!
To see the devil in the darkness
is due to an illusion in your mind,
and all illusions are due to a delusion.
In the mind without beginning and end,
one day you came closer
and became a transient mind like a cloud drifting.
As you tire of loneliness,
with an attachment to being yourself,
and make the devil in the darkness ···.
If you really stand aloof from everything,
with an innocent freedom,
as you become the wind without a delusion,
without distinguishing between dark and light,
or differentiating a devil from an angel,
and become a pure, innocent wind,
to be everywhere,
and not to stay anywhere—
it might be the wind.

7. 생존게임

176. 어느 날 갑자기 평화롭던 초원에 낯선 모습의 사자가 등장한다. 이 지역을 다스리던 늙은 사자는 새로운 침입자를 응징하러 달려간다. 조용하던 초원에 물러설 수 없는 한판의 사투가 벌어진다. 물고 물리는 치열한 접전 끝에 마침내 새로 나타난 강자에게 밀린 늙은 사자는 자신이 지배하던 영역을 포기하고 떠날 수밖에 없다. 이제 새로 등극한 젊은 사자가 이 지역의 새로운 지배자가 된 것이다. 사투 현장을 숨죽이고 지켜보던 암사자 무리와 새끼들은 새로운 지배자를 숨죽이며 바라본다. 그들의 얼굴에는 앞으로 다가올 운명을 초조하게 기다리는 눈빛이 역력하다. 새로 등극한 지배자는 피 묻은 모습 그대로 어슬렁거리며 사자 새끼들에게 다가선다. 사자 새끼들은 숨을 죽이고 땅바닥에 엎드린 채 다가오는 운명을 무방비 상태로 바라본다. 새로운 지배자는 사자 새끼들에게 다가가 하나둘씩 잔혹하게 물어 죽인다. 이때 암사자가 새끼를 보호하려고 살육의 현장에 끼어들었다가는 암사자마저 생명을 보장할 수 없기에 암사자들은 살육의 현장을 침묵하며 속수무책으로 바

7. Survival Game

176. One fine day, a strange lion suddenly appears in a peaceful meadow. The old lion governing this area runs to defeat the new invader. A desperate struggle, unable to step back, occurs at the calm meadow. At last the old lion, defeated by the strong, cannot help leaving his territory after grappling in mortal combat. The young lion newly ascending to the throne becomes the new ruler of this area. A lot of lionesses and their cubs watching the desperate struggle look at the new ruler with breathless attention. There is clearly a fretful look—awaiting their coming fate—on their faces. The new ruler with a bloody feature as is approaches, strolling closer to the cubs. Cubs look at the coming fate in a defenseless state, lying on their faces with breathless attention. The new ruler approaches closer to the cubs and cruelly bites them to death. A lioness only looks at the scene of slaughter helplessly because she cannot also assure her safety if she breaks into the scene to save her cub. At last the new ruler gets rid of all sources of future troubles and finishes preparations to breed his cubs. Now a night

라볼 뿐이다. 마침내 새로운 지배자는 후환을 깨끗이 없애고 자신의 씨를 뿌릴 준비를 마무리한다. 이제 공포와 살육의 밤이 지나고 새날이 밝아온다. 초원에 구름이 일고 비가 뿌려진다. 새로 등극한 지배자 주위에 암사자들이 모여들고 지배자는 암사자들과 하나씩 교미한다. 새로운 강자의 종족 번식이 시작된 것이다. 힘에 밀려 쫓겨난 늙은 사자의 행방은 알 길이 없다. 작열하는 태양에 증발하여 바람으로 돌아갔으리라. 자연은 강자를 선택한다. 진정한 강자는 머물지 않고 항상 새롭게 불어오는 바람과 같다. 낡은 것은 가고 새로운 바람꽃이 피어난다.

177. 모든 생명체는 주위와 끊임없이 교감하며 생명을 이어가고 있다. 생명의 오고 감이 흐르는 바람과 같으니 생존이란 태어나서 둘로 나뉘었다가 죽어서 하나로 돌아가는 게임이다. 생존게임에는 언제나 상대가 있게 마련이다. 남녀 간의 사랑에도 상대가 있고 기업 간의 경쟁에도 상대가 있다. 생존게임이란 혼자서는 할 수 없기에 친구든 적이든 누군가 함께 해야만 한다. 생존게임에서 먼저 해야 할 것은 뜻을 같이할 파트너를 선택하는 것이다. 생존게임에서 게임 룰에 능숙한 파트너를 만났다면 이미 게임의 절반은 이긴 것이다. 그러나 당초 기대와 달리 게임에서 패할 경우도 있으니 이는 생명이 진화하는 과정에서 겪어야 되는 아홉 수의 운명이다. 생존게임에서 좋은 파트너를 만나고 행운마저 함께하여 승리했다고 하여도 게임이 끝난 것은 아니다. 지금의 친구가 내일의 적이 될 수 있기에 언제나 긴장의 연속이다. 생존게임에는 짝사랑이란 없기 때문에 파트너가 떠나가기 전에 끊임없이 스스로를 변화시켜야 한다. 생존게임에서 좋은 파트너를 선택하는 것도 중요하지만 더욱 중요한 것은 스스로를 항상 새롭게 변화시키는 힘이다. 과거의 바다에 닻을 내린 상대에게 어느 누가 신선한 매력을 느끼겠는가? 생명은 바람과 함께 오는 것이니 항상 새롭게 변하는 것이 생존의 기본이다.

of fear and slaughter passes, and a new day breaks. Clouds gather, and it rains in the meadow. A lot of lionesses gather around the new ruler, and this ruler mates with a lot of lionesses one by one. Just like that, a new, strong species starts breeding. There is no way to find traces of the expelled old lion. He might be gone with the wind by evaporating in the scorching sun. Nature chooses the strong. The strong is really like the wind, not to stay but to blow newly. The old goes away, and a new windflower blooms.

177. All creatures live, responding to each other continuously. As the coming and going of life is like a blowing wind, survival is a game dividing into two from birth and uniting into one after dying. There is always a counterpart in the survival game. There is a counterpart in love, and there is also a counterpart in competition between companies. As the survival game cannot be done alone, someone should be accompanied regardless of friends or enemies. The first thing to do in the survival game is to choose a congenial partner. If you meet a proficient partner skilled in the rule of the survival game, you've already won half of the game. However, according to circumstances, you can fail to win contrary to your first expectation; that is the ninth fate, which a creature should endure in the course of evolution. Though you win the survival game together with a good partner and fortune, it doesn't mean that the game is up. The tension always continues because a friend now becomes an enemy. Now that there is no unrequited love in the survival game, you have to change yourself endlessly before your partner leaves you. It is important to choose a good partner in the survival game, but the power to change your own is more important. Who will be freshly fascinated by a partner anchoring in a past ocean? As life comes together with the wind, it is the basis of survival to change fresh.

178. (시 23)
배는 떠나가고
바다 저편 황혼마저
한 점이 되고 있다.

구할 것이 무엇이던가?
이미 행복이고
바람이 아니던가?

모든 것은 지나가고
지금은 영원한 순간
살아있음이 꿈이었나니.

179. 모기가 매우 하찮은 생물이지만 일상생활에서 신경을 쓰이게 하는 것처럼 주변에 하찮은 존재가 의외로 고통을 줄 수 있으니 주변 환경을 우선 잘 선택하고 선택한 주변에 대해서 도리를 깨우치게 교육하고 상벌로 다스려야 한다. 하찮은 것이라고 소홀히 하다가 전체가 무너지고 많은 사람이 고통을 당하게 된다.

178. (Poem 23)
A boat left,
and even a red sunset beyond the ocean
is becoming a spot.

What is to be pursued?
It is happiness as it is,
and the wind, isn't it?
As everything passed away,
and now is an everlasting moment,
it might be a dream to be alive.

179. Although a mosquito irritates human nerves in daily life, nevertheless it is a trifling creature that troubles you unexpectedly. Therefore, first you have to choose your surroundings well. Then educate those around you to have a sense of duty, and evaluate them with rewards and punishments. If you disregard them because they are trivial, the whole will collapse, and a lot of people will suffer pain.

180. 지구상의 자원은 일정 규모로 한정되어 있다. 한정된 자원을 얻기 위해 자연의 정글 속에서 동식물들이 경쟁하듯 도시의 정글 속에서 사람들 간에 제한된 부를 놓고 경쟁한다. 내가 가지면 누군가가 갖지 못할 것이고 누군가가 가지면 내가 갖지 못할 것이다. 사람들은 도시의 정글 속에서 경쟁하고 있지만 그 결과는 언제나 부족하고 불만족하다. 설사 오늘 행운이 찾아와 일시적으로 만족할지라도 전체적으로 부족하다는 생각은 떠나지 않는다. 바람꽃은 1할의 행운을 얻기 위하여 9할의 불행과 조바심과 분노와 좌절을 감내하며 도시의 정글 속을 헤쳐가고 있다. 내가 편한 만큼 남이 힘든 것이고 내가 힘든 만큼 남이 편한 것이고 내가 많이 가질수록 남이 적게 갖는 것이고 내가 적게 가질수록 남이 많이 갖는 것이다. 모든 사람을 만족시킬 만한 충분한 물질이 지구상에 없을 뿐 아니라 사람들의 마음에 여유가 없는 것이 더욱 삶을 궁핍하게 한다. 그런 줄 알면서도 최선을 다하여 노력하는 것이 생존의 미덕으로 남아 있다. 그러나 노력의 결과는 시운에 따라서 결정되고 노력하는 과정만 의지로 남는다. 종의 진화과정에서 구축되어 있는 먹이사슬처럼 도시의 정글 속에 구축되어 있는 빈익빈, 부익부의 고리를 끊고 분배의 질서를 바로잡기란 쉬운 일이 아니다. 철학자가 사색하는 시간을 갖기 위하여 노예가 철학자의 밥을 지어야 하는 것이라면 이는 당연한 처사인가 부당한 처사인가? 그에 대한 해답은 사람마다 처한 위치에 따라 다르다.

180. Resources on earth are limited to a certain amount. Like how animals and plants in the jungle compete to get limited resources, people compete to get the limited fortunes in the urban jungle. If I get something, someone cannot get as much as I get, and inversely, I cannot get as much as someone gets if someone gets something. People compete with each other in the urban jungle, but they always feel a shortage and are not satisfied with the results. Even if they are temporarily satisfied with the fortune of today, they always think that it is totally not enough. A windflower pushes its way through the urban jungle, enduring 90 percent misfortune, irritation, anger, and frustration to get 10 percent fortune. Others have difficulty as much as I feel comfortable, and others feel comfortable as much as I have difficulty. The more I have, the less others have, and the less I have, the more others have. The fact that materials are not enough to satisfy all people on earth, not to mention that people are narrow-minded, makes life poorer. Even so, utmost efforts remain a virtue of survival. However, the result of efforts is decided according to the tide of the times, and only a will remains while endeavoring. It is not easy to break the chain of the poor getting poorer and the rich getting richer, built up in the urban jungle like a food chain built up in the course of the evolution of species, and to set the distribution of wealth in order. Is it a reasonable conduct that a slave serves in preparing meals for a philosopher to have a time of speculation or not? The answer about that varies according to the situation of each person.

181. 새는 직선으로 빠르게 난다. 나비는 팔랑거리며 천천히 난다. 나비가 빠르게 나는 새를 피할 수 있는 것은 팔랑거리며 나는 나비 몸짓을 직선으로 나는 새가 가늠할 수 없기 때문이다. 이처럼 사람마다 태어남이 다르니 같을 수 없고 같을 수 없으니 사는 것이 다를 수밖에 없다. 그러나 다르다는 것은 자존이지 차별의 대상이 아니다. 그러므로 모든 것은 차별을 넘어서 하나에 이른다.

182. 아홉이 무너져야 하나가 일어서는 시련 속에서 살아가는 열악한 인생들에 후회는 없다. 사업이나 국가경영이나 역사 속에 자취만을 남길 뿐 무덤에 가져갈 것은 아무것도 없다. 사자와 악어 간에 싸움이 벌어진다면 누가 이길까? 들판에서 싸우면 백번 사자가 이길 것이고 늪지에서 싸우면 백번 악어가 이길 것이다. 저마다 처한 환경과 재능이 다르니 어찌 하나만을 보고 승패를 가늠하랴! 달은 차면 기울고 영원한 승자는 없는 법이니 저도 졌다 하지 말고 이겨도 이겼다 하지 마라. 아홉 개의 무덤 사이로 바람이 불어도 한 송이 바람꽃은 언제나 피어난다.

181. A bird flies fast in a straight line, but a butterfly flutters slowly. A butterfly can avoid fast-flying birds because the straight-flying birds cannot take aim at the fluttering butterfly. Like this, people cannot be the same because they are born in different circumstances, and their lifestyles are naturally different because they are not same. However, to be different is not the object of distinction but self-respect, so all things return to one beyond distinction.

182. There is no regret for the poor lives enduring the trials that they'd win one time after collapsing nine times. A business as well as a governmental administration leaves only a trace in history, and there is nothing to bring to the tomb. If a lion has a fight with a crocodile, who will win? If they fight in the field, a lion will win as a matter of course. On the other hand, a crocodile will win if they fight in the swamp. As each has different talents and circumstances, how can a victory be decided by only one thing! As the moon will wane if it waxes in full, and there is no everlasting winner in the world, don't say that you are a loser if you lose, and don't say that you are a winner if you win. Though a wind blows among nine tombs, a windflower always blooms.

183. (시 24)
황소 몰고 저녁노을 태우며 간다.
고개 넘어 황톳길 터덜터덜 간다.

꼬부라진 오솔길 꾸부정한 발걸음
피리소리 바람 타고 돌아서서 간다.

"이제는 그만 가야지."
"이제는 그만 가야지."

"돌아가는 이 길을
이제는 그만 가야지." 하면서

달 뜨는 언덕에 피리 불며 간다.
고개 넘어 황톳길 터덜터덜 간다.

꼬부라진 오솔길 꾸부정한 발걸음
피리소리 바람 타고 돌아서서 간다.

184. 지구상에서 벌어지는 종교 간, 민족 간의 이념전쟁이나 석유를 둘러싼 경제 전쟁이나 그로 인한 테러나 정치인들 간의 당파논쟁이나 부익부 빈익빈으로 왜곡된 사회적 반목이나 개인 간의 사사로운 갈등들이 인류 역사의 큰 틀에서 본다면 찰나적인 오해일 뿐 그때 그 시절이 지나고 나면 모두 다 돌아와 거울 앞에서 스스로 되돌아보게 된다. 그때 즈음이면 어느 산마루 능선 한 점에 나목으로 서 있는 자신들의 벌거벗은 모습을 바라보며 달팽이 뿔 재기와 같았던 지난날의 미혹을 흙에 묻고 바람꽃이 되어 있으리라.

183. (Poem 24)
One goes together with a bull, burning with the setting sun.
One plods along the ocher road over a ridge.

With meandering steps on the winding path,
one goes back beating time to the sound of a flute.

"No longer go now."
"No longer go now."

"On the way to return to."
Saying, "No longer go now."

One goes down the hill of moonrise playing a flute.
One plods along the ocher road over a ridge.

With meandering steps on the winding path,
one goes back beating time to the sound of a flute.

184. An ideological war between religions and between races occurring in the world, an economic war or terror related to oil, a party dispute between politicians, a social hostility distorted by the poor and the rich, and a private discord between persons—all are but a misunderstanding of the moment in view of human history, so all returns looking back upon themselves in front of a mirror after time and tide pass by. Looking at their true selves like a bare tree on the ridge at that time or so, they will become windflowers after burying their transient delusion of the past in the ground.

185. 세계 주요 도시에서는 출산율이 떨어지고 할 일 없는 노인들이 증가하여 이대로 가다가는 결국 빈곤한 노인들로 득실거리는 황량한 지구가 되고 말 것이다. 이러한 악순환의 고리를 끊기 위해서 직장인들이 정년까지 지구환경을 이용한 개발사업에 종사하고 정년 이후에는 지구환경을 회복하는 개선사업에 종사할 수 있도록 하여 건강한 지구, 건강한 노후 생활이 되도록 하고 한 여성이 평균 두 명의 자녀를 출산하도록 하며 산소 호흡기에 의존하여 비정상적으로 노인의 생명을 연장하는 의료행위는 자제하도록 하여 순리에 따라 생사가 순환되도록 하여야 한다. 오는 것을 막지 않고 가는 것을 잡지 않는 자연의 섭리에 따라 봄, 여름, 가을, 겨울이 순환하듯이 인위적인 삶에서 자연적인 삶으로 회복 시켜 나가야 한다.

186. 현대 문명의 생활방식이 세분화되고 이웃 간의 인정이 단절되면서 각박한 현실에 적응하지 못하고 자살하는 사람들이 증가하고 있다. 치열한 생존의 법칙하에 도시의 정글 속을 살아가는 사람들이 정글의 법칙을 벗어나 자살로 극적인 인생역전을 시도하는 것은 대단한 아이러니가 아닐 수 없다. 자살하는 사람들의 입장에서 본다면 세상은 그만큼 부조리하다. "생명을 부지하고 살 만한 가치가 무엇인가?" 하는 삶에 대한 근원적인 물음과 함께 "서둘러 가야 할 이유는 무엇인가?" 반문하면서 한편으로 "산소마스크를 쓰면서 모질게 생명을 연장하는 노인들은 무엇인가?" 되묻게 하는 것이 삶의 계층 간 아이러니다. 그러나 누구나 한 번쯤은 벗어야 할 육체이기에 자살하는 것만으로 인생역전이 이뤄지는 것이 아니다. 죽음은 누구나 맞이하는 삶의 일부이므로 사는 동안 서두르지도 멈추지도 않고 스스로를 향하여 돌아가는 여유로움을 깨우쳐야 한다.

185. As birthrate is reduced and jobless old people are on the increase in the major cities of the world, at this rate, the earth will be deserted and swarmed with poor, old people. In order to cut this vicious circle, businessmen should be asked to work on recovering the global environment while they work on developing and taking advantage of the globe until they retire, so the globe becomes sustainable and environmentally sound, and these retired men can live healthily in their old age. In addition, a woman delivers two babies on average, and medical treatment unusually extending the lives of old people by aerobic respiration is self-controlled, so life and death should be circulated in a rational manner. Natural life should be recovered from an artificial life, as the four seasons circulate according to the dispensation of nature not to block the coming and not to hold the going.

186. People committing suicide are increasing in number because the lifestyle of the modern culture is subdivided, and communication with neighbors is cut off. It is clearly an irony that people living in the urban jungle under the law of severe survival commit suicide, getting out of the law of the jungle. The world is absurd in view of people committing suicide. The original question of life is, "What is worth bearing life?" And there's a cross-question, "What is the motive to end life in a hurry?" Then a question to throw back on the other hand is, "What is the purpose of old people trying to extend their wretched life with aerobic respiration?" There is an irony between the classes of life, but life is not reversed with suicide because everybody is fated to leave their body given for a while. As all die and death is a part of life, people have to realize their presence of mind, going back toward themselves without hurry or stopping during their lifetime.

187. (시 25)
경쟁 그리고 기록의 뒤안길로
영웅을 앞세우고 뛰어간다.

유행 속에 떠오른 허상으로
군중은 고독 속에 환희하고

다시 돌아와 눕는 자화상에
속절없이 마주하는 그림자

브레이크 없는 게임 속으로
스스로를 잊으며 달려간다.

187. (Poem 25)
Beyond competition and record,
a crowd runs with a hero at the head.

With a virtual image arising in fashion,
a crowd is delighted in loneliness.

With a self-portrait lying again in return,
the shadow is resignedly opposite.

In the game without brakes,
a crowd runs forgetting themselves.

188. (시 26)

족속들이 유행을 만들고
그 족속들의 도시가 밀려온다.
아메바 물결치는 군중 속으로
무수히 흩어지는 사념들
욕망에 묶여 몰려가는 홍수 속에
하늘 바다 구분 없이 혼돈하고
머리와 꼬리가 뒤엉키고
달을 삼키고 별을 삼키고
유행을 넘어서 유행으로
족속을 넘어서 족속으로
무리 져 헤엄치는 유령의 도시여!
울음도 아니고 웃음도 아니고
서로가 부대끼는 소음 속으로
좌표 없는 시간 속에
브레이크 없는 도시는 밀려간다.

188. (Poem 26)

A lot sets the fashion,

and the city of a lot surges.

In crowds waving like amoebas,

a lot of thought scatters.

By floods overflowing with desires,

the heavens and the ocean are chaotic without division.

Heads get entangled with tails,

and the moon as well as the stars is swallowed.

With fashion over fashion,

and with a lot over a lot,

what a city of ghosts pawing the air in a group!

Neither crying nor laughing,

struggling with each other in uproar.

In time out of coordinates,

a city is pushed without brakes.

189. (시 27)

청설모 달아나는 가지 사이로
하얀 목련 곱게 떨어지고
꽃잎 띄운 연못가에
소나무 그림자 거울같이 맑다.

먼 산 넘어 봉봉이
구름에 젖가슴 풀어헤치고
굽이도는 계곡 사이로
어우르는 바람 소리 적막하다.

190. (시 28)

벼루에 뜬 둥근 달이 임의 얼굴 같아서
먹을 갈고 마음을 갈고

벼루에 이는 물결이 임의 숨결 같아서
먹을 갈고 마음을 갈고

벼루에 스치는 바람이 임의 노래 같아서
먹을 갈고 마음을 갈고

벼루에 고인 세월 속에 임을 부르니
마음이 씻겨간 빈자리에 학이 날아오르네.

붉은 해를 입에 물고 날아오르네.
날갯짓에 먹물 한 점 날아오르네.

189. (Poem 27)
Between branches on which a chipmunk runs away,
the white petals of a magnolia flutter down lovely.
In a pond scattered with petals,
the shadow of a pine tree is reflected clearly.

Peak to peak along the ridge,
unveil their bosoms into clouds.
In the valley turning around,
the echo of wind resounds alone.

190. (Poem 28)
As a full moon rising on the ink stone is like a face of love,
cultivate a mind, rubbing an ink stick.

As a wave rising on the ink stone is like a breath of love,
cultivate a mind, rubbing an ink stick.

As a wind blowing on the ink stone is like a song of love,
cultivate a mind, rubbing an ink stick.

By calling love in the time remaining with an ink stone,
in the void beyond a mind does a crane fly up.

It flies up with the sun in its bill.
A dot of ink flies up, flapping its wings.

191. (시 29)

텅 비어 막힘이 없으니 진이요

하나 되어 다툼이 없으니 선이요

있는 그대로 꾸밈이 없으니 미로다.

192. (시 30)

하늘 바다에 수많은 낙조 물들고

기슭에서 기슭으로 세월이 흘러도

빈 배는 그대로 기다리고 있다.

하늘 바다에 수많은 그림자 기울고

안갯속으로 임은 떠났어도

빈 배는 그대로 기다리고 있다.

193. 1이라는 숫자가 갖는 의미는 어떠한가? 0과 1로 이뤄진 이진법이 반도체의 혁명을 가져오고 0으로써 상징되는 무와 1로써 상징되는 존재가 메모리칩에서 수없이 반복을 계속하며 오늘날 일상생활에서 있고 없음을 좌지우지하기에 이르렀다. 이와 같이 있고 없음이 선택 아닌 일상의 흐름인데 모두 다 1등이 되어 잘 먹고 잘살아야 하는 것이라면 2등 이하는 무얼 먹고 살아야 하는가? 2등 이하는 아무것도 아닌 0이란 말인가? 1등의 위치에 잠시 서 있는 자는 특별히 선택되었다는 착각에서 벗어나 다수가 있기에 1등이 있음을 헤아려야 한다.

191. (Poem 29)

It is True because of no barrier in the void.
It is Good because of no quarrel by uniting into one.
It is Beauty because of no affectation as is.

192. (Poem 30)

The setting sun glows in the sky and ocean,
and the time and tide flow from bank to bank.
Nevertheless an empty boat is still waiting.

A lot of shade sinks in the sky and ocean,
and thou leave into the mists of time.
Nevertheless an empty boat is still waiting.

193. What is the meaning of the number one? The binary system consisting of zeros and ones brought the revolution of semiconductors. Nothing symbolized by zero and existence symbolized by one are continuously repeated in memory chips, so those came to lead existence and nothingness in daily life at present. Just like that, since existence and nothingness are not a choice but a daily routine, if all people have to live well by taking the first place, how does a class lower than the second live? Do they deserve to live as nothing? The one taking first place temporarily should get out of the illusion of being selected specially and know that he can only take the first place because there are a number of common people.

194. 남편을 죽인 여인은 자신이 낳은 아들에게 죽임을 당하고 저주받은 그 아들마저 스스로 죽음에 이르니 피보라 치는 욕망의 불길은 마침내 재가 되어서야 끝이 난다. 이와 같이 미망에서 깨어나면 꿈인 것을 삶에서 깨어나면 무엇인가? 부어도 넘치지 않고 퍼내도 비워지지 않는 허공에 걸인이 아랫도리 벗고 대변을 본다. 그런 후 열 걸음도 안 되는 나무그늘에 돌아와 누워 잠을 청하니 허공과 걸인 사이에 경계가 있는가? 없는가?

195. 식과 성을 제외하고 인간이 할 수 있는 것이란 무엇인가? 생로병사로부터의 해탈을 구하는 것인가? 대륙을 정복하는 꿈을 키우는 것인가? 종교를 만들고 신을 찾는 것인가? 예술에 도취되고 과학문명에 몰입하는 것인가? 이처럼 인간은 다양한 방법으로 육체를 넘어서 식과 성으로부터 해방되려고 한다. 그러나 진정한 삶은 육체를 동반하는 생존의 긴장 속에서 피어나는 것이기에 바람꽃은 하늘 바다에서 육체의 닻을 들고 영혼의 돛을 펼쳐나간다.

194. A woman killed her husband and was killed by her own son, and the son inheriting a curse killed himself. The flame of bloody desire ends by becoming ash at last. What is to awake from life, whereas it is a dream to awake from an illusion like this? As a beggar moves bowels into the void, which is not full by pouring and is not empty by dipping out, he falls asleep coming back to the shade within ten steps. Is there any confines between the void and the beggar or not?

195. What can humans do except to eat and to have sex? Is that to be delivered from birth, old age, sickness, and death? To dream of conquering the continent? To seek God by making a religion? To be intoxicated with art? Or to be immersed in scientific civilization? Like this, humans try to be free from eating and having sex in several ways. However, a windflower goes spreading the sail of the soul while getting up the anchor of the body to heaven and the ocean, because real life is lived together with a body amid the tension of survival.

196. 하루와 일 년은 지구가 자전하는 것과 태양 주위를 공전하는 천체 운행에 맞춰 정해진 것이고 한 달은 달이 지구 주위를 공전하는 천체 운행 주기에 맞춰 정해진 것이지만 일주일은 천체 운행과 상관없이 사람들의 노동과 휴식을 위하여 정해진 주기다. 생존하기 위해서 노동이 필수적인 것이지만 살아가기 위해서 휴식이 또한 필수적이다. 그래서 노동의 정도에 따라 휴식기간이 다르기는 하지만 대부분 사람들은 일주일에 하루를 쉬고 문명이 발달하면서 이틀을 쉬는 경우가 많아졌으며 앞으로는 사흘 쉬는 경우도 많아질 것이다. 또한 사람들이 함께 일하고 함께 쉬려면 일정한 날에 휴일을 정해 놓을 필요가 있으나 지구는 자전하기 때문에 반대편과 12시간 시차가 있으니 어차피 세계인이 공통으로 똑같은 요일에 휴일을 맞이할 수는 없다. 하루의 절반은 차이가 날 수밖에 없다. 따라서 휴일이란 무슨 요일을 택할 것인가 하는 데 의미가 있기보다는 어떻게 올바른 휴식을 취할 것인가 하는 데 의미가 있다.

197. 덩치가 작은 쥐나 덩치가 큰 코끼리나 거의 비슷하게 평생 동안 이억 번 정도의 호흡을 하고 팔억 번 정도의 심장박동을 하다가 생을 마감한다. 따라서 분당 백오십 번 호흡하는 쥐의 수명은 삼 년에 불과한 데 비하여 분당 여섯 번 호흡하는 코끼리는 오륙십 년을 산다. 이와 같이 호흡과 심장박동수에 따라 수명은 상대적으로 변하는 것이니 모든 살아있는 생명은 한 호흡의 의미를 소중히 새겨야 한다. 삼라만상 모든 것은 한 호흡에 펼쳐지고 한 호흡에 사라지는 바람 속의 춤과 같다.

196. A day and a year are determined by the earth's rotation and revolution, respectively, and a month is determined by the moon's revolution, but a week is a period determined for human labor and rest regardless of the movement of heavenly bodies. Labor is essential for survival, but rest is also essential to living. Therefore, even though a rest period is different according to the degree of labor, most people take a rest for a day every week. There are also many cases in society, amid our advanced civilization, where people have two days off. Three days is to be expected in the future. It is also necessary to determine a rest day for working and resting together with fellow workers, but all cosmopolitan cannot have a rest day on the same day because there is a twelve-hour difference in time between one side and the other side of the rotating globe. There is no way to overcome a difference of half a day. Therefore a rest day has meaning with regard to how to take a rest properly, rather than what day is taken in a week.

197. Both a small rat and a big elephant breathe two hundred million times, and both their hearts beat eight hundred million times in their lifetime. The average life span of a rat breathing about 150 times per minute is only three years, while the average life span of an elephant breathing about six times per minute is fifty to sixty years. As above, considering that a lifetime becomes relatively different according to the number of breaths and heartbeats, all lives alive should catch the meaning of a breath carefully. All creation is like a dance of wind, spreading with an exhalation and disappearing with an inhalation.

198. 인간복제를 자연에 대한 도전이라고 우려하는 것은 행여나 실수로 괴물을 만들어내지 않을까 우려하기 때문이다. 하지만 이미 주변에는 수많은 복제가 이뤄지고 있다. 광고나 매스컴을 통하여 오락과 스포츠와 패션과 온갖 유행을 통하여 정신적, 심리적인 복제가 무의식적으로 이뤄지고 있다. 할아버지의 할아버지가 손자의 손자일 적부터 홀로그램의 영상처럼 흡수되고 반사되어 스스로를 기억하고 외모에서부터 정신적인 영역에 이르기까지 알게 모르게 복제되고 복제하며 서로가 하나 되어 살고 있다. 짐승들도 서로 몸을 비비며 체취를 나누는 것은 서로가 하나임을 표현하기 위한 것이다. 무릇 만물은 한시적인 개체에서 보편적인 전체로 변화되는 과정에서 서로 껴안고 서로 느끼며 있는 그대로의 개체가 지속되기를 바라고 있는 것이다. 이는 개체가 죽어서 전체와 화합한 후에도 없어지지 않고 전체와 함께하기를 바라기 때문이다.

199. (시 31)
직선을 휘어서 원을 그으니
안과 밖이 나뉘고
안은 원 안이요 밖은 원 밖이다.
원을 그렸으되 원은 어디 있는가?
경계만 남아
안은 안이 아니고 밖은 밖이 아니니
선마저 묘연하다.
이름하여
원은 원이로되 무한량이로다.

198. Concerned about creating a monster possibly by mistake, people worry about human cloning as a challenge to nature. However, a lot of duplication is already performed all around us. Mental and psychological duplication is performed unconsciously by means of fashion, amusements, and sports as well as advertisements and mass communication. People live in harmony duplicating or being duplicated—figuratively up to the spiritual sphere—without knowing, and humanity remembers itself from generation to generation by absorbing and reflecting images like a hologram. It is also to express themselves, united into one, that animals share their body smell by rubbing on each other. As a general rule, all creations want to exist continuously as is while hugging and feeling each other in the course of changing from the momentary individual to the universal whole, because they don't want to disappear. They want to be with the whole even after being united into the whole by dying.

199. (Poem 31)
As a circle is drawn by curving a straight line,
the inside and the outside are divided.
And the inside is inside the circle, and the outside is outside the circle.
Even if a circle is drawn, where is the circle?
Because of the only confines remaining,
the inside is not the inside, and the outside is not the outside.
So a line is also missing.
As named,
though a circle is a circle, it is infinite.

200. (시 32)
뚫어져라 바라보니 공산(空山)이요
마음 안에 머무르니 생멸(生滅)이라.

저 건너에 무엇이 있을까 하니
허공 앞에 벽이로다.

오고 간 것 없이 무구하고
바람 소리에 공산이 와르르

깨어보니 온 데 간 데 벽은 없고
황소타고 가는 것은 웬 놈인가?

201. (시 33)
공산에 달 뜨니 어둠은 푸르르고
교교한 달빛에 대지는 고요한데
공산에 걸린 가슴 오가지 못하고
잃어버린 꿈들로 긴 밤 지새우다
달빛에 흠뻑 젖어 구름이 된다.

202. 공산(空山)에 색(色)이 깊으니 빈 거죽이 도(道)일세.

203. 인생이란 바람 속에서 피어나는 꽃. 소유할 수 없기에 사랑스럽고 머물지 않기에 더욱 아름다운 꽃.

200. (Poem 32)
There is an empty hill if I stare into space,
and it is birth and death if I stay in mind.

As I think what is over there,
it is a wall before the void.

As it is eternal without coming and going,
the empty hill crumbles with the sound of the wind.

As soon as being awakened, the wall is missing,
then who is the guy riding on a bull?

201. (Poem 33)
As the moon rises over an empty hill, the bluish dark deepens,
and Mother Earth is calm, bathing in the bright moonlight.
While a mind hanging over the empty hill is bewildered,
and passes all night with a lost dream,
it becomes a cloud by wetting with the moonlight.

202. As lust deepens in the void, the empty substance might be
the truth.

203. Life is a flower blooming in the wind. Life is lovely because
it cannot be possessed, and it is more beautiful because it does not
stay.

204. 인생은 생각하는 것처럼 그렇게 중요한 것도 그렇다고 허망한 것도 아니다. 얻는다고 행복해지고 잃는다고 불행해지는 것도 아니다. 인생은 오색의 마법에 걸린 인형도 아니고 오감에 흔들리는 허수아비도 아니다. 괴성과 몸부림에 잃어버릴 영혼은 더욱 아니다. 텅 비어 막힘이 없고 하나 되어 다툼이 없고 있는 그대로 꾸밈이 없으니 가히 바람꽃 그대로다.

205. (시 34)
인생에서 오고감이 무엇인가?
쉼 없는 세상 번잡에서 놓여나니
허공 속에 한 점 바람이라.

오지 않는 인연에 애달파하지 않고
다가서는 인연에 마다하지 않으니
있는 그대로 여유로운 삶이어라.

206. 무릇 생명은 물이 흐르는 가운데 살아가고 물이 메마르면 생명은 시들어 버린다. 사람도 몸과 마음이 메말라서는 넉넉하고 여유로운 삶을 누릴 수 없다. 물이 흐르듯이 몸과 마음이 여유로워야 삶에 생기가 솟아난다. 인생은 시련 속에서 살고 있지만 가슴속 심연에 한 줄기 강물이 흐르고 있기에 향기로운 것이다.

204. Life is not so important and not so nonsensical as to be thought. It doesn't make you happy if you get something, and it doesn't make you unhappy if you lose something. Life is not a doll bound by a spell of the five cardinal colors, not a scarecrow shaken by the five senses. Furthermore, it is not a soul lost by a strange sound and a violent struggle. It is really a windflower itself because there is no barrier in the void, no quarrel by harmonizing with one thing, and no affectation as is.

205. (Poem 34)
What is the meaning of coming and going in life?
As soon as one is released from the triviality of the restless world, there is a wind rising in the void.

Not to long for the ties not coming,
and not to refuse the ones approaching,
that is the composure of life as is.

206. All of life is living in a place where water flows, while life fades if water is dry. Also man is not able to live in comfort if his mind and body are dry. Vitality springs up in life when the body and the mind have enough to flow like water. Though we are living with trials, our lives are beautiful because a river flows in the abyss of mind.

207. (시 35)

아직 살아 있다는 그것만으로 위안을 삼는다면
자신을 속이는 슬픈 일이다.

살아있음이려니 죽지 않음에 삶의 의미를 둔다면
널 속에 잠자는 몸일 뿐

길가에 주검을 보며 죽음은 어느 때고 다가오려니
매달리는 여인인 양 버려두고

붙잡지 않으면 날아가는 파랑새인 양
우선 삶에 매달려

일방으로 스쳐 가는 시간 속에서
죽음은 무상 삶은 유상이라고 지레짐작하고

아직 살아있다는 그것만으로 위안을 삼는다면
자신을 속이는 슬픈 일이다.

창고에 쌓인 식량처럼 어느 때고 꺼내먹는 삶이라면
순간순간 솟아나는 향기는 어디에 있을까?

다가설수록 멀어지는 허상일 뿐
삶은 창고에 싸놓는 것이 아니요

가꾸는 대로 향기 피어나서
순간순간 채워지는 안개 꿈과 같은 것
그래서 더욱 아름다워지는 것이 삶이리라.

207. (Poem 35)
If you find consolation only in surviving still,
it's a pity to deceive your own.

If the meaning of life is only not to die,
life is nothing but a body sleeping inside a coffin.

Seeing a corpse by the roadside, you think of death coming
anytime,
and throw away death like a clinging woman.

Like a blue bird that flies away if not held,
by being addicted to life first.

In time changing evanescently,
guessing that death is worthless, and life is worth it.

If you find consolation only in surviving still,
it's a pity to deceive your own.

If life is to eat anytime, like food stocked in a warehouse,
where is the fragrance of life spreading every second?

That is only a false image, getting away contrary to getting near.
Life is not about stocking in a warehouse.

As the fragrance spreads according to attention,
life is like a foggy dream filled up every second.
Thus it is life to become more beautiful.

208. (시 36)

새가 날아오르는 것은
숲이 그립기 때문입니다.

새로울 것 없는 계절은
여름인 양 푸르고

아이가 창공을 날아가니
생사는 단순하였습니다.

바람인 줄 어찌 모르고
삶이라 하겠습니까?

순간은 그런 것이려니
침묵은 하늘이 되었고

달이라 품어 안던 세월은
기다림뿐이었습니다.

고개 넘어 장승도
부질없는 이름뿐이었습니다.

이제 무영탑을 돌아보니
그림자는 보이지 않습니다.

아무것도 없는 것은
네가 늘 곁에 있음이려니

208. (Poem 36)
A bird flies up
because it longs for a forest.

The season as usual
is full of vigor like summer.

As a juvenile flew into the heavens,
life and death were simple.

Without knowing of the wind,
how can it be called life?

A moment might be like that,
so a silence became the heavens.

Time and tide hugging the moon—
that was nothing but to await.

A totem pole over the hill—
that was also nothing but a name in vain.

On looking back at the astral tower now,
its shadow is not seen there.

The reason why there is nothing
is that you are always nearby.

209. (시 37)
오늘 하루가 너에게 묻고 있다.
"인생을 낭비하지 않았느냐?"

수많은 날들이 기억 속에 지워지며
사소한 일들로 흘러간 세월들

어느덧 황혼이 어둠에 묻히고
낯선 얼굴로 돌아와 눕던 날

너에게 맡겨진 한 폭의 캔버스에
무엇이 그려져 있을까?

210. (시 38)
비 오는 날 태어난 하루살이는
온종일 빗속에서 일생을 보내고

청명한 날 태어난 하루살이는
온종일 햇빛에서 일생을 보낸다.

빗속의 일생도 한 생이요
햇빛 속의 일생도 한 생이니

어인 분별로 하루해를 탓하리?

209. (Poem 37)
You are asked today,
"Didn't you waste your life?"

So many days disappeared from memory,
and time and tide were taken up with trifles.

On the day when twilight falls into the darkness before you are
aware of it,
and you lie down coming back with a strange feature,

on the canvas left in your keeping,
what will be drawn?

210. (Poem 38)
An ephemera born on a rainy day
spends its whole life in the rain.

And another ephemera born on a sunny day
spends its whole life in the sun.

As life in the rain is a life,
and life in the sun is also a life,

how can a day be blamed with distinction?

211. (시 39)
앞서지 마라.
가벼움에 방황하리라.

구하지 마라.
무거움에 고뇌하리라.

평상심에
삶은 여유로우리니.

212. (시 40)
삶은 순간 속에 피고 지고
침묵은 그대로 변함없으니

오늘을 맞이하기 위하여
어제와 작별하지 않아도 되리라.

하늘은 오래전에 열리고
강물은 지금도 흐르나니

세월은 빈 배가 되어
기슭에서 기슭으로 저어가리라.

211. (Poem 39)
Don't be far ahead,
or you will wander with lightness.

Don't pursue,
or you will suffer the weight.

With presence of mind,
life will be calm and composed.

212. (Poem 40)
As life blooms and fades every moment,
and silence is constant as it is,

for greeting today,
it is not necessary to say farewell to yesterday.

As the heavens is open long ago,
and the river flows still,

time and tide become an empty boat,
and it will row from bank to bank.

213. (시 41)

떠나간다. 가는 곳 몰라도 떠나간다.
색과 향을 따먹으며 그런 양 떠나간다.

즐거움도 괴로움도
하루 햇살 부서지는 마른 가지에 걸쳐 놓고

비밀을 모르는 아이처럼
이것이 세상인 양 몸이 나인 양 떠나간다.

하루 이틀 지나고 이제는 수많은 날들이러니 돌아보면
숨소리만 세월을 헤이고 모든 것이 그대로 있음을 본다.

헛되고 헛된 꿈을 가슴에 묻고
떠나간 길이 되돌아오는 길임을 본다.

오색의 유혹도 한 줄기 빛에 실려 그림자 뒤로 사라지고
싱싱한 피와 살도 풍상에 베인 껍질 속에서 철이 든다.

그리고 그것들이 꿈이었다 할지라도 서러워 않는 것은
온갖 상념이 들로 하늘로 날아가 버려

오가는 인생에 부질없는 나이테만 늘어가지 않도록
스스로를 바라보기 때문이다.

213. (Poem 41)

I start off. Though I don't know where to go, I start off.
Taking colors and flavors, I start off like that.

While pleasure as well as annoyance is left,
hanging over a dried branch with the sunlight of a day,

like a child not knowing of a secret,
as if this is the world, and a body is me, I start off.

On looking back into the past after one or two days passed,
only with the sound of breathing counting time, I see all things as
is.

Burying a transient, evanescent dream in my heart,
I realize that the left way is a returning way.

The temptation of five colors disappears behind the shadow with a
streak of light,
and the fresh blood and flesh are also mature together with the skin
bearing hardships.

And then, even if those were a dream, I don't feel sorrow
because all thoughts scatter in the plain and sky.

And in the coming and going life, I look at myself,
not to go on increasing only with an annual ring uselessly.

214. (시 42)

지난여름 목련꽃 피기 전에 오신다던 손님은 오지 않고
꽃잎 저버린 텅 빈 정원에 낙엽마저 바람에 쓸려갑니다.

어리던 짐승도 이제 함께 늙었는지 모퉁이에 졸고 있고
낡은 집만큼이나 무거워진 육신이 겨울나기 힘들어
지난해 떠난 임이 더욱 그립습니다.

자리에 일찍 누워 겨울밤을 뒤척이니
반백 년이 훌쩍 지난 추억만 벽에 걸려 아른대고
밤이 되니 주위는 침묵에 쌓여 작은 짐승들 소리만 들립니다.

내일이면 행여나 오실까 일찍 불 지피고 정원도 손질하리라
이따금 바람 소리에 문풍지 우짖는 밤

꿈속의 햇살을 해진 가슴에 안아보니 아직은 부를 임이 있고
봄이 되면 가볼 무덤이 있고 기다리는 손님이 있습니다.

214. (Poem 42)

There is no news from the guest expected to come before a magnolia bloomed last summer.

In the empty garden where flowers fade, even the fallen leaves blow away with the wind.

As an animal that used to be young seems old now, it is falling asleep at a corner.

As a body depressed like an old house does not easily pass through the winter,

thou who passed away last year art more and more missed.

While going to bed early, tossing and turning all night in winter,

only an old memory, passed on for more than half a century, is haunting, hanging on the wall.

As night falls, there is only the sound of little animals in silent surroundings.

A firepot will be lit early, and a garden will also be cared for, for the guest who may drop by tomorrow.

At night when a windbreak is sometimes howled with the wind.

On hugging the sunlight of dream to the worn heart, there is still thou to call.

And there are a grave to visit in the coming spring and a guest to wait for.

215. 인간은 이성적이며 동시에 감성적이다. 감성이 이성의 통제를 벗어난 극한의 상태는 혼돈 내지는 혼수의 상태이다. 거기에는 이미 이성은 존재하지 않고 질서를 기대할 수도 없다. 아무 데나 대소변을 보고 헛소리를 하는 지경에 이르고야 만다. 이성이 무너지고 질서가 무너지는 것은 그리 어려운 일이 아니다. 찬란히 빛나던 별이 급기야 폭발하여 우주의 어둠 속으로 재가 되어 사라져버리는 것이 자연의 모습이다. 이성은 자연의 질서가 혼돈상태로 치닫지 않도록 끊임없이 존재에 긴장을 부여하지만 이성이 변화무쌍한 감성을 언제까지나 통제하리라고 기대할 수는 없다. 그러기에 주검을 둘러메고 고갯길을 넘어가는 상여 소리가 이승에서 맴돌지 저승에 이를지는 삶에 남겨진 여백이다.

216. 얼굴이란 그 사람의 얼을 나타낸다. 사람은 눈과 입을 통하여 상대에게 자신의 생각과 감정을 미세한 부분까지 표현한다. 눈빛은 그 사람의 지성을 나타낸다. 눈빛에 총기가 있으면 정신이 맑고 사고력과 판단력이 빠르다. 총기가 없는 눈빛에서 맑은 정신을 기대하기란 어렵다. 미소는 그 사람의 감성을 나타낸다. 입가에 미소 띤 모습은 상대에게 호의를 나타내고 마음의 여유를 보여준다. 초롱한 눈빛은 그 사람의 깊은 사고력과 맑은 지성을 나타내고 우아한 미소는 고운 심성과 아름다운 감성을 나타내준다. 눈빛이 빛날지라도 미소가 결여된 얼굴은 자칫 차갑고 배타적인 지성에 빠지기 쉽다. 반면에 입가에 미소를 머금어도 눈빛에 총기가 없다면 자칫 초라해질 수 있다. 초롱한 눈빛과 우아한 미소가 한데 어우러진 얼굴에서 바람꽃의 향기를 느낄 수 있다.

215. Man is rational as well as sensitive. The extreme state that sensibility gets out of reason is the state of chaos or coma. There is already no reason, and any order cannot be expected. It stands on the brink of relieving nature anywhere and talking in delirium. It is not so much difficult that reason and order collapse. It is the figure of nature that a brightly shining star suddenly explodes, disappearing into the darkness of the universe after becoming ashes. Reason constantly gives strain to existence so that the order of nature is not in chaos, but it cannot be expected that reason controls changeable sensibility forever. Therefore it is a blank space left in life, whether a bier carrier's song, passing over the peak together with the corpse, echoes in this world or reaches to the other world.

216. Man's face expresses his soul. People reveal their thoughts and feelings delicately with their eyes and mouth. Glittering eyes show intellect. If the eyes are glittering bright, the spirit is clear, and thinking power and judgment are speedy. A clear spirit cannot be expected from eyes without brightness. A smile shows emotions. This smiling feature shows a friendly feeling for partners and shows something plentiful in mind. Glittering eyes show their thinking power and clear intellect, and a graceful smile shows a good mind and a beautiful emotion. However, glittering eyes without a graceful smile are liable to become chilly and exclusive, whereas a graceful smile without glittering eyes is liable to become poor. Therefore the scent of a windflower can be smelled only from a face in harmony, with glittering eyes and a graceful smile.

217. 꽃이 아름다운 것은 향기가 있기 때문이고 육체가 아름다운 것은 영혼이 깃들어 있기 때문이다. 영혼의 향기는 남녀 간에 사랑으로 느껴지기도 하고 부모와 자식 간에 혈육의 정으로 느껴지기도 하고 사물 간에 일체감으로 느껴지기도 한다. 향기는 주위에 대한 배려이며 누군가에 대한 그리움의 표현이다. 꽃의 향기가 벌을 부르듯이 영혼의 향기는 주위에 교감을 불러일으킨다. 향기는 주는 즐거움이다. 홀로 간직한 향기는 의미가 없다. 주위를 즐겁게 해줄 수 있기에 향기로운 것이다. 사람이나 사물들로부터 발산하는 향기들은 한데 어우러져 천지간에 두루 퍼져있다. 거리의 응원에서 수많은 인파가 박자에 맞춰 열광하는 것이나 창공을 무리 지어 나는 철새 떼의 장대한 군무는 서로 간에 조화를 이루며 교감할 수 있기에 가능한 것이다.

218. 하루해가 수만 번 지나도록 한 것이라곤 부질없는 이름 석 자돌 위에 새겨 놓고 낡은 몸 거죽 흙에 묻었으니 바람꽃 지는 날 무엇이라 할까? "허공이여! 비우고 또 비웠으니 이제 비울 것이 없소." 그러면 허공은 대답하리. "무명지박(無名之樸)이면 이미 족하니라."

217. Flowers are beautiful because they have a scent, and a body is beautiful because it has a spirit. The scent of a spirit is smelled through love between a man and a woman, affection between people of the same flesh and blood (between parents and children), or a sense of unity between things. This scent is a reminder to have regard for one's surroundings and to express longing for somebody. The scent of a spirit arouses sympathy from the surroundings, like how the scent of flowers attracts bees. This scent is pleasure being given away. It's meaningless to keep the scent itself. It's called scent because it makes one's surroundings happy. Scents diffused from people and things are spread, harmonizing together in the heavens and on earth. A crowd wildly excited and keeping time with the cheering in the street, or a magnificent group dancing of migratory birds flying in the blue heavens—all these are possible because they share each other's feelings of harmony.

218. As all I have done after days have passed tens of thousands of times is to carve a useless name in a tombstone and to bury an old body in the ground. What shall I say on the very day a windflower is gone? "Dear void! I have emptied myself again and again, so there is nothing remaining to empty anymore."
Then the void will reply, "It is already enough if your life was like a nameless, rough pine's."

219. 천년을 아무것도 하는 일 없이 산다. 불어오는 바람에 흘러가는 구름처럼, 쉬지 않고 흐르는 계곡의 물처럼 몸은 허공에 벗어 던지고 뜻 모를 이름 석 자 지우고 있는 그대로 산다. 들숨에 살고 날숨에 꿈꾼다. 씨앗이 싹을 틔워 고목이 되고 옹달샘이 물길을 열어 바다가 되도록 없었던 사람들이 태어나고 죽는다. 해는 동쪽에서 솟아나 서쪽으로 황도를 달리고 하늘이 어둠과 밝음을 호흡하는 동안 천년의 메아리가 허공에 여울진다. 그렇게 천년이 하루같이 흐른다.

220. 하얀 수염이 텁수룩한 남자가 콘크리트바닥에 앉아서 성자처럼 정좌하고 있다. 전에는 공장에서 일한 적도 있지만 지금은 힘든 일은 할 수 없고 결혼을 하지 않아 처자도 없다. 얼마 전까지 부랑자 합숙촌에서 지내다가 지금은 노숙하고 있고 미래에 대한 기약도 없다. 그가 할 수 있는 것이란 출퇴근길에 거리에 나와서 앉아있는 것이 전부다. 쉬운 일은 없고 힘든 일은 할 수 없고, 수중에는 돈 한 푼 없으니 춥고 배고프다. "믿으라! 그렇지 않으면 지옥에 가리라!" 차 안에서 누군가가 피곤한 시민들의 잠을 깨운다. 이미 침묵은 깊고 노숙자이건 거리이건 지옥은 어디에나 있어 왔다. 살아있다는 것은 존재의 긴장이며 죽음을 넘나드는 게임이다. 병렬로 갈지 직렬로 갈지 게임의 방향은 스스로 정해야 한다. 자유로운 영혼이여! 주저할 것이 무엇인가?

219. One lives doing nothing for a millennium. He lives as it is—like a cloud flying with the blowing wind and a creek flowing in the valley ceaselessly—throwing a body away into the void and rubbing out a meaningless name. He lives while inhaling and dreams while exhaling. While a seed grows to become an old tree and a small fountain flows to become the ocean, nonexistent people are born, and then they die. While the sun rises from the east, moving to the west ecliptically, and the heavens breathe darkness and brightness, the millennium echoes in the void. The millennium passes away like a day.

220. A man wearing a white whisker sits erect on his knees, on the concrete floor, like a saint. He worked in a factory before, but he cannot do hard work now, and he has no wife and children because he didn't get married. He stayed in a vagabond camp a few months ago, but now he sleeps in the open and has no hope for the future. All he can do is to sit on the street in time when people go to work and again during closing hours. There is no easy work, and he cannot do hard work and has no money in his hands, so he feels cold and hungry. "Believe! Or you will go to hell!" Somebody awakes the tired citizens in an electric train. A silence already deepens, and hell used to be everywhere, regardless of vagabonds or streets. Survival is the tension of existence and the game ready to die. People have to choose the direction of a game—whether to go in a row or go in a series by themselves. What a free spirit! Why do you hesitate?

221. (시 43)

풍상에 서걱이는 돌먼지 날리고
황토 냄새 배어나는
나무뿌리 추스르던 언덕에
임자 없는 집 한 채 휘돌아서면
처마 사이 구름 한 조각 흘러가고
능마루에 햇살 삼삼히 부서져
스산한 겨울바람 낡은 깃발에 파닥이고
늙은 소나무 허리 틀고 서 있는 양지 비탈에
얼어붙은 물줄기 해동을 기다리던 곳
부스스한 하늘이고 마른 풀잎 흩날리다
겨우내 배고픈 짐승들 발자국 소리에
함께 짐승 되어 헤맨다.

222. (시 44)

가고 없는 아이 옆에
늙은 성자 굽어보고

어미도 함께 서서
창밖에 가을은 그리운데

바람꽃은 말없이
허공에 향기만 그윽하다.

221. (Poem 43)
Raising dust crumbled in the wind and frost,
and smelling of ocher soil,
on the hilltop where roots of trees were picked up,
while turning around an ownerless shanty,
a piece of cloud floats between eaves.
As the sunlight shines in the ridge,
a worn flag flutters in the piercing winter wind.
At the sunny slope where an old pine stands, twisting its waist,
a place where a frozen stream was awaiting a thaw⋯.
While dried grasses scatter in a rather cloudy day,
by the touch and sound of beasts starved during wintertime,
I wander together with them.

222. (Poem 44)
Beside a child gone away,
an old saint is looking down.

As a mother also stands up,
the fall outside the window is missed.

While a windflower is in silence,
the void is fragrant only with blossoms.

223. 누구나 태어난 곳이 있고 스스로를 향한 회귀본능이 있기에 향수와 그리움은 있게 마련이다. 그리움이란 자기 자신의 내면에 던져진 물음이다. 그래서 마음속 고향을 그리워한다. 자신의 존재를 함께 나눌 수 있는 친구가 있기에 고향이 그리운 것이다. 친구는 개체로 태어난 생명이 전체에 이르는 통로이다. 친구는 대지에서 태어난 모든 생명들이 본래로 향하는 길목에서 만나게 되는 동반자다. 그러기에 친구는 삶 속에서 부딪히는 모든 만물 속에 깃들어 있으면서 자신의 모습을 보여주는 거울이다. 그 거울을 보면서 고향을 느끼고 스스로의 회귀본능에 안기게 된다. 홀로 태어나서 홀로 떠나야 하는 인생에서 행복할 수 있는 것은 돌아갈 고향이 있고 함께할 친구가 있기 때문이다. "돌아갈 고향은 어디이며 함께할 친구는 누구인가?" 언젠가는 묻게 되는 질문이다.

223. Since everybody has his hometown and the instinct to return to himself, homesick and nostalgia remain by definition. Nostalgia is a question thrown into the inner world, so people long for their hometown in the inner world. They long for home because there is a friend to share their existence. A friend is a passage that allows an individually born life to arrive whole. A friend is a companion that all lives born on earth meet on their way to return to the origin. Therefore a friend dwells in all things met in life and is also a mirror to reflect oneself. People feel home while looking in the mirror, and they are steeped in their homing instinct. People can be happy in life born alone and left alone because there are hometowns to return to and friends to accompany. "Where is a hometown to return to, and who is a friend to accompany?" That is a question arising someday.

224. 지하철에 주말 행락객이 분빈다. 전철에 육십 대 남자와 사십 대 여자가 앉아 있다. 포마드 기름으로 머리를 매끈하게 빗어 넘기고 검정 가방을 든 육십 대 남자는 날카로운 눈매를 번득이며 사십 대 여자에게 훈계하듯이 무엇인가 말하고 있다. 그때마다 여자는 상체를 앞뒤로 흔들며 연신 불안한 듯 미간을 찌푸린다. 남자는 툭툭 여자를 건드리면서 설교하듯이 어른다. "하나님의 딸을 누가 감히 해코지하겠느냐?" 그래도 여자는 연신 불안한 눈빛이다. 남자는 그런 여자의 얼빠진 표정을 하나도 놓치지 않고 읽으면서 대화 사이사이로 갈고리 눈매를 번뜩인다. 남자는 먹이를 어떻게 요리할지 이미 머릿속에 구상이 끝난 듯이 고압적이면서도 여유 있는 태도로 실눈을 가늘게 뜨고 주위 동정을 살핀다. 허약한 심기로 흔들리는 여자, 그 영혼을 구제하겠노라고 충동질하는 포마드 기름 머리의 남자, 여자는 먹이가 되어 잡아먹힐지라도 우선 당장 심신이 괴로우니 어쩔 수 없다는 표정이고 남자는 먹이를 앞에 놓고 잡아먹기 전에 마지막 마무리를 어떻게 할지 궁리한다. 먹이가 하나님이고 하나님이 먹이가 되어 잡아먹고 잡아먹히려는 생존게임을 남녀 간에 벌이고 있다.

어느덧 전철이 역에 도착하자 많은 행락객이 쏟아져 내린다. 산행을 시작한 지 몇 시간쯤 지나 정상에 이를수록 길은 가파르고 코앞에 보이는 정상은 멀기만 하다. 마지막 정상은 화강암 바위로 급경사를 이루고 있어서 가까이 다가갈수록 멀어지는 느낌이다. 다리근육에 무리가 느껴지지만 모두 오르는 정상을 놔두고 되돌아온다는 것은 패배감을 안겨줄 것만 같아 기를 쓰고 오른다. 인생이란 이와 같다. 막상 정상에 오르고 나면 다시 내려와야 하건만 한번 출발한 것이니 남들이 다 가보는 정상에 나도 한번 가보고 싶은 것이 인생이다. 마지막 정상에 이르는 코스는 바위투성이에 가파른 경사를 이루고 있어 가깝

224. There is a large number of weekenders crowded in the subway. A man about sixty and a woman about forty sit together in the electric train. The man has hard eyes and pomaded hair and is holding a black bag and talking to the woman as if he is admonishing her to do something. Whenever he talks to her, she knits her brows, shaking her upper body backward and forward as if feeling uneasy. The man coaxes, touching her as if he is preaching to her. "Who will dare hurt a daughter of God?" However, the woman expresses her uneasiness continuously through her eyes. The man's hard eyes glitter, watching her abstracted look during the conversation. The man observes the movement of their surroundings, narrowing his eyes with nonchalant attitude, as if he had already shaped an idea on how to cook a prey. The woman sways with a weak temper, and the man with pomaded hair pretends to relieve her soul. The woman makes an expression that she has no choice even though she is caught as a prey because her body and mind are very tired now, and the man thinks of a way to finish before catching his prey. While the prey becomes god, and God becomes the prey, a survival game is played between the man and the woman.

The electric train arrives in the station before they are aware of it, and lots of weekenders pour out. The closer they reach the summit after a few hours passed since climbing the mountain, the farther the summit is, though it is straight ahead before their eyes. The closer they reach the summit, the farther they feel the summit is, because the summit made of granitic rocks forms a steep slope. In spite of their leg pains, they continue climbing because they don't want to taste defeat by returning before the summit, which challenges everybody. Life is like this. If they reach the summit, they have to come down. Even so, it is common in life that people want to reach the summit since they already started climbing.

게 보이지만 막상 쉽게 정상을 드러내 주지 않는 것이 산이다. 도심의 각박한 인심도 산에서만큼은 너그러워지는지 가파른 정상에 이르는 좁은 길목을 사람들 간에 서로 양보하고 기다려주는 아량을 베푼다. 산은 사람들의 마음을 여유롭게 해주는 힘을 가지고 있다. "지자는 물을 좋아하고 인자는 산을 좋아한다."라는 말이 이를 두고 하는 말이다. 전철에서 보았던 남녀도 하나님과 먹이를 사이에 두고 올라갔다 내려와야 하는 인생을, 피었다가 지는 바람꽃을 생각하며 어느 정거장에서 내렸을 것이다. 천지간에 바람 아닌 것이 없으니 모든 것은 바람으로 와서 바람으로 돌아가리라.

225. (시 45)
나는 계단 위로 올라가고
너는 계단 아래로 내려온다.

너와 나 사이에
얼마나 침묵이 흘렀을까?

행복의 성을 찾아
안갯속 꿈길을 헤매려니

네가 가리키는 거기에
이미 내가 있었구나.

The final course to reach the summit forms a steep, rocky slope. A mountain doesn't allow people to reach its summit easily though it looks close. As even coldhearted people in urban areas change their mind to be generous in the mountains, so they show themselves to be magnanimous and make mutual concessions on the narrow route to reach the steep summit. A mountain has the power to make people's mind generous. Like this, there is a saying that goes, "A wise man likes water, and a humane man likes mountains." The man and the woman seen in the electric train would also get off at a certain station, thinking of life coming down after going up between God and a prey, then thinking of a windflower fading after blooming. Since there is nothing but wind between heaven and earth, everything will come with the wind and be gone with the wind.

225. (Poem 45)
I go up the stairs,
and you come down the stairs.

Between you and me,
how long does a silence continue?

To search for the castle of happiness,
wandering along a dreamy way in a fog,

at the place where you point out,
I have already been there.

226. (시 46)

분별없는 욕망이 사라지던 날
눈 부신 햇살처럼 날으리라.

낯선 모습이 잔잔한 미소 되어
삶 저편 너머 바람이 되기까지

나의 껍질과 텅 빈 허공을
하루에서 한 생으로 반추하며

자유로움에 행복이려니
바람꽃 향기가 그윽하구나.

226. (Poem 46)
On the day that a thoughtless desire disappears,
I will fly like a brilliant sunlight.

As a strange figure smiles tenderly,
until it becomes wind beyond life,

while my exterior and the empty void
are ruminated over from day to life.

As it might be happy to feel free,
the smell of windflower is fragrant.

제3편
삶의 5대 불가사의

〈육체에서 흙으로 , 수묵담채화〉

꽃 빛깔이 저마다 다르듯이 삶에 대한 해답도 사람마다 다르다. 불가사의한 삶에 다가서는 비밀의 열쇠는 시대에 따라 현인들의 가르침에 따라 천차만별 다르기에 스스로 찾아야 한다. 살아생전에 누구든지 알고 싶어도 아무도 가르쳐주지 않는 불가사의한 삶의 비밀은 어떤 것일까?

Chapter 3

The Five Mysteries of Life

As each flower's color is different, the answer to life varies according to each person. People have to find the key to the secret, approaching closer to the mysterious life by themselves, because the key to the secret varies multifariously with the times and wise men's instructions. What is the secret of mysterious life that nobody teaches though everybody wants to know while alive?

8. 신이란 무엇인가?

227. 대부분 사람들이 신을 믿는다고 하지만 시대와 지역에 따라 사람마다 느끼는 신에 대한 개념은 천차만별 다르다.

228. 신은 시대와 종교에 따라 다양한 개념으로 변천되어 왔으나 공통점은 자아를 확장하려는 자유로움에 있다. 개체가 전체와 하나 됨은 지복이요, 이러한 믿음 가운데 신이 함께한다.

8. What Is God?

227. Most people say that they believe in God, but the concept of God felt by all sorts of people differs according to the times and regions.

228. God has changed into various concepts according to the times and religions, but a characteristic common to all takes the liberty to enlarge itself. Uniting an individual with the whole is supreme bliss, and God is together with such faith.

229. 이해는 객관적이고 이성적이며 쌍방향적이어서 증명할 수 있지만 믿음은 주관적이고 감성적이며 일방적이어서 증명할 수 없는 것이다. 신은 증명할 수 있는 것이 아니라 오로지 믿음 속에서 살아 있는 것이다.

230. 세상에는 다양한 종류의 믿음이 있고 같은 종교라 하여도 믿는 사람들에 따라 믿음의 방향과 깊이가 각기 다르므로 온전한 믿음을 깨우치는 것이 곧 행복에 이르는 길이다.

231. 미약한 개체가 장대한 전체와 화합하여 영속하리라는 염원이, 인간의 믿음도 이러한 염원에서 출발하는 것으로 개체를 확장하는 힘이다. 이 힘은 외부에서 오는 것이 아니라 각각 개체의 믿음 속에서 자라나는 것으로 이렇게 자라난 힘이 곧 신이요, 전체에 이르는 길이요, 그 길을 함께 갈 벗이다.

232. 사는 동안 하루하루가 현실이지만 지나고 나면 한순간의 꿈과 같다. 수십 년의 세월도 하룻밤의 꿈과 같이 느껴지는 것이다. 꿈은 현실에 뿌리를 내리고 시공을 넘나들며 상상의 세계를 보여준다. 꿈이라는 경험을 통하여 상상력을 발전시킨 것으로 민속신앙이나 우상숭배, 미신 등이 있다. 고대 그리스나 인도에서는 상상력을 동원하여 많은 신들을 만들어서 일상 속에 영속성을 부여하였고 그 후 중동지역에서 많은 신들을 유일신으로 단일화하여 신앙심에 더욱 강력한 결속력을 갖게 하였다. 현재 세계에 널리 분포되어 있는 여러 종교의 신들은 역사적인 사실을 바탕으로 상상력에 영속성을 부여한 것인데 아이러니하게도 상상력이 경전에 묶여 본래의 의도와 달리 경직되거나 맹

229. Understanding can be proven because it is objective, rational, and interactive, but faith cannot be proven because it is subjective, emotional, and one-sided. God is not to be proven but to be alive solely in faith.

230. As there are various forms of faith in the world, and the direction and depth of faith differ according to believers even though they believe in the same religion, so it is just the way to reach happiness, to awake to sound faith.

231. The wishes of a weak individual to last forever by harmonizing with the huge whole is the power to enlarge an individual, since human faith also originates from this kind of wish. As the power is not to come from the exterior but to grow itself in the faith of each individual, power grown like this is just God, a way to reach the whole as well as the friend going the same way.

232. Every day is realistic for a lifetime, but it seems a dream in a moment after it passed by. Even a few decades can feel like a dream of a night. A dream takes root in reality and shows the imaginary world while frequenting space-time. It is folk belief, idol worship, superstition, etc., to develop an imagination through an experience called a dream. People in ancient Greece and India bestowed perpetuity on daily life, establishing a lot of gods by mobilizing the imagination, then unifying all these gods. The one and only God spread in the Middle East could make people united more closely in faith. The gods of various religions distributed widely in the world at present are based on historical facts, and they bestowed perpetuity on the imagination. Ironically, as imagination is bound by scriptures, it becomes stiff contrary to

신을 강요하기도 한다. 신앙심이 추구하는 궁극적인 목적은 죽음의 단절로부터 자유로운 영속성을 얻는 데 있다. 사람들은 신을 통해 영원히 살 수 있기를 바라는 것이다. 신이란 삶의 영역을 넓히고 확장하는 과정에서 만나게 되는 개념이다. 작게는 나를 의미하기도 하고 너를 의미하기도 하고 크게는 너와 나를 포함한 우주 전체와 그 너머를 의미하기도 한다. 또한 과거에 있기도 하고 현재에 있기도 하며 미래에 있기도 하는가 하면 과거, 현재, 미래에 걸쳐서 동시에 있기도 한다. 시간과 공간에 제한이 없고 주객에 제한이 없으며 개별적인 동시에 포괄적이다. 따라서 한시적인 삶을 살고 있는 인간에게 신은 매우 매력적인 존재로 다가온다.

원시시대의 주술 신에서부터 그리스 신화에 나오는 여러 신들을 거쳐 현대의 종교에서 추구하는 유일신에 이르기까지 믿는 주체에 따라 모습은 달리 하지만 그 근본 취지는 시간과 공간의 제약을 벗어나 자유로움을 확장해 나가려는 데 있다. 삶은 한시적이고 긴장된 순간의 연속이므로 우리는 시공간의 제약을 극복하고 긴장의 피로감에서 벗어나 평온한 안식을 얻기 위해 신을 상상하고 신과 함께하기를 원한다. 신은 형이상학적인 개념이지만 그 출발은 사람마다 개별적인 사고에서 출발한 것으로 형이하학적인 것을 포함한다. 성전이나 우상 등은 형이하학적인 것이면서 동시에 형이상학적인 상징이기도 하다. 일개의 형상이 의미하는 바는 그 너머 형이상학적인 자유로움을 함께 상징하는 것이기에 형상에 얽매여 전체를 놓쳐서는 안 된다. 신을 향한 확장은 우리를 생존의 긴장과 한시적인 제약으로부터 자유롭게 한다. 신은 결코 외부에서 다가오는 존재가 아니다. 신은 믿으려는 자의 마음속에서 함께 성장하는 것이기에 믿는 방향과 깊이에 따라 신의 향기도 형상도 제각기 다르다. 지금 늦은 밤 풀벌레 소리가 평화롭게 느껴

the original intention, and sometimes blind belief is forced. The ultimate objective that faith pursues is to get perpetuity, free from extinction by death. People want to live forever through God. God is the concept to be met in the course of widening and enlarging life's boundaries. It means either me or you in a narrow sense, or the whole universe or beyond that, including you and me, in a broad sense. In addition, it is either in the past, in the present, or in the future—or over all time simultaneously. It is not limited in time and space, regardless of host and guest, and is individual as well as comprehensive. Therefore God as an attractive existence approaches humans living with a limited life.

According to believers, God has changed from an enchanter of primitive ages to the one and only God pursued by modern religions via a lot of gods in the Greek myths, but the fundamental purpose is to enlarge freedom out of the limits of time and space. As life is transient, and continues with every tense moment, we imagine God and want to be together with Him in order to overcome the limits of time and space, and to take rest peacefully, out of tiredness from the tension. God is a metaphysical concept, but this concept includes physical science because it starts from each individual thought. A temple and an idol are not only physical matters but also the metaphysical symbols. Since a form symbolizes the metaphysical freedom beyond it, the whole meaning should not be lost while bound to it. The extension toward God lets us feel free from the tension of survival and transient restrictions. God is not existence coming from the exterior. As God is to grow Himself together with the mind of a believer, God's scent and form are various according to the direction and depth of a particular faith. If you peacefully feel the singing of crickets late at night now, it is due to your faith that God is together with you. What is faith for? Faith is for life—that is, faith is for all

지고 있다면 이 모든 것은 신이 함께하고 있다는 믿음 때문이다. 무엇을 향한 믿음인가? 삶을 향한 믿음이다. 지극히 한시적이고 제한적이고 긴장된 생존으로부터 평화와 안식을 얻고 지엽적인 나로부터 벗어나서 우주적인 대아로 확장되어 나가는 만물일체라는 믿음이다. 형이하학적인 이해로부터 만물일체라고 하는 형이상학적인 믿음으로 확장해나가는 과정에서 신이 함께한다. 나의 울타리가 없어지고 만물이 하나 되는 것이 곧 신의 경지다.

things united into one, to take peace and rest from a very transient, restrictive, and tense existence, then to expand to the universal self out of the minor self. God is together with us in the course of expanding to a metaphysical faith, for all things in one, from physical comprehension. It is just God's state that my boundaries disappear, and all things are one.

233. 존재 중에 특이한 존재가 인간이고 인간은 생명을 지녔기에 더욱 특이한 것이며 생명은 유한하기에 더더욱 특이하여 이렇게 특이한 존재가 보편적인 전체로 합일하는 것은 매우 뜻깊은 일이다. 특이한 것은 한시적이고 보편적인 것은 영속적인 것이기에 특이한 개체에서 보편적인 전체로 확장해 나가는 것은 자연의 이치다. 삶은 긴장과 시련의 연속이지만 그럼에도 불구하고 삶을 사랑하기에 개체가 죽음을 극복하고 전체와 합일하려는 믿음을 갖게 된다. 믿음이 개체의 가슴에서 시작하여 그 믿음이 벽을 넘고 이승에서 저승으로 개체에서 전체로 다다르는 길에 신이 함께한다. 신이란 만물이 하나로 확장되어 나가는 통로다. 수많은 존재 가운데 한시적인 개체가 유한함을 극복하는 과정에서 믿음이 쌓이고 그 믿음 속에서 신이 함께 성장한다. 개체가 죽은 후 새로운 모습으로 변할지라도 없어지지 않고 전체와 함께 지속되기를 바라는 것은 산 자의 시각에서 바라보기 때문이며 이처럼 개체는 제각기 삶을 사랑하고 있는 것이다. 신은 개체가 살아서나 죽어서나 전체와 합일하거나 분화하거나 개체이거나 전체이거나 상관하지 않고 있는 그대로 믿음이 있는 곳에서 모두를 사랑하는 벗으로 함께한다.

233. As humanity has a peculiar existence among all existences, a human being is more peculiar because he is alive. It is even more peculiar that life is mortal, so it is very meaningful that such a peculiar existence is united with the universal whole. Since a peculiar thing is momentary and a universal thing is everlasting, it is a natural law that a peculiar individual expands into the universal whole. Life continues amid the tension and trials. Nevertheless, an individual loves his life, so he has faith to overcome death and unite with the whole. Faith starts from the heart—and there is God, in a way that allows faith to get over its confines—and reaches from this world to the other world and from an individual to the whole. God is a passage through which all individual things expand into one. When a momentary individual, among a lot of existences, overcomes his limit, he comes to have faith, and God grows from this faith. It is exciting to continue together with the whole, not disappearing, though an individual may change into a new aspect after dying because he looks from the viewpoint of the living. Like this, an individual loves his life respectively. Regardless whether an individual lives or dies or is united with the whole or divided—or it is an individual or the whole—God exists as a friend who loves all things, as it is in the place where faith is.

234. 어느 신도가 흐르는 강물에 몸을 누이고 뜬 채로 합장하며 한 시간가량 견딘 후에 물으로 나오자 구경하던 많은 사람들이 그녀의 신심에 존경을 표한다. 그녀는 믿음이 깊으면 누구나 할 수 있노라고 말하지만 일반인들은 믿기지 않는다는 표정들이다. 사람들은 상식을 벗어나는 현상에 대하여 쉽게 종교적인 의미를 부여하려고 한다. 고금동서에 무속인이 많은 것은 기복신앙에 의존하려는 불안한 심리 때문이다. 이처럼 사람들은 일상이 허전하고 뉴스에 굶주리고 유행으로 외로움을 달래려 하고 그런 가운데 스포츠 영웅을 만들기도 하고 스크린 영웅을 만들기도 하고 심지어 사이버 영웅을 만들어 놓고 열광하며 대리만족한다. 사람들은 마약과 알코올에서 환각을 느끼며 스트레스를 달래보기도 하고 섹스와 도박으로 일상의 무료함을 달래어 보기도 한다. 그러나 그러한 것은 유행 따라 사라지는 일시적인 것이다. 언젠가는 스스로 거울 앞에서 마주해야 할 시간이 온다. 온갖 유희 속에서 피난처를 찾을지라도 결국 자신으로부터 도피할 수는 없다. 도락과 환희로 스스로를 만족시킬 수는 없다. 잠시 스스로를 망각시킬 수 있을지언정 스스로에 대한 해답은 아니다. 무엇인가를 구하기 위하여 고뇌하고 그 고뇌에서 도피하려고 온갖 잡기나 유행에 몰려다닐 필요가 없는 것이다. 평상심으로 스스로 막힘 없이 사노라면 만물은 어느새 다가와서 하나가 되어 있으리라.

235. 마음을 벗으면 선이요 마음에 매이면 악이다.

234. A certain believer no sooner went out shoreward after floating in a flowing river by joining her palms together for an hour than a lot of people seeing the sight respected her faith. She said that anybody who is deeply faithful can do that, but the public put on a surprised expression. People easily intend to put religious meaning on a phenomenon beyond common sense. There is also a lot of shamans for all ages and countries because of unstable psychology, being dependent on faith to invoke a blessing. Like this, people feel empty in daily life, are hungry for news, and overcome loneliness by following fashion, during which time they are contented by proxy and extremely excited by making either sports stars, movie stars, or even cyber heroes. People try either to relieve stress by hallucinating with a drug and alcohol or to soothe the daily tedium with sex and gambling, but those things are transient like fashion. Someday all people have to face themselves in the mirror. People cannot escape from themselves after all, even though they are eager to take refuge in all sorts of amusements. People cannot satisfy themselves with pleasures and joy. Those things are not the solution to them, though they can forget themselves temporarily. It is not necessary that people anguish to pursue something and lapse into a lot of amusement and fashion to escape. If you live by opening yourself with your composed mind, all things will become one together with you, after getting near you in no time.

235. It is good if one frees oneself from one's mind, and it is evil if one is bound by one's mind.

236. (시 47)

변함없는 벗이여!

그대는 오랜 세월 나를 부르고

그대 흘린 피 강물을 이루니

핏빛 강물에 배를 띄우고

그 위에 신전을 세웠노라.

그 피로 말미암아 육신 거듭나고

믿음이 그대를 구원하리라고

기쁨의 눈물을 흘리는 그대여!

그대는 육체에 갇혀

영생의 채찍으로 스스로를 때렸노라.

내 이름을 경배하는 그대여!

광란의 춤에 빠진 벗이여!

영원히 미칠 수만 있다면

차라리 행복하련만

적막 속에 공허함은 찾아오고

다시 혼자가 되는 그대가 아니더냐?

경전 속에 문자 보고 울고 싶거든

차라리 짐승의 슬픔을 바라보아라.

그대를 위한 것은 아무것도 없다.

그대가 할 수 있는 유일한 길은

자신을 복제하는 것일 뿐

나는 이제 그대 피를 마시기에 지쳤다.

그대의 신이 되는 것이 괴롭구나.

추락하는 꿈속에 날개가 없다는 걸

236. (Poem 47)

My consistent friend!

As thou hast called me for a long time,

and the river has been flooded by thy blood,

thou set a ship afloat on the bloody river,

and had a temple built there.

Thy body would be born again due to the blood,

and faith would rescue thee.

Dreaming like that, how joyfully dost thou shed tears!

Thou art bound by thy body

and lash thyself with the whip of eternal life.

Thou who bow respectfully to my name!

Thou friend who indulge in frantic dancing!

If thou canst be crazy forever,

Thou wouldst be happy.

However, thou feel hollow in loneliness.

Art thou not the one who becomes alone again?

If thou want to cry by seeing text in the scripture,

it would be better to see the sorrows of beasts.

There is nothing for thee.

The unique way thou canst do

is only to duplicate thyself.

I am too exhausted to drink thy blood.

It is hard for me to become thy God.

There is no wing in the falling dream.

If thou awake to all of these truly,

thou ought to be alone.

Even if thou feel lonely,

be contented to know that is thee.

Making another thee everywhere thou wend,

while thy heart beats under the influence of blood,

진실로 이 모든 것을 깨닫거든
그대는 혼자이어라.
그리고 외롭다 하여도
그것이 그대임을 알고 자족하여라.
가는 곳곳에 또 다른 그대를 만들고
그 피에 취해 심장 뛰다가
그것들이 자신이 아님을 깨닫거든
수많은 그림자에 그대 가슴 밟히며
허공에 나비를 날리거라.

237. 신에게 어떤 이름을 붙이든 신을 어떤 형태로 묘사하든 그것은 종교마다 주어진 표현의 자유다. 그래서 종교마다 경전에 신을 묘사하고 표징을 세워 위엄을 상징하여 신도들의 믿음을 확고히 하려 한다. 그러나 그러한 상세한 표현이 때때로 오해와 편견을 불러일으키기도 한다.

238. 지구상 모든 종교의 공통점은 사랑과 자비이며 그 배경은 만물이 하나 됨이다. 만물은 허공 속에서 하나다. 허공은 아무것도 추구하지 않는 순수함이다. 무엇인가 추구하면 이미 그것은 집착이다. 진정한 종교는 허공 속에 자유롭게 펼쳐지는 믿음 속에서 찾을 수 있다. 신은 추구하는 것이 아니라 자유롭게 펼쳐지는 믿음 속에 항상 함께하는 것이다.

once thou realize that is not thyself,
while thy bosoms are trampled by a lot of shadows,
let loose a butterfly in the void.

237. It is freedom of expression given to each religion, what God is called and how to describe God. Therefore every religion tries to place the faith of believers on a firm foundation by describing God in the scripture and symbolizing His majesty with a sign, but sometimes such a detailed expression arouses both misunderstanding and prejudice.

238. A common point of all religions in the world is love and mercy, and its background is that all things become one. All things are one in the void. The void is the purity to pursue nothing. To pursue something is already an adherence. True religion can be found in the faith spreading freely in the void. God is not to be pursued but to be always present together with the faith spreading freely.

239. 빛과 어둠이 교차하는 거리에 신의 깃발이 펄럭이고 그 깃발 아래 전사들이 모였다. 영혼을 흔드는 리듬이 육체에서 육체 사이로 박자에 맞춰 울린다. 정열은 머나먼 전설을 넘어서 핏빛으로 펄럭이고 낯선 자들이 신의 이름으로 경배한다. 엄숙과 침묵 속에 반전되는 육체의 흔들림이 영혼의 울림으로 지속된다. 고개 숙인 자들의 기도가 타협을 거부하는 깃발 아래 흔들리고 칼을 상징하는 징표와 구원을 상징하는 징표가 광란 속에 교차한다. 치켜든 손과 발이 전율하는 주술 속에서 눈과 입이 허공을 향해 외친다. 눈동자와 입술, 굽은 등과 팔다리가 뒤엉키는 육체와 육체 그 너머 영혼으로 울부짖는 신의 모습이 침묵 속에서 메아리친다. 아무도 묻지 않는 율법과 행위로 이어지는 착각 속에서 신성함은 칼을 품고 입술을 떨며 전율한다. 신은 누구인가? 태양의 그림자를 가로지른 회당 아래 경배하는 자들의 울부짖음은 무엇을 향한 포효인가? 침묵 속에 퍼져가는 배타적인 울림이 삶의 마지막 숨소리가 되어 어둠에 피를 뿌린다. 위태로운 삶이여! 아무것도 없는 지금 이 순간 무엇을 향한 기도인가? 삶과 죽음이 합일하는 순간 그대로 있음에 침묵하는 위태로움이여! 오만이여! 오만 속에 드러나는 텅 빔이여!

피로 물드는 이 밤이 지나기 전에 신의 전사들은 어둠을 불사르며 상대의 눈동자 속에 비친 자신의 모습을 바라보고 잃어버린 스스로를 찾아 헤맨다. 환희 속의 광란이여! 믿음의 욕망이여! 영원한 순간이여! 꿈속의 삶이여! 육체는 장난이 아닌 것을. 고통과 희열이 교차하는 기로에서 영혼은 순간처럼 머무나니. 신의 전사들이여! 경배와 침묵과 외침과 전율이 한데 어우러져 영혼을 흔들고 육체를 채찍질하건만 사랑과 죽음은 언제나 함께하고 있다. 피는 흘러 대지를 적시고 거죽과 해골은 이제 바람을 기다린다. 눈물은 마르고 끊어지는 숨소리에 마

239. Warriors flocked to God's standard flying in the street, intersecting with light and dark. The rhythm shaking souls resounds in measured time from body to body. Passion flutters in bloodred by going beyond the remote legend, and strangers bow respectfully with God's name. The shakes of bodies reversed with gravity, and silence continues as an echo of souls. The prayer of bowers flutters under the slogan of rejecting compromise, and the sign symbolizing the sword and the sign symbolizing the relief intersect in frenzy. The raised hands and feet shiver under a charm, and eyes and a mouth shout toward the void. The figure of God is shouting as a soul beyond body to body entangled with pupils, lips, a hunched back, arms, and legs echoes in silence. Sanctity shivers by concealing the sword and by trembling lips under the illusion continued with religious precept and act that nobody asks. Who is God? What is the shout of those bowing respectfully in the chapel, crossing the shadow of the sun? The exclusive shout spreading in silence sheds much blood in the dark by becoming the last breath of life. What a dangerous life! What is the prayer for the present time when nothing exists? What a peril in silence, as it is at the moment when life and death unite into one! What haughtiness! What a vacancy emerging from haughtiness!

God's warriors wander, hovering, looking for their lost selves by seeing their figures reflected on the pupils of companions while burning the dark before the night flooded with blood passes by. What madness with joy! What a desire of faith! What an everlasting moment! What a life in a dream! Seeing that a body is not just for fun, a soul stays in a moment at the crossroads where pain and joy intersect. God's warriors! Even though a respectful bow, a silence, a shout, and a shiver entangled each other, shaking souls and lashing bodies, love and death are always together. The ground wets with blood streaming down, and the flesh and

지막 흩어지는 생명의 불꽃이여! 바람은 꿈을 꾸며 내일을 기약하지 않아도 되려니 지금 이 순간 모든 것을 아름다움이라 불러라. 모든 것을 용서하라! 고통과 희열과 침묵과 광란이 하나 되는 지고함을 어찌 모르고 삶이라 하겠는가? 순간 속에 피고 지는 삶이여! 머물지 않고 흐르는 바람이여! 이제 신은 가고 칼도 깃발도 함성도 함께 가고 없으니 바람이 스쳐 간 침묵 속에 한 송이 꽃은 피어나리라.

240. 아동학대와 같은 범죄를 고해성사하면 사제는 면죄하지 말고 법에 알려야 한다는 여론이다. 그러면 아무도 고백 안 할 것이고 종교의 역할은 축소될 것이다. 죄인을 처벌하는 것은 당연하지만 일부 국가통수권자나 종교단체에서는 죄인에게 특별사면이나 면죄부를 주곤 한다. 죄인에게 참회의 기회를 주는 것은 의미 있는 일이지만 범죄를 처벌하지 않으면 범죄가 증가할 것은 분명하다.

241. 정신병자는 자체적인 뇌 손상으로 조절이 안 되는 것이고 신들린 자는 망령이나 맹신에 의해 조절이 안 되는 것으로 분명 각기 다르기는 하지만 비정상적이라는 점에서는 같다. 비정상적인 자가 정상적인 자와 분명 다르기는 하지만 하늘 아래 함께한다는 점에서는 또한 같다. 그러니 이단, 이교도라 하여 업신여기지 마라. 결국 같은 하늘 아래 함께 살아가는 형제들이다.

skeleton wait for a wind now. Tears dried up. What a flame of life scattered with the last breath! As the wind doesn't need to promise tomorrow, having a dream, call all things at the present moment a beauty. Forgive all things! How can it be called life without knowing the sublimity that pain, joy, silence, and madness unite into one? What a life blooming and fading in a moment! What a wind blowing without staying! As God went, and swords, standards and shouting also went together. Being no more, a flower will bloom in the silence that a wind blew over.

240. If sinners confess their sins like child abuse, public opinion says that the priest should not remit their sins and report them to the police. If so, nobody will confess, and religion's role will be reduced. Criminals deserve to be punished, but some nations' presidents or some religions used to grant amnesty or indulgence to criminals. It is meaningful to give the chance of confession to criminals. However, there is no doubt that the number of criminals increases if they are free from penalty.

241. A psychopath cannot control himself due to his brain malfunction, and a possessed person cannot control himself due to a departed soul or a religious frenzy. They are different from each other distinctly, but they are the same in terms of being abnormal. An abnormal person is different from a normal person distinctly, but they are also the same in terms of being together in the world. Therefore, don't look down on them though they are unorthodox or heathens. All of them are our brothers and sisters living together in the world after all.

242. 지구상에 다양한 종교로 인하여 갈등이 빚어지고 전쟁이 끊이지 않고 있다. "너의 종교는 죽어야 하고 나의 종교는 살아야 한다."라는 광신이 전쟁을 일으키고 있다. 종교 간의 통합으로 갈등을 해소하고 전쟁을 억제하리라고 기대할 수도 있지만 획일화된 단일 종교가 인류를 지배한다는 것은 다양성을 추구하는 자연의 이치에 부합하지 않는다. 종교 간의 통합보다는 종교 간의 화합이 현실적이다. 모든 종교가 공통점을 서로 이해하고 존중하여 각자의 특성에 따른 다양성을 인정한다면 종교 간의 화합이 가능하다. 단일 종교는 아닐지라도 여러 종교가 뿌리를 함께하는 것이 가능하다. 뿌리라 함은 사랑과 자비를 의미한다. 인류가 적어도 서로를 죽이는 종교는 면할 수 있는 것이다. 그러나 종교가 죽지 않고 살아있기 위해서는 영적인 자유가 획일화된 경전 속에 문자로 갇혀서는 안 된다. 사랑과 자비가 영적으로 교류하며 순간마다 새로워지는 종교가 살아있는 종교다.

243. 신경성 위장약이나 정신병 치료약 중에는 위약이라는 것이 있는데 실제 성분은 아무것도 아닌 약을 의사는 환자에게 처방해주는 것이다. 그런데 놀랍게도 환자는 이 위약을 먹으면 증세가 호전되고 먹지 않으면 증세가 악화된다. 이처럼 환자의 증세는 그 약의 성분보다도 그 약에 대한 환자의 믿음에 의해서 좌우된다. 믿음이 깊을수록 병을 치료하는 데 더욱 효과를 발휘한다. 신경성 위장약이든 정신병 치료약이든 어느 약을 먹든 간에 어느 종교를 믿든 간에 믿음이 깊을수록 삶의 시련을 극복하는 데 더욱 효과를 발휘한다. 이와 같이 모든 신앙의 핵심은 믿음이요 믿음 가운데 신이 있고 믿음이 사라지면 신도 함께 사라진다.

242. Several kinds of religions in the world cause discord and go to war continuously. Fanaticism—"Your religion should die, and my religion should live"—causes war. It can be expected that the unification of religions copes with trouble and restrains war, but it is not suitable to the natural law of pursuing diversity, when a single uniform religion governs the human race. Harmony of religions is more realistic than the unification of religions. Harmony of religions is possible if all religions respect each other by comprehending a common point, admitting the diversity according to each specific character. It is possible that various religions are rooted in the same soil though they are not a single religion. Root means love and mercy. The human race can avoid religions killing each other at least. However, spiritual freedom should not be confined as text in the uniform scripture in order that a religion is not dead but alive. It is a living religion that interchanges love and mercy spiritually, to become new every moment.

243. There is a placebo among the medicines for a nervous stomach or a mental disease, and a doctor prescribes this medicine that is not composed of medically effective ingredients for the patient. However, the marvel is that the patient's condition takes a turn for the better when he takes the medicine, and takes a turn for the worse when he does not. The patient's condition depends on the patient's belief in the medicine rather than the ingredients. The deeper a belief is, the more effective it is in treating a disease. Regardless whether you take a medicine for a nervous stomach or a mental disease, or what kind of religion you follow, the deeper your faith is, the more effective it is in overcoming the trials of life. Like this, the core of all religions is faith, God exists in faith, and God disappears if faith fades away.

244. 모든 생명체는 생존에 다른 긴장감을 항상 안고 살아가고 있으며 특히 어둠에 대한 불안감은 이러한 긴장감을 가중시킨다. 이런 상황에서 시각이나 청각에 남은 잔상과 기억이 상상하는 방향으로 증폭되면 누구에게나 환영과 환청이 일어날 수 있다. 그러므로 평상시 긴장을 이완시키도록 하고 어둠 속에서 불안전한 활동은 자제하도록 하며 잔상과 기억이 남지 않도록 환영, 환청을 일으킬 만한 모형, 그림, 이야기, 영상물 등 제반 시청각 대상물을 가까이하지 말고 공포를 조장하는 주술적, 또는 종교적인 편견이나 모임에 빠지지 않도록 하여 사물에 대한 올바른 인식과 건전한 상상력을 길러야 한다.

245. 인간의 천사도 인간이고 인간의 악마도 인간이다. 이와 같이 유유상종하니 천사도 악마도 지상에 함께 있는 것이다.

246. 믿음은 나의 확장이다. 믿음을 통하여 유한한 나로부터 무한한 나로 확장된다. 무한한 나는 육체의 감옥에 갇혀있지 않는 참 나 즉 허공이요 신의 모습이다.

247. 예술을 학습해서 흉내 낼 수는 있어도 훌륭한 작품을 만들 수 없듯이, 신앙도 학습하여 흉내 낼 수는 있어도 믿음이 깊어지는 것은 아니다. 배움이 없는 촌부라 할지라도 그대로 믿음이 깊으면 그것이 곧 깨달음이요 올바른 신앙이다.

244. All creatures are always living with the tension of survival, along with a sense of uneasiness, especially as the dark increases such tension. In this situation, anybody can see a phantom and hear an auditory hallucination if the remaining visual afterimage and aural memory are amplified into the direction of imagination. Therefore people should reduce tensions at ordinary times, contain themselves from being active unsafely in the dark, and keep away from such audio-visual materials as models, pictures, stories, and movies capable of raising a phantom and an auditory hallucination in order that any afterimage and memory do not remain. They should also cultivate right awareness of things and sound imaginative power, not falling into magic or religious prejudice or gathering evoking horror.

245. The angel of humans is a human being, and the devil of humans is also a human being. Like attracts like, so the angel and the devil are together on earth.

246. Faith is to expand myself. My limited self is expanded into my infinite self through faith. My infinite self is my true self, not confined in this prison called a body—that is, the void as well as God's image.

247. As a person who cannot create a great work of art can imitate art by studying, so can he imitate faith by studying even when he cannot have deep faith. It is just an awakening as well as having the right faith, if he has deep faith, though he is an illiterate countryman.

248. 하나에서 시작하여 둘에 이르니 하나는 둘이 되고 둘은 하나를 품게 되어 마침내 둘은 하나가 된다. 나에서 시작하여 너에 이르니 나는 네가 되고 너는 나를 품게 되어 마침내 너와 나는 하나가 된다. 삶에서 시작하여 믿음에 이르니 삶은 믿음이 되고 믿음은 삶을 품어 마침내 신과 인간은 하나가 된다.

249. 지금 여기 평범한 인생들은 새로운 무엇을 보다 나은 삶을 꿈꾸며 살고 있다. 그러나 지금 여기가 없다면 꿈은 언제, 어디에서 출발할 것인가? 믿음으로 신을 벗 삼고 이승을 떠나야만 개체가 전체에 이르는 것도 아니다. 사는 동안에도 마음 한번 바꾸면 만물이 하나요, 여기가 천국이다.

250. 인간의 삶은 육체가 활동하는 물질의 세계와 꿈이나 상상력이 활동하는 의식 또는 무의식적인 정신의 세계와 영화나 게임을 통한 가공의 세계로 이뤄진다. 이들 세계는 각각 독자적인 위치를 지니면서 동시에 함께 작용하여 인간 삶의 삼위일체를 구성한다.

248. One becomes two as it starts from one and arrives at two, and then two become one because two bear one. I become you as it starts from me and arrive at you, and then you and I become one because you bear me. Life becomes faith as it starts from life and arrives at faith, and then God and humans become one because faith bears life.

249. Common people live here now, dreaming of something new and a better life. However, if the present and this place do not exist, when and where will the dream start? Only to leave this world with God as a companion through faith is not the way that an individual reaches to the whole. Once a mind changes even while living, all things are one, and here is heaven.

250. Human life consists of the physical world, where the body is active; the spiritual world, where dreams or imaginations are active consciously or unconsciously; and the fictitious world, through movies or games. These worlds not only have a peculiar domain respectively but also work together simultaneously, so they form the trinity of human life.

251. 영혼의 모습을 본 적이 있는가? 영혼의 목소리를 들은 적이 있는가? 본 적도 들은 적도 없어도 영혼은 우리에게 매력적인 존재로 다가온다. 영혼은 우리에게 시간 밖의 죽음으로부터 시간 속의 삶으로 다가와 시공을 넘나든다. 천사 같은 모습의 영혼은 누구나 친구로 사귀고 싶은 대상이다. 무당이 무아경에 몰입하면 영혼을 부를 수 있다는데 그것이 어떤 것인지는 무당만이 알 뿐 입증할 길이 없다. 입증할 길이 없다 해도 문제 될 것이 없다. 동정녀가 아이를 잉태했다 하여도 사람들이 부인하지 않는 것은 초월적인 존재와 가까워지고 싶은 마음 때문이다. 우리의 몸은 지구의 중력권 안에서 살지만 마음만은 하늘을 자유롭게 날고 싶은 것이다. 현실이라는 굴레에서 벗어나 영혼과도 친구하고 천국에도 가보고 싶은 것이다. 자유로움이 모든 것을 꿈꾸게 한다. 자유로움 그 자체가 바로 영혼이고 신이고 천국이고 꿈이다. 우리의 삶은 현실에서 보면 꿈이고 꿈에서 보면 현실이다. 그러니 꿈이 꿈이 아니고 현실이 현실이 아니라 하여 이상할 것이 없다.

252. 육체와 대치되는 개념으로 영혼을 생각하게 되는데 영과 혼은 유사한 개념으로 혼동해서 사용하고 있지만 엄밀히 구분하면 영과 혼은 다른 의미를 지닌다. 영은 인간의 영역 밖에 있는 정신적인 기운이며 혼은 인간 영역 안에 있는 정신적인 기운이다. 이들 간에 활동 영역이 다를지라도 영과 혼이 소통함으로써 한 개체로서의 인간이 우주 전체와 합일하게 된다.

251. Have you ever seen the soul? Have you ever heard the voice of a soul? Even if neither has been seen nor heard, the soul comes as an attractive existence to us. The soul comes and goes from death outside time to life inside time and beyond space-time. The soul, like a feature of an angel, is an object with which everybody wants to be acquainted. An exorcist insists that she can call a soul in ecstasy, but there is no evidence for that. Even if there's no evidence, there is no problem. People don't deny the fact that a virgin got pregnant because they want to be acquainted with a transcendent existence. Even if our bodies live in a state where the earth's gravitation exists, our minds want to fly the sky freely. We want to free ourselves from the restraints of reality, be acquainted with a soul, and go to heaven. Freedom makes us dream everything. Freedom itself is just a soul, God, heaven, and a dream. Our life is a dream in view of reality, and reality in view of a dream. Therefore it is not strange that a dream is not a dream and reality is not reality.

252. We think a spirit and a soul are concepts contrary to the body, but there is a discrepancy between these two concepts, though they are understood similarly. The soul is a mental vigor existing outside each individual domain, while the spirit is a mental vigor existing inside each individual domain. Even if they are different vigor in view of mental activity, humans as individuals can unite with the whole universe by coming to a mutual understanding between the spirit and the soul.

253. 미래라는 꿈은 실상은 지금이다. 수많은 미래를 꿈꾸어 왔지만 항상 지금이 아니었던가? 지금이란 멈추지도 않고 잡을 수도 없는 순간으로 항상 영원한 지금이다. 그러므로 순간은 지금을 통해서 영원에 이른다.

254. 현자들의 가르침에도 불구하고 사람들은 고뇌에서 해방되지 못하고 역사적인 인물들이 나타나 현실에 만족하지 못하는 사람들에게 구원을 충동질하였지만 실상은 그들에게 괴로움을 가중시켰을 뿐이었고, 스스로 메시아라고 자칭하는 교주와 잡기로 신통함을 내세워 보이는 무속인, 초능력자 등이 나타나 사람들의 마음을 현혹시켜 왔다. 그러한 구원과 기적에도 불구하고 그들이 제시한 사상과 신념들은 일시적인 환상만을 안겨줄 뿐 꿈에서 깨고 나면 사라져버리는 거울 속의 그림자와 같은 것이었다. 그들의 가르침은 삶의 이면에 드리워진 그림자를 보여줄 뿐 지금 묻고 있는 개개인의 삶에 대한 해답은 아니었다. 삶의 지혜는 그림자가 아니고 빛이다. 그러나 빛 자체는 손에 잡히지 않는 것이며 어둠과 침묵을 가르는 찰나적이고 불완전한 존재의 표현이다. 온전함, 행복감은 각자의 느낌에 의해서 달성되는 순간적인 것이며, 그런 느낌마저도 지속하고자 하는 욕망으로 바뀌게 되면 곧 삶의 우상이 되고 허상이 되어 사람들을 고뇌하게 한다. 애당초 존재의 심연은 허공이다. 존재는 없음에서 출발하여 있음이 곧 그대로 없음이요 없음이 곧 그대로 있음이다. 각자의 깨달음이 곧 존재의 신비이며, 바람꽃이다. 가르침은 말뜻 그대로 삶의 신비를 향한 가리킴일 뿐 그 이상의 것이 아니다. 가르침은 손가락에 불과하며 삶의 신비는 손가락이 가리키는 그 너머 바라보는 달빛이다. 나무, 미풍, 별빛처럼 주변에 흐르는 침묵 속에서 스스로 깨우쳐야 할 신비가 숨 쉬고 있다.

253. A dream by the name of future is actually the present. Even if people have dreamed of so many futures, those are always in the present, aren't they? The present is always the everlasting present because it is a moment that does not stop, is not caught. Therefore a moment comes to the everlasting through the present.

254. In spite of the precept of wise men, people couldn't be free from anguish, and historical personages appeared urging those people not satisfied with realities to accept their salvation, but they actually only added anguish to the people. The founder of a religious sect styling himself the Messiah as well as an exorcist and a person with preternatural power showing marvelousness with various arts and craft appeared, confusing the minds of the people. In spite of such salvation and miracle, their thoughts and beliefs offered only a temporary illusion to the people, and they were the same as a shadow in the mirror, disappearing after awaking from a dream. Their precepts showed only a shadow hanging behind life, but they didn't show a solution to the lives of individuals asking now. The wisdom of life is not a shadow but a light. However, light itself cannot be caught, and it is an expression of an instant incomplete existence flying through the darkness and the silence. Soundness and happiness are achieved in an instant by the feelings of each person. If a feeling becomes a desire that we want to last, the desire makes us agonize because it becomes an idol and illusion of life. The abyss of existence is originally the void. As existence starts from the void, to be itself is just not to be, and not to be is just to be. Each person's awakening is just the mystery of existence, and it's just a windflower. The precept is nothing but an instruction for the mystery of life, and it is nothing more than itself. The precept is nothing but an index finger, and the mystery of life is the moonlight viewing over there. The mystery to be awakened by each person is breathing in the silent atmosphere, such as trees, wind, and twinkling stars.

255. (시 48)

그리스 신화보다 더 오래전부터
수많은 사람들이 임을 부르고 또 부르건만
나는 임을 부를 수가 없습니다.

임이 어디 있는지 볼 수도 들을 수도 없거니와
임이 사는 전설의 땅은 아득히 멀기만 하고
임의 이름을 찾을 길이 없습니다.

수많은 사람들이 임을 부르고
그들 속에서 임은 수천 년이 넘는 세월을 살아오건만
히말라야 동굴 속에서도 하늘 저편 별들 사이에서도
임을 찾을 수가 없으니
그런 나를 부르는 임의 사랑이 가엾습니다.

임이 나를 삼키기도 전에 내가 임을 삼킨 것이라면
내 속에서 임을 찾을 수 있으련만
임은 끝내 내 속에 있음을 침묵하노니

임은 이미 임이 아니고 나는 이미 내가 아니요
그 옛날 헤어진 조각이 다시 하나가 되리라는 소망으로
임을 구별하지 않고 사는 것이
임에게 가깝게 가는 것임을 이제야 깨닫습니다.

255. (Poem 48)
From a long time before Greek myths,
a lot of people call and call thee continuously,
but I cannot call thee.

I can neither see nor hear where thou art.
Far away is the legendary land where thou live,
and I have no way to look for thee.

A lot of people call thee.
Though thou hast lived among them for thousands of years,
either in the caves of the Himalayas or between stars in the sky,
I cannot look for thee,
so thy love calling me is regretful.

If I swallowed thee before thou swallowed me,
I could look for thee inside me,
but thou keep silence after all concerning that thou art inside me.

Thou art already not thee, and I am already not me,
as I hope that the pieces separated long ago unite into one.
To live not distinguishing thee is to be close to thee.
That I do realize just now.

256. 어느 날 아침 삼형제가 길을 나섰습니다. 한참을 걷다가 첫째가 말했습니다. "어디서 향기가 나네."

그러자 둘째가 말했습니다. "향기라니 내가 보니 가시인데."

그러자 뒤따라오던 셋째가 말했습니다. "붉은색이야."

길섶에서 조용히 이 말을 듣고 있던 자이언트 장미가 내심 생각했습니다. "너희들은 똑같은 나를 두고 제각기 다르게 느끼는구나."

삼형제는 온종일 길을 걷다가 해가 서산에 기울기 시작하자 지쳐서 첫째가 말했습니다. "자이언트 장미는 도대체 어디에 있는 것일까?"

둘째가 말했습니다. "혹시 길을 잘못 든 것은 아닌가."

그러자 셋째가 말했습니다. "우리가 이미 지나쳐버렸는지도 모르잖아."

삼형제는 가던 길을 되돌아서며 생각해보았습니다. "향기가 나고, 가시가 있고, 붉은색이라면 바로 그것이 우리가 찾고 있던 자이언트 장미가 아닌가!"

삼형제는 뒤늦게 깨닫고 자이언트 장미를 찾았지만 이미 날은 저문 뒤였습니다. 사랑과 자비의 신은 똑같은 하나이므로 무슨 종교를 믿느냐, 어떤 이름으로 신을 부르느냐보다는 우리의 믿음과 함께하고 있는 신을 올바르게 이해하는 깊은 안목이 중요한 것입니다.

256. One morning, three brothers started on a journey. While walking for a long time, the first brother said, "What a fragrance!"

And then the second brother said, "It's not a fragrance but a thorn."

And then the third brother said, following along behind, "It's a red color."

A giant rose thought at heart, listening to their dialogue silently on the roadside, "Each of you feels the very same me differently."

While walking along the way, the three brothers were no sooner tired than the sun began to set behind the hill, so the first brother said, "Where in the world is a giant rose?"

The second brother said, "Maybe we took a wrong way."

And then the third brother said, "Perhaps we already passed by it."

The three brothers thought, turning back, "Since we breathed fragrance, felt thorn, and saw a red color, it must be the giant rose we've been looking for!"

But night already fell while the three brothers looked for the giant rose after realizing it late. As love and mercy, God is the same. It is important to take a deep view comprehending God together with our faith rightly, rather than what religion we follow or how we call God.

9. 모든 존재는 어디서 왔는가?

257. 허공에 바람이 일어 꽃이 피니 바람꽃이라. 바람은 꽃이 되고 꽃은 바람이 되어 어디에나 있고 어디에도 머물지 않는 바람꽃이라.

258. 아름다움은 머물지 않고 흐르는 것이며 그 변화가 조화로울 때 더욱 아름다운 것이다.

259. 인도 경전에 아그니라는 불의 신이 있다. 아그니는 한 몸에 머리가 둘 달린 모습을 하고 두 개의 머리는 각각 불을 주관하는 신이자 스스로 불이 되어 타오르는 상징적인 의미를 지닌다. 순간의 존재가 창조주이자 피조물인 것이다.

9. Where Does All Existence Come From?

257. Once the wind rises in the void, a flower blooms with the wind; that is the windflower. As the wind becomes a flower and a flower becomes the wind, to be everywhere and not to stay anywhere, that is the windflower.

258. Beauty is not to stay but to flow, and it is more beautiful when a change is harmonious.

259. There is a god of fire called "Agni" in Indian scripture. Agni has two heads. One head symbolizes God governing fire, and the other head symbolizes fire burning itself. It means that existence in a moment is not only the creator but also a creature.

260. 창조와 진화는 어떤 관계인가? 신이 개입된 것을 창조라고 하고 주변 환경의 요인이 상호작용하는 것을 진화라고 하는데 모든 존재는 자유의지와 주변 환경의 영향이 복합적으로 작용하여 이뤄지는 것으로 창조와 진화는 대치적이라기보다 상보적이다. 모든 생명체는 시간과 공간상에서 연속적인 진화를 거듭하기도 하고 경우에 따라서는 일시적인 단절을 극복하고 불연속적인 진화를 거듭하기도 한다. 불연속적인 진화란 곧 창조를 의미한다. 진화 속에서 창조가 일어나고 창조 속에서 진화가 일어난다. 우주상의 만물은 주객의 입장을 넘어서 창조적인 진화와 진화적인 창조를 거듭하며 변하고 있다.

261. 우주에서 바라본 허공의 모습을 일컬어 어둠의 침묵이라 한다. 어둠의 침묵은 반존재로서 존재의 배경을 이루고 존재는 시간과 함께한다. 존재가 없으면 시간도 없으며 시간과 존재는 상보적인 관계다. 존재한다는 것은 어둠의 침묵만으로 텅 비어있던 공간이 움직이기 시작한다는 것이고 시간과 함께하고 있다는 것을 의미한다. 존재한다는 것은 시간과 함께 존재한다는 제한적인 개념으로 시간으로부터 자유로운 절대적인 존재는 없다. 변하지 않거나 시간과 함께하지 않는 것은 존재하지 않는다. 오직 우주 경계 밖에서 시간이 정지된 어둠의 침묵만이 존재의 배경을 이루고 있을 뿐이다. 만일 어떤 존재가 시간이 정지된 상태에 있다면 그것은 이미 존재가 아니다. 또한 존재는 어둠의 침묵을 배경으로 하므로 어둠의 침묵으로부터 떨어져 나온 별개의 것이 아니다. 모든 존재는 지면에 붙어 있지도 떨어지지도 않고 굴러가는 바퀴처럼 어둠의 침묵과 상호 작용하면서 시간과 함께한다. 반존재인 어둠의 침묵이 파동하면서 에너지 흐름이 형성되고 에너지가 수축·팽창하는 과정에서 존재가 출현한다. 어둠의 침묵으로부터 파동

260. What is the relationship between creation and evolution? It is called creation when a divine intervenes, and it is called evolution when environmental factors interact. As all things are to exist by acting compositely with free will and the influence of circumstances, so are creation and evolution complementary rather than contrary. Sometimes all creatures repeat a continuous evolution in time and space, and sometimes they undergo discontinuous evolution by overcoming the temporary interruption. Discontinuous evolution means creation. Creation rises in evolution, and evolution rises from creation. All things in space are changing by repeating a creative evolution and an evolutionary creation beyond the position of host and guest.

261. The picture of the void seen in the universe is called the silence of the dark. The silence of the dark forms the background of existence as anti-existence, and existence is together with time. There is no time where there is no existence, so time and existence are complementarily related. To be existent means that an empty space with only the silence of the dark starts to move, and something is together with time. To be existent means the limited concept existing together with time, so there is no absolute existence free from time. There is no existence that does not change or is not together with time. Only the silence of the dark in time at a standstill forms the background of existence outside the universe. If a certain existence is in time at a standstill, it is no longer existence. Furthermore, existence is not another thing to be separated from the silence of the dark, because existence sits in the silence of the dark. All existence is together with time, interacting with the silence of the dark, as a wheel rolls neither attached to the ground nor separated from it. While the silence of the dark as anti-existence waves, a stream of energy forms, and existence appears while energy condenses or expands. The movement waving from the silence of

하는 출렁임이 시공간에 존재의 출현을 알리는 것이다.

어둠의 침묵에서 존재가 출현하는 데 에너지가 필요할 뿐만 아니라 존재에서 다른 존재로 변하는 데도 에너지가 필요하다. 에너지는 어디에서 오는 것인가? 존재가 변하기 위해서는 에너지를 필요로 하며 에너지가 소모되는 과정에서 무효화되는 에너지의 자취가 남긴 피사체를 일컬어 에테지(에테르와 에너지의 합성어)라 한다. 에테지는 어둠의 침묵을 통해서 다시 에너지로 부활하는 것으로 물리법칙 또는 자연법칙에 국한되지 않고 형이상학적 개념을 어우르는 존재생성의 메신저 역할을 한다. 에테지에 의해 어둠의 침묵이 파동하고 어둠의 침묵이 파동하면서 생성되는 에너지로 존재가 출현하고 존재가 에너지를 소모하며 변하는 과정에서 배출되는 에테지로 어둠의 침묵이 파동하는 것으로 상호 간에 지속 가능한 순환고리를 형성한다. 존재가 에너지를 사용하는 과정에서 에테지를 배출시키는 반면 배출된 에테지는 어둠의 침묵을 파동시키는 과정에서 흡수·소멸되고 어둠의 침묵이 파동하면서 에너지를 방출하므로 어둠의 침묵과 존재 사이에 평형을 이룬다. 죽은 자의 영혼이 그 시신을 먹은 히말라야 독수리를 통해서 다시 하늘을 날듯이 에테지가 어둠의 침묵을 파동시키고 어둠의 침묵이 파동하는 과정에서 다시 에너지가 생성된다. 에테지가 어둠의 침묵을 통하여 에너지로 부활하는 것이다.

어둠의 침묵이 파동하면서 생성된 에너지가 존재를 출현시키는 것은 물리법칙에 따른 것이지만 에테지가 어둠의 침묵을 파동시키는 것은 물리법칙을 넘어서는 형이상학적인 개념이다. 물리법칙은 형이하학적인 우주 안에서만 적용할 수 있는 보편적인 전제일 뿐이며, 예를 들어 빛의 속도가 운반체의 속도와 상관없이 항상 일정하다는 것도 전제다. 존재의 근원을 규명하기 위해서는 우주 안에서 이뤄지는 전체와

the dark is announced as the appearance of existence.

Energy is necessary for existence not only to appear from the silence of the dark but also to change into another existence. Where does energy come from? Energy is necessary for existence to change, and the subject left by the trace of energy invalidated in the course of consuming energy is called *ethergy*, which is a portmanteau of *ether* and *energy*. Since ethergy is to be revived as energy through the silence of the dark, it plays the role of messenger to create existence, with the metaphysical concept not confined to physical or natural laws. Ethergy waves the silence of the dark, existence appears from the energy created while the silence of the dark is waved, and the silence of the dark is waved by ethergy emitted while existence changes, consuming energy. Like this, they form a sustainable cycle with each other. All existence emits ethergy while consuming energy. On the other hand, the emitted ethergy is absorbed while waving the silence of the dark, and the silence of the dark emits energy while waved, so the silence of the dark and all existence are kept in equilibrium. As the spirit of the dead flies through the heavens again, through a Himalayan eagle eating its corpse, ethergy waves the silence of the dark, and energy is created again while the silence of the dark is waved. Ethergy is to revive as energy through the silence of the dark.

It is based on physical laws that energy is created while the silence of the dark is waved, but it is a metaphysical concept beyond physical laws when ethergy waves the silence of the dark. Since physical laws are a universal premise, only applicable in the universe of physical science—e.g., it is also a premise that the speed of light is constant regardless of the speed of the carrier—the silence of the dark beyond the universe, as well as the changes to the whole and individuals happening in the universe, should be clearly defined in order to find out the origin of existence. Our daily life depends on physical laws, but the metaphysical concept is necessary to find out the origin of

개체의 변화는 물론이고 우주 밖의 어둠의 침묵도 함께 규명해야 한다. 우리의 일상은 물리법칙에 의존하지만 존재의 근원을 규명하기 위해서는 형이상학적인 개념이 필요하다.

어둠의 침묵이 파동할 때 시간이 증가하는 +방향으로 파동하면서 생성되는 에너지는 우리가 살고 있는 팽창하는 우주의 존재를 형성하고 시간이 감소하는 -방향으로 파동하면서 생성되는 에너지는 수축하는 우주의 존재를 형성하므로 어둠의 침묵이 +와 -를 반복하며 파동하기 때문에 그 합은 항상 0이다. 또한 어둠의 침묵의 파동에 따라 존재가 +와 -를 반복하며 변화하기 때문에 존재의 변화의 합도 항상 0이다. 존재가 변하기는 변하되 그 결과는 변한 것이 없다는 것이다. 결국 제자리걸음하는 그리스의 시시포스 신화와 같다. 존재는 변화하는 그 자체로서 의미를 다 한 것이며 존재의 변화에 방향성이 없는 것으로 존재의 변화에 어떠한 가치를 부여할 수 없는 것이다.

생명이 진화하는 것은 지구와 같은 생태계 내에서 극히 제한적이고 한시적인 방향성을 보여주지만 생태계 밖의 외계에서 거시적으로 보면 제자리에 머물러 있는 것과 같다. 우리의 눈높이에서는 수평선이 일직선으로 보이지만 바다로 둘러싸인 지구표면이 둥근 것처럼 각 개별적인 존재들이 일방향성으로 변화하는 듯하지만 거시적으로 보면 존재의 변화의 합은 어둠의 침묵을 배경으로 항상 원점에 와 있다. 존재는 자유로움 자체이며 귀한 것도 천한 것도 악한 것도 선한 것도 아닌 지극히 보편적이고 평범한 것이다. 그 배경은 어둠의 침묵이며 원점으로 회귀하는 파동에 의해 존재는 존재에서 존재로 변화하는 순간 속에 있다. 존재란 일정한 형태를 갖추고 있는 것 같지만 실상은 없는 것이며 존재에서 존재로 순간순간 변화를 나타내고 있을 뿐이다. 시간은 지금 속에 살아 있지만 엄밀히 말하면 수백분의 일초도 지금이

existence.

The energy created while the silence of the dark is waved in the plus direction of increasing time forms the inflating universe in which we are living, and the energy created while the silence of the dark is waved in the minus direction of decreasing time forms the deflating universe. The sum of the waves is always zero while the silence of the dark is repeatedly waved in the plus and minus directions. Also the sum of the changes in existence is always zero while all existence changes repeatedly in the plus and minus direction according to the wave motion of the silence of the dark. It means that there is nothing changed in the result though all existence changes. It is like Sisyphus of Greek myth about climbing and falling down repeatedly in the same place. As existence has its meaning by changing itself, and there is no direction in change, so any kind of value cannot be given to the change of existence.

The evolution of life shows a very limited, momentary direction in the ecosystem, like the earth, but it is the same as a standstill in view of the macroscopic, external world outside the ecosystem. The horizon looks like a straight line in our view, but the earth covered with ocean is round. Like this, each individual existence looks like it's changing in one direction; however, from a macroscopic view, the sum of the changes in existence is always at the starting point, with the silence of the dark for a background. Existence is freedom itself, is neither noble nor base, is neither virtue nor vice, and is very universal and common. Its background is the silence of the dark, and existence is in a moment changed from existence to existence by the wave motion revolving around the starting point. Existence looks like having a certain form, but it is actually nothing except showing changes from existence to existence momentarily. This is the same reason why time flies in the present; however, strictly speaking, there is no present, even a hundredth of a second—only the past or the future. Time cannot show itself, but it shows itself through a change in existence. To be existent means that time flies, and energy is the

란 없는 것이며 과거 아니면 미래만이 있는 것과 같은 이치다. 시간은 스스로를 보여 줄 수 없지만 존재의 변화를 통해서 자신을 보여준다. 존재한다는 것은 시간이 흐른다는 것이며 파동에 의한 에너지의 흐름에서 존재가 출현하는 것으로 에너지가 곧 존재이자 시간인 셈이다. 존재의 근원은 어둠의 침묵을 배경으로 하고 어둠의 침묵과 우주 사이에 경계만 있을 뿐 우주의 끝은 가변적이며 존재는 시작도 끝도 없이 항상 지금 순간에 있다.

존재란 어둠의 침묵을 배경으로 시간과 함께 있는 것이다. 어둠의 침묵이 없다면 존재도 없고 존재가 없다면 시간도 없다. 어둠의 침묵과 존재와 시간은 제각기 상보적인 관계에 있다. 존재한다는 것은 어둠의 침묵을 배경으로 하기에 가능하며 시간과 함께 변하기 때문에 가능하다. 만일 어둠의 침묵이라는 배경이 없다면 존재할 공간이 없는 것이다. 어둠의 침묵으로부터 존재할 공간이 마련된다. 그렇다고 어둠의 침묵이 곧 공간은 아니다. 존재가 없는 어둠의 침묵은 단지 어둠의 침묵일 뿐이다. 존재는 어둠의 침묵을 배경으로 하고 어둠의 침묵은 존재하도록 공간을 구성한다. 또한 존재는 시간 속에서만 가능하다. 시간이 정지되어 변할 수 없는 존재는 과거의 그림자처럼 이미 사라지고 없는 존재다. 시간은 스스로 흐르는 것이 아니고 존재를 통해서 흐른다. 존재는 흐르는 시간 속에 있으며 시간은 존재의 변화를 통하여 흐른다. 어둠의 침묵과 시간과의 관계는 어떠한가? 존재는 어둠의 침묵을 배경으로 시간과 함께하므로 존재를 사이에 두고 어둠의 침묵과 시간은 상호 연관되어 있다. 존재는 어둠의 침묵에 붙어 있지도 떨어져 있지도 않은 채 시간과 함께 돌고 있는 바퀴와 같다. 만일 시간이 멈추고 존재도 없이 어둠의 침묵만은 가능한 것일까?

어둠의 침묵이란 존재의 배경으로서 의미가 있는 것으로 존재가 없이

same as existence and time because existence appears in the flow of energy created by the wave motion. The origin of existence is together with the silence of the dark for a background, and the limit of the universe is variable except there is only a boundary between the silence of the dark and the universe, and existence is always in the present without beginning and end.

Existence set in the silence of the dark is to be together with time. No silence of the dark, no existence. No existence, no time. The silence of the dark, existence, and time are complementary to each other. It is possible for existence to be because existence is with the silence of the dark for a background and is together with time. If there is no silence of the dark for a background, there is no space to exist. The space to exist is set up from the silence of the dark. Even so, the silence of the dark is not just a space. The silence of the dark without existence is merely the silence of the dark. Existence is with the silence of the dark for a background, and the silence of the dark transforms the space into existence. Existence is also possible only in time. An existence unable to change in time at a standstill is already nothing, disappearing like a shadow of the past. Time is not to fly by itself but to fly through existence. Existence is in the flying time, and time flies through existence. What is the relationship between the silence of the dark and time? Since existence set in the silence of the dark is together with time, the silence of the dark is connected with time, both being on the other side of existence. All existence is like a wheel rolling together with time, neither attached to the silence of the dark nor separated from it. Is it possible only for the silence of the dark to be if time stops and there is no existence?

As the silence of the dark has a meaning as a background for existence, it is meaningless if there is only the silence of the dark without existence. It is not only to show the void when a certain prophet holds up a lotus while preaching a sermon. The beautiful lotus set in the void is to make the void profound. Time flies

그 배경만 있다면 아무런 의미가 없는 것이다. 어느 선각자가 설법 중에 연꽃을 들어 올린 것은 허공 때문만이 아니다. 허공을 배경으로 피어난 아름다운 연꽃이 허공의 깊이를 더하고 있는 것이다.

시간은 시작도 끝이 없이 존재의 변화에 따라서 순간순간 흐른다. 우주가 언제 탄생했느냐 존재가 언제 시작되었느냐 하는 것은 매우 지엽적인 질문이다. 시간에 시작과 끝이 없듯이 존재에도 시작과 끝이 없다. 우리가 생각하는 시간은 우리 일상에 맞춰 임의로 정한 것이며 시간은 빠른 것도 느린 것도 아니고 시작이나 끝이 있는 것도 아니다. 어느 개체가 태어나면 시작이고 죽으면 끝이다 하는 것은 오직 그 개체에 한정된 것일 뿐이다. 우리는 일상생활에서 편의상 시간을 정해놓고 하루해가 뜨고 하루해가 지는 것을 바라보며 시간의 시작과 끝을 관습적으로 생각하고 있지만 시간은 상대적인 것이어서 존재의 변화 또는 존재와 존재 간의 변화에 따라 다르게 흐르며 한 개체의 탄생과 죽음에 의해 시작과 끝을 말할 수는 있지만 시간 자체는 시작도 끝이 없이 무한궤도처럼 존재와 함께할 뿐이다. 순간이 시작이고 순간이 끝이니 시작이 곧 끝이고 끝이 곧 시작이 되어 시작과 끝은 매 순간 반복된다.

역설적으로 어둠의 침묵과 존재를 바꿔서 생각할 수도 있다. 어둠의 침묵이 실체라면 지금 보이는 이 모든 존재들은 무엇인가? 어둠의 침묵을 보이기 위한 배경이자 허상으로 배경을 여럿으로 구분하는 것은 무의미하다. 허상이 여럿으로 보일지라도 그것은 배경이라는 하나의 의미를 갖고 있을 뿐이다. 결국 모든 존재들이 어둠의 침묵이라는 실체 앞에서는 동일하다. 대소도 동일하고 생사도 동일하다. 대소가 구별되고 생사가 구별되는 순간 어둠의 침묵은 사라지고 어둠의 침묵이

momentarily without beginning and end according to the change in existence. It is a very important side question—when the universe was created or when all existence began. As there is no beginning and end in time, so there is no beginning and end in all existence. The time that we think of is arbitrarily fixed in order to suit our daily lives, time is neither fast nor slow, and there is neither beginning nor end in time. It is limited only to an individual—it is a beginning if he is born, and it is an ending if he is dead. We customarily think of the beginning and end of time while looking at the sunrise and sunset, by setting time for convenience's sake in our daily lives, but time flies differently according to the change in existence or the change from an existence to another existence because time is relative, and time itself is only with existence without beginning and end, like an endless track, even though a beginning and an end can be shown by the birth and the death of an individual. Since a moment is the beginning and a moment is the end, the beginning is just the end, and the end is just the beginning. Therefore the beginning and end repeat in a moment.

Paradoxically speaking, we can think of the silence of the dark and existence reversely. If the silence of the dark is substantial, what is all existence seen at present? Those are a background and a virtual image in order to show the silence of the dark, so it is meaningless to divide a background individually. Even though the virtual image is individually seen, it has only the meaning of a background. All existence is the same in front of the substance called the silence of the dark after all. Great and small sizes are the same, and life and death are also the same. At the moment, great and small sizes as well as life and death are distinguished, the silence of the dark disappears, and all kinds of existence appear in the place where the silence of the dark disappears. All existence is also one in front of the silence of the dark, just as the silence of the dark is one, not to be

사라진 자리에 온갖 존재들이 발현한다. 어둠의 침묵이 구분할 수 없는 하나이듯이 모든 존재들도 어둠의 침묵 앞에서는 하나이다.

결국 어둠의 침묵과 존재가 모두 하나 되는 경지에 이르면 어둠의 침묵과 존재를 구분하는 것조차 의미가 없게 되고 어둠의 침묵이 존재가 되고 존재가 어둠의 침묵이 된다. 이 경지에서는 시간도 구분하는 의미가 없게 되어 아무것도 없으면서 아무것이나 있게 된다. 밤하늘에 반짝이는 별빛처럼 있는가 하면 순간에 없고 없는가 하면 순간에 있는 것이다. 어둠의 침묵과 존재가 하나인 듯 둘인 듯 서로 오고간다.

262. 모든 존재를 바람꽃에 비유하면, 어둠의 침묵과 존재의 관계는 바람과 꽃의 관계라 할 것이다. 바람은 어둠의 침묵에서 일어나는 파동처럼 모든 존재에 펼쳐지는 자유로움을 상징하며, 꽃은 삼라만상 다양한 모습으로 펼쳐지는 존재의 자기완성을 상징한다.

263. 모든 자연계는 사람들에게 이미 알려진 자연과 아직 알려지지 않은 자연으로 구성된다. 천지간 모든 존재는 자연 그대로이며 자연을 벗어난 초자연이란 어둠의 침묵이라는 존재의 배경 이외에는 없다. 다만 알려지지 않은 자연을 사람들이 초자연으로 혼동하고 있는데 흔히 말하는 영혼이란 비물질적인 것으로 알려지지 않은 자연 현상 중의 하나이다. 모든 존재란 물질과 비물질을 포함하는 것으로 존재가 변할 때 물질에서 물질로의 변환만이 있는 것이 아니다. 모든 생물에 깃든 생명력은 비물질적이지만 물질적인 비를 맞고 성장하는 것처럼 물질에서 비물질, 비물질에서 물질로의 변환도 있다. 그러나 어둠의 침묵은 존재의 배경으로 물질도 비물질도 아닌 형이상학적인 개념이다.

divided.

If the silence of the dark and existence reach the stage of becoming one after all, it is meaningless even to divide the silence of the dark and existence, so the silence of the dark becomes existence, and existence becomes the silence of the dark. Since it is meaningless to even divide time in this stage, there is everything while there is nothing. Like starlight twinkling at night, it disappears and in a moment appears, and it appears and in a moment disappears. The silence of the dark and existence come and go toward each other, and they seem either to be one or two.

262. Comparing all existence with a windflower, the silence of the dark is to all existence as the wind is to a flower. The wind symbolizes freedom spread in all existence, like the wave rising with the silence of the dark; and a flower symbolizes the perfection of existence itself, spreading with various figures of nature.

263. The natural world consists of nature that is already known and the part of nature still unknown to people. All existence in the heavens and the earth is nature itself, and there is no supernatural beyond nature except the background of existence called the silence of the dark. People just confuse the still-unknown nature with the supernatural. The commonly known soul is one of the unknown natural phenomena in the universe, an immateriality. As all existence includes both material property and immaterial property, so there is not only the change from matter to matter when all existence changes. The life force existing in all creatures is immaterial, but it grows in the material rain. Like this, there is also the change from materiality to immateriality and from immateriality to materiality. However, the silence of the dark as the background of existence is a metaphysical concept, which is neither material nor immaterial.

264. 청동독수리가 꿈속에서 들려오는 메아리 소리에 날개를 퍼덕인다. 꿈속으로 날아갈 수 있는 것은 오로지 자신의 모습을 바라볼 수 있는 거울을 통해서만 가능하다. 독수리는 삶과 꿈 사이를 넘나드는 통로를 찾기 위해 오랜 침묵의 세월을 기다리다가 마침내 마주치는 눈동자 동공 속에 비쳐진 자신의 모습을 바라보고 꿈속으로 날아든다. 무거운 청동 날개가 어느새 바람을 일으키는 거대한 날개가 되어 아득한 계곡 사이의 머나먼 기억을 넘어서 날아간다. 독수리가 날갯짓을 할 때마다 기나긴 침묵은 안개처럼 걷히고 텅 빈 허공 속으로 광활한 시공이 펼쳐진다. 어둠 속에 잠들어 있던 정지된 시간이 흐르기 시작한다. 하늘과 땅이 열리고 어둠을 가르는 빛이 광야에 펼쳐진다. 태양과 물과 나무들이 노래한다. 독수리는 펼쳐진 날개를 자연의 흐름 속에 맡긴다. 하는 바 없이 불어오는 바람 따라 독수리의 비상이 시작된다. 꿈이 펼쳐진 것이다. 꿈속에서 거울을 잃고 자신의 모습을 보지 못하게 되면 독수리는 시공의 굴레에 갇히게 되고 자아를 잃어버린 독수리는 꿈 밖에서 청동의 날개를 접고 괴목 위에 멈춘 채로 영원한 순간을 부동의 침묵 속에서 보내야 한다. 눈동자에 비친 모습을 통하여 스스로를 있는 그대로 바라보게 될 때 다시 독수리는 자신의 모습을 찾아서 날게 된다. 청동 날개의 독수리여! 삶의 무게를 넘어 바람 속에 꿈의 나래를 펼쳐라!

264. Immediately upon hearing echoes resounding in a dream, a bronze eagle flutters its wings. It is possible for the eagle to fly into a dream only through a mirror capable of looking at itself. Waiting for a long time of silence to find a passage going and coming often between life and dream, at last the eagle flies into a dream by looking at itself, reflected on the pupil of eyes confronting itself. The heavy bronze wings fly beyond the far-off memory in the deep valley, becoming huge wings, raising the wind in no time. Whenever the eagle flaps its wings, a long silence lifts like a mist, and the vast space-time spreads itself in the empty void. Time at a standstill, sleeping in the darkness, starts flying. The heavens and the earth open, and light passing through the dark spreads itself in the wilderness. The sun, water, and trees sing along. The eagle leaves its spread wings with the flow of nature. The eagle begins to fly according to the rising wind without doing anything. At last a dream comes true. If the eagle cannot look at itself by losing the mirror in a dream, the eagle is confined in a spatiotemporal trap, and the self-effaced eagle has to pass the everlasting moment in the motionless silence, standing on a wooden prop with folded bronze wings outside the dream. When the eagle looks at itself as is through the feature reflected on its pupils, the eagle gets to fly again, realizing itself. What an eagle with bronze wings! Spread wings of dreams in the wind beyond the weight of life!

265. 독수리가 비상할 때 양쪽 날개를 함께 펼치는 것처럼 존재가 출현하는 데 어둠의 침묵과 존재가 함께 펼쳐진다. 반면에 독수리가 양 날개를 접으면 독수리의 비상이 정지되듯이 반존재인 어둠의 침묵과 존재가 하나로 합치되면서 서로 상쇄되어 모든 것은 사라지고 만다. 날개를 펼치면 만물이 나타나고 날개를 접으면 모든 것은 사라지는 것이니 없는가 하면 있고 있는가 하면 없는 것이 존재의 속성이다.

266. 우리는 변화하는 존재 속에서 살면서 매일같이 일출 일몰을 경험하며 한시적인 삶에 익숙해져 있다. 그래서 달리던 차는 언젠가 멈추는 것이 당연하다고 생각한다. 그러나 지구를 벗어난 우주공간에서는 멈추는 것이 이상한 것이다. 출발했으면 영원히 달리는 것이 정상적이다. 지구상의 생명체가 중력을 받으며 육체와 함께 생존하는 것은 존재 전체에서 보면 특이한 경우로서 한시적이다. 우리는 한시적인 특이 조건에서 살면서 연대의식과 유전정보를 발전시켜 한시적인 삶을 극복하려고 한다. 그러나 한시적인 삶에서 영원을 추구하려는 것은 모순이다. 한시적인 삶은 한시적인 그대로 즐기는 것이며 보편적인 전체와 합일하는 순간에 영원이 우리와 함께한다.

265. As an eagle spreads both wings when it flies, the silence of the dark and existence spread together when existence appears. On the other hand, as the eagle stops flying if it folds both wings, everything disappears by offsetting each other if the silence of the dark as anti-existence and existence unite into one. Since all things appear if the wings are spread and everything disappears if folded, it is in a moment not to be, and it is not in a moment to be. That is the property of existence.

266. We are familiar with the limitedness of life while living in a changing existence, while experiencing the sunrise and the sunset daily. Therefore we think it is right that a running car will stop sometime in the future. However, it is strange if it stops if it is in outer space. There, it is normal to run forever once started. In view of the whole existence, it is limited and is a peculiar case, as creatures on earth exist with a body under the influence of gravity. We try to overcome this limited life by developing a sense of solidarity and gathering information of inheritance while living under these limited, peculiar conditions, but it is a contradiction to pursue eternity in a limited life. This limited life is for enjoying itself as is, and eternity is together with us at the moment, uniting with the universal whole.

267. 무는 아무것도 없다는 가정하에 도입된 개념으로 존재와 대치되는 것으로 혼동되고 있다. 그러나 존재와 대치되는 개념은 무가 아니라 반존재인 어둠의 침묵이다. 존재와 반존재가 상쇄되면 그것이 무이다. 어둠의 침묵이 존재가 아니라는 의미에서 무와 혼동될 수도 있다. 그러나 어둠의 침묵은 무와 다르다. "어둠의 침묵이란 오감으로 체감할 수도 없는 칠흑 같은 어둠과 끝없는 침묵뿐이니 이것이 곧 무가 아니냐?"라고 반문할 수도 있으나 어둠의 침묵은 보이지 않는 공간을 품고 있는 존재의 배경으로서 아무것도 없다는 의미의 무와는 다르다. 존재가 없다면 어둠의 침묵도 없고 시공간이 없는 오로지 무일 뿐이다. 존재가 있는 곳에는 어둠의 침묵이 항시 함께한다. 어둠의 침묵과 존재는 분리될 수 없는 빛과 그림자와 같다.

268. 너의 시간과 나의 시간은 다르지만 너와 내가 우리가 되어 함께하면 너와 나의 시간은 같아지고 반대로 너와 내가 헤어지면 시간은 제각기 흐른다. 제3자의 시간도 우리의 시간과 다르지만 제3자와 우리가 함께 하면 제3자의 시간은 우리의 시간과 같아지고 헤어지면 다시 달라진다. 어디에서나 똑같이 흐르는 절대적인 시간이란 없으며 존재의 변화 또는 존재와 존재 간의 변화에 따라서 시간이 다르게 흐른다.

267. As nothingness is an introduced concept on the assumption that there is not anything, so it is confused with the thing opposed to existence. However, the concept opposed to existence is not nothingness but the silence of the dark as anti-existence. It is just nothingness if existence and anti-existence offset each other. As the silence of the dark is not existence, so it might be confused with nothingness, but the silence of the dark is different from nothingness. Somebody could ask back, "Since there is only the darkness not felt with the five senses and the endless silence, the silence of the dark is just nothing, isn't it?" However, as the silence of the dark is the background of existence, bearing the invisible space, it is different from nothingness, with the meaning that there is not anything. If there is no existence, there is no silence of the dark, and there is only nothingness, without time and space. The silence of the dark is always together with existence as long as there is existence. The silence of the dark is to existence as light is to shadow—not separated.

268. Though your time is different from my time, your time comes to be equal to my time if you and I are together by becoming us. Inversely, if you and I are parted from each other, time flies separately. The time of a third party is also different from our time, but it comes to be equal to our time if a third party is together with us, and it comes to differ again if a third party is parted from us. There is no absolute time flying equally anywhere, and time flies differently according to the change in existence or the change between existence and existence.

269. 별이 빛나는 것을 볼 수 있는 것은 타오르는 별의 에너지가 광원이 되어 그 광원으로부터 방사되는 빛의 입자가 관측자까지 도달하기 때문이다. 그뿐만 아니라 별에서 방사되는 빛이 우주공간 모든 방향으로 퍼져나가므로 관측자가 별을 어느 방향에서도 볼 수 있는 것이다. 즉 우주공간 어디에서나 그 별로부터 방사된 빛이 충만해 있는 것이다. 그럼에도 불구하고 관측자가 별의 위치를 혼동하지 않고 식별할 수 있는 것은 빛이 우주공간에서 최단 코스로 직진하기 때문이다. 우주공간에는 수많은 별들로부터 방사되는 빛들로 충만한데 이들 간에 서로 충돌한다면 별빛이 관측자에 도달하기 전에 사라지고 없을 것이다. 그러나 빛과 빛은 서로 간섭하며 투과하기 때문에 충돌하지 않고 진행할 수 있는 것이다. 또한 백오십억 광년이나 떨어진 빛을 현재 관측할 수 있다는 것은 빛의 수명이 무한에 가깝기 때문이다. 즉 별은 이미 백오십억 년 전에 에너지가 고갈되어 사라지고 없어졌을지라도 그 별에서 방사된 빛은 백오십억 년이 넘도록 우주공간을 직진하고 있다. 빛이야말로 어둠의 침묵을 배경으로 존재하는 모든 것 중에서 가장 보편적인 것으로 존재를 대표하는 꽃이라 할 만하다. 모든 존재는 빛을 통하여 자신의 아름다움을 표현한다.

269. It is possible to see a twinkling star because the energy of the burning star becomes a light source, and particles of light emitted from the light source arrive to an observer. Furthermore, light emitted from a star travels, spreading in all directions of space so that an observer can see the star from any direction—that is, space is full of light emitted from the stars. Nevertheless, an observer can distinguish the position of a star without confusion because light travels straight, taking a shortcut. Since space is full of light emitted from a great number of stars, this light will disappear before arriving at an observer if they collide with each other. However, light can travel without collision because it penetrates, interfering each other. In addition, even light fifteen billion light-years away can be observed because the life span of light is almost infinite—that is, light emitted from a star travels straight in space for more than fifteen billion years though the star had already disappeared accordingly as its energy became exhausted before fifteen billion years. Light is most universal among all existence set in the silence of the dark, so it deserves to be the flower representing all existence. All existence expresses their beauty through light.

270. 일백억 광년 떨어져 있는 별이 폭발하여 사라지는 장관을 지금 여기에서 관측하였다면 사실상 그 별은 일백억 년 전에 이미 사라지고 없는 별이며 폭발하는 모습은 일백억 년 전의 과거를 보는 것에 불과하다. 더욱 재미있는 것은 일백억 광년보다 더 멀리 떨어져 있는 곳에서 바라본다면 그 별은 아직 폭발하지 않고 반짝이는 모습으로 보인다. 이미 죽은 자가 아직 살아있는 것이다. 이와 같이 가시적인 현상계는 이미 사라지고 없는 빛과 지금 보이는 빛과 아직 보이지 않는 빛의 흐름 속에서 동시적으로 존재한다. 현상계의 모든 존재는 어둠 속에 깜박이는 빛이 되어 과거와 현재와 미래를 하나로 관통하며 흐른다. 사라지고 없는 수많은 별들을 현재 모습처럼 보고 있으니 순간의 존재는 영속적인 시간의 틀에서 벗어나 있다. 순간의 존재마다 제각기 다른 시간 속에서 살고 있기에 영속적이고 절대적인 시간은 없다.

271. 차는 지나가면 뒷모습을 볼 수 있지만 빛은 한번 지나가면 다시 볼 수 없다.

270. If you observe the grand spectacle when a star fifteen billion light-years away disappears with an explosion at present, the star already disappeared fifteen billion years ago, and the exploding spectacle is nothing but the past, fifteen billion years ago. It is more interesting that if you observe the sight at a place farther than fifteen billion light-years, the star won't explode yet but will instead twinkle. The already dead is still alive. Like this, the visible phenomenal world exists simultaneously in the stream of the already disappeared light, the presently shown light, and the not-shown-yet light. All existence in the phenomenal world becomes the light shining in darkness, and it passes through the past, the present, and the future in line. Since you see a great number of stars disappearing as if they exist in the present, existence in a moment is out of permanent time. There is no permanent, absolute time because each existence in a moment is living in a different time.

271. If a car passes through, we can catch sight of the car's back. However, once light passes through, we cannot see the light anymore.

272. (시 49)

태초에 어둠이 갈라지고
천지간에 아무런 이름도 없더라.
주인도 없고 객도 없이
침묵 속에 한 줄기 바람 일어
생명이 잉태하니
눈을 뜨고 비늘 입고
고독을 부르며 헤매더라.
삶의 뿌리 찾아
흙을 잊지 못하고 잊지 못해
물고기 한 마리
화석이 되고 나무가 되어
어느 장인의 손에서
목어가 탄생하니
지금도 태초의 꿈속을 헤매더라.

273. 빛과 어둠의 침묵이 존재와 반존재로서 진행되다가 상쇄되어 무
가 되듯이 삶이란 죽음을 배경으로 진행되다가 삶과 죽음이 합치되면
서로 상쇄되어 사라진다. 만물은 마음의 의식 또는 우주적 전체의식
이라는 거울을 사이에 두고 하나가 둘인 듯이 서로 마주 보고 있다.

272. (Poem 49)

Since darkness breaks to pieces in the beginning,
there is no name between the heaven and the earth.
Without a host and guests,
by the blowing of wind in silence,
as a life is born,
it opens its eyes and wears scales
and wanders, calling out to the loneliness.
Looking for the root of life,
not to forget and not to forget soil,
as a fish becomes a fossil,
and becomes a tree,
by the hand of a craftsman,
a wooden fish is born.
It is still wandering in the dream of the beginning.

273. While light and the silence of the dark progress as existence and anti-existence, they become nothing by offsetting each other. Like that, while life progresses in the background of death, life and death disappear by offsetting if they unite into one. All things face each other in the mirror called the consciousness of the mind or the consciousness of the universal whole as if one is two.

274. 일상에서 느끼는 온기, 열기, 습기, 냉기, 한기, 사기, 혈기, 살기 등 감각적인 기운에서부터 전자파, 장파와 단파, 초단파, 엑스선, 감마선 등 감각적으로 인지되지 않으나 물리적으로 작용하는 기가 주위에 운기한다. 또한 물체 간에 작용하는 전기력, 자기력이나 우주공간에서 작용하는 중력, 또는 원자 구조와 같이 미시적인 세계에서 작용하는 강력이나 약력 등이 있고 청각적으로 감지되는 소리의 음파와 시각적으로 인지되는 가시광선이나 태풍, 폭풍, 미풍과 같은 바람의 기운도 있다. 이런 모든 것들은 물질과 물질 사이를 연결시키고 물질과 정신 간에 작용하는 힘을 지닌다. 이러한 힘들을 총칭하여 기라 한다. 기란 무엇인가? 기는 모든 존재에 개별적으로 내재하는 힘이자 만물 간에 작용하는 힘이다. 기가 개체에 작용할 때는 개별적이지만 동시에 전체와 연결될 때는 전체적이다. 기는 만물에 질서를 유지하고 항상 유동적이다. 우주에 충만하게 퍼져있는 기는 모든 물체에 작용하는 힘의 흐름이자 물질에 질서를 부여하는 의식의 흐름이다. 개체마다 충만된 기를 자신의 힘과 의식으로 삼고 활동하다가 개체가 소멸하게 되면 개체에 내재되어 있던 기는 다시 전체에 합일한다.

275. 해와 달, 박테리아와 모기 등 모든 존재마다 주어진 시간은 제각각 다르며 천차만별 사람들 간에도 느껴지는 시간은 다르다. 섹스 중인 남녀의 시간과 독방에 갇힌 죄수의 시간은 결코 같을 수가 없고 갓 태어난 아기의 시간과 임종을 앞둔 노인의 시간은 같을 수가 없다. 모든 존재의 변화가 다르듯 모든 존재에게 적용되는 시간은 제각기 다르다.

274. There are several kinds of energy acting in circumstances—from the sensible mood felt in daily life, such as warmth, heat, humidity, chill, cold, miasma, vigor, and bloodthirstiness, to the physical force not felt sensually, such as electronic waves, long and short waves, microwaves, X-rays, and gamma rays. Furthermore, there are electric and magnetic forces acting between material objects, gravity acting in space, strong and weak forces acting in the microscopic world like in atomic structures, sonic waves perceived aurally, visible rays perceived visually, and wind power, like typhoons, storms, or breezes. All of them hold the power connecting a material object and another material object, as well as acting between a material object and a spirit. These kinds of power are called energy generically. What is energy? Energy is the power immanent in all existence individually as well as the power interacting with all things. Energy is individual when it acts on an individual, but it is whole when it is connected to the whole. Energy maintains order in all things, and it is always mobile. Energy spread fully in space is the stream of power acting on all material objects as well as the stream of consciousness keeping order in substances. Each individual acts with full energy as its power and consciousness, during which time energy immanent in an individual returns, uniting with the whole if an individual becomes extinct.

275. The time given to all existence—like the sun, the moon, bacteria, a mosquito, etc.—is different from each other, and all sorts of people feel time differently. The time of a couple having sex is not equal to the time of a prisoner in solitary confinement, and the time of a newborn baby is not equal to the time of an old man at the moment of death. As the change in all existence differs, the time applied to all existence differs from each other.

276. 미생물의 수명은 수초도 안 걸리지만 태양, 지구, 달의 운행에 변화가 있으려면 수십억 년도 더 걸린다. 작은 것에 주어진 시간은 순간이지만 큰 것에 주어진 시간은 무한에 가깝다. 큰 공간의 존재는 긴 시간 속에 있고 작은 공간의 존재는 짧은 시간 속에 있다. 시간과 공간은 비례한다. 공간이 미세하게 쪼개질수록 미세한 공간 속에는 찰나적인 순간만이 존재한다. 찰나적인 순간에 찍힌 한 장의 사진 속에는 존재의 변화가 없고 그 사진 속의 시간은 정지되어 있다. 그러나 활동사진처럼 여러 장의 사진을 연결하면 변화하는 존재들과 함께 시간이 다시 흐르는 것처럼 보인다. 엄밀히 말하면 시간이란 존재의 변화를 표현한 것일 뿐, 시간 자체가 스스로 흐르는 것이 아니다.

276. The life span of microbes is less than a few seconds, but it takes more than a few billion years to change the movement of heavenly bodies—like the sun, the earth, and the moon. The time given to a micro thing is only an instant, but the time given to a macro thing is almost infinite. The existence of a big space is in the long term, and the existence of a small space is in the short term. Time and space are in proportion. The more minutely space is sliced, the more instant time exists in the sliced space. There is no change in existence in the picture taken in a moment, and the time inside the picture is at a standstill. However, if several pictures are connected like a picture sequence, time seems to fly again with the changing existences. Strictly speaking, time does not fly itself but only expresses the change in existence.

10. 나는 무엇인가?

277. 내가 나를 죽이고 내가 나를 살리는 것이다. 내 속에 모든 것이 다 있다. 그래서 나 자신을 잃지 말고 나 자신을 알라는 것이다.

278. 주위에 휩쓸려 꼭두각시처럼 놀아나는 모습을 바라보며 꿈에서 깨고 나니 꿈속의 나는 벌레같이 하잘것없는 존재였다. 남들 따라 살고 있는 모습이 너무나 허망하고 가치 없고 의미 없는 그런 꼭두각시 놀음 같았다. 분위기에 휩쓸려 살다가 꿈에서 깨고 보니 하잘것없는 일에 허둥대며 살고 있는 모습이 정말 바보스럽다. 도대체 본래의 내 모습은 어디에 두고 그렇게 살고 있었던 것일까?

10. What Am I?

277. It is me not only to kill me but also to let me live. Everything is inside me. Therefore I have to know myself in order not to lose myself.

278. I had a trivial existence, like an insect in my dream after awaking from sleep, while looking at myself acting as a puppet depending on the circumstances. It looked like a very vain, worthless, meaningless puppet play that I lived following others. It is really foolish that I was flustering myself over trivial matters after awaking from a dream in which I lived according to the circumstances. Where on earth did I leave my true self while living like that?

279. 나는 누구인가? 한 인간의 몸과 마음을 나라고 하고 그 주변의 모든 것은 내가 아니다. 그 주변의 누군가도 똑같이 그렇게 생각한다. 수없이 많은 내가 곳곳에 있다. 이쪽에서 보면 나인데 저쪽에서 보면 내가 아니다. 나라는 것은 오로지 주관적으로만 가능한 것이며 객관적인 나는 어디에도 없는 것이다. 수많은 사람들이 주관적으로 나라고 생각하고 있지만 객관적으로 보면 어디에도 나는 없다. 본래 나라는 것은 없는 것이며 주관적인 생각이 만들어낸 환상일 뿐이다. 나라는 환상이 사라졌을 때 혜안이 눈을 뜬다. 나라는 환상에서 깨어나고 나라는 집착에서 벗어나면 그것이 곧 천국이요 깨달음이다.

280. 나는 생물학적인 부분과 정신적인 부분으로 구성된다. 생물학적인 부분은 몸을 의미하고 정신적인 부분은 생각, 마음, 정신, 주변 환경 등을 의미한다. 생물학적인 나와 정신적인 나는 분리될 수 있는 것이 아니다. 생로병사는 생물학적인 육체에 국한된 것이지만 정신적인 부분은 육체를 넘어서는 무한한 개념이다. 일상생활은 생물학적인 육체를 기초로 하지만 그것이 나의 전부가 아니다. 오히려 정신적인 부분이 나의 대부분을 차지한다. 생물학적인 나는 하나의 개체로서 지극히 주관적이며 한시적인 존재인 반면에 정신적인 나는 매우 광대하고 무궁하다.

281. 생물학적인 한 인간은 가능한 것이지만 생물학적인 나는 주관적인 환상일 뿐 객관적으로는 없는 것이다. 반면에 정신적인 나는 지고하고 무한한 것이지만 그 무한함이 생물학적인 나에 갇혀 있으면 생물학적인 한 인간의 죽음과 함께 소멸되고 열려 있으면 전체에 이르는 것이다.

279. What am I? Once the body and the mind of a certain person are called me, all things except me in the circumstances are not me. Somebody else in similar circumstances also thinks the same way. There are a lot of me everywhere. It is me in my sight, but it is not me in another sight. It is only subjectively possible to be myself, and there is not me objectively anywhere. A lot of people think that it is me subjectively, but there is not me anywhere objectively. I am primarily not to be, and it is only an illusion made by a subjective thought. When an illusion by the name of me disappears, quick-sighted wisdom arises. It is just heaven as well as a spiritual awakening if one awakes from an illusion by the name of me, then gets out of an attachment by the name of me.

280. I consist of a biological part and a mental part. The biological part means my body, and the mental part means my thoughts, mind, spirit, and surroundings. The biological part and the mental part of me are unable to separate into two parts. Birth, old age, sickness, and death are confined to the biological body, but the mental part is an infinite concept beyond the body. Daily life is based on the biological body, but that is not the whole of me. On the contrary, the mental part takes most of me. The biological part of me is a very subjective, temporary existence as an individual, while the mental part of me is vast and eternal.

281. Though a biological human is possible, a biological me is only a subjective illusion, and there is not a biological me in an objective sight. On the other hand, the mental me is supreme and infinite, but the mental me becomes extinct together with the death of the biological me—if the infinity is confined to the biological me and it arrives to the whole if the infinity is open.

282. 각각의 개체가 주변과 조화로운 질서를 유지하는 가운데 전체 우주를 구성하고 있는데 그들 중에서 주관성을 지닌 한 개체가 바로 나다. 그런 내가 전부인 양 생각하는 환상이 나에 대한 집착을 가져오게 한다. 내가 없는데 내 것이 어디 있는가? 몸, 재산, 주변의 것들을 잠시 관리하다가 다 놓고 가는 것이 인생이다. 나는 임시적인 관리인이지 영원한 소유주가 아니다.

283. 나와 너는 대치적인 개념인데 나와 우리는 공동체 개념이다. 그러나 우리가 세분화되어 우리 속에서 너를 발견하면 공동체 개념이 대치적인 개념으로 바뀐다. 그래서 무리를 이루는 사회가 때로는 협동과 투쟁으로 혼란스러움에 빠진다.

284. 육체가 어느 날 갑자기 시공간 한 점에 감옥이 되어 나를 세상으로부터 격리시켰다. 육체는 감옥에 갇힌 나에게 소리 없이 다가와 친구가 되어 주겠노라고 속삭인다. 나는 감옥에 왜 갇히게 되었는지 이유도 모르고 육체와 함께 살기 시작했다. 그로부터 육체는 나의 친구가 되어 세상을 보여주고 항상 그림자처럼 동행하며 속삭이곤 하였다. 육체는 마치 나인 양 행동하였고 나는 그러한 육체를 당연하게 생각했다. 나는 어느덧 육체에 익숙해지고 매사 육체를 통하지 않으면 안 되게 되었다. 나는 육체 없이 아무것도 할 수 없었고 육체가 나 자신이라고 생각하였다. 그렇게 한세월 흐르다 보니 어느덧 감옥의 창살이 비바람에 흩날리고 해진 천정으로 밤이면 별이 보이고 창틈으로 바람이 흘러들었다. 육체는 이제 해진 모습이 되어 나를 떠나려고 한다. 나는 육체가 떠나면 홀로 외로움을 어찌할까 괴로워하는데 막상 육체가 떠나자 그동안 격리시켰던 감옥도 꿈처럼 사라지고 모든 것은 하나가 되어 있었다.

282. The universe is composed of individuals while each individual is in harmonious order with the circumstances, and an individual having subjectivity among them is just me. The illusion to think of such me as the whole causes an attachment to me. Where is mine while I am not? It is a life to leave all things after managing a body, a mind, and surroundings for a while. I am not a permanent owner but a temporary manager.

283. You and I are based on a confrontational concept, while we and I are based on a common concept. However, the common concept changes into the confrontational concept if we are subdivided and you are found among us. Therefore, sometimes a society forming groups falls into confusion with collaboration and struggle.

284. One day a body suddenly became a prison at a point in time and space, then isolated me from the world. A body silently approached me, confined, and whispered to me to become a friend. I began to live together with a body without knowing why I was confined. Then the body became my friend while showing me the world, and it used to whisper going with me like a shadow always. The body acted as if it was me, and I thought that such a body was right. I was accustomed to a body before I was aware of it, and I couldn't help doing everything through this body. I couldn't do anything without a body, and I thought that the body was my own self. With the lapse in time like that, the iron bars of a prison were exposed to the weather, stars were seen through the worn-away ceiling at night, and the wind blew through a chink in the window while I didn't realize it. Now the body becomes a feature worn away, and it is ready to leave me. I am worried how I should overcome loneliness if this body leaves me, but the prison that isolated me for a while also disappeared like a dream, and all things united into one as soon as the body left me at last.

285. 푸른 신호등, 붉은 신호등을 구분하는 삶 속에 살면서 너와 내가 하나 되는 것은 쉽지 않다. 너는 멈추고 나는 가는 것이다. 그러나 불이 꺼지면 어둠 속에서 손에 손을 잡고 우리는 함께 원점으로 돌아간다.

286. 무엇인가 구하려면 무엇인가 잃게 마련이고 그렇게 얻어 본들 결국 모든 것을 놓고 가는 것이 인생이거늘 그럼에도 불구하고 평생을 하루같이 살다가 어느새 원점으로 돌아와 나목으로 서 있는 자신의 모습을 보고서야 비로소 철드는 것이 인생이다.

287. 육체가 시공의 덫에 걸려 있다. 육체에 갇힌 사람들 사이에 공간의 덫이 걸리고 과거의 기억과 미래의 환상은 시간의 덫이 되어 생명을 억압한다. 육체는 나를 꿈꾸고 전부를 가장하지만 본래 나는 없고 육체는 형상일 뿐이다. 과거와 미래가 영원을 꿈꾸고 지속을 가장하지만 순간을 잃어버린 껍질 속에서 드넓은 하늘을 찾을 길이 없다. 덫에 걸린 육체가 생존 속에서 몸부림치다가 마침내 껍질을 벗고서야 한 송이 꽃으로 피어난다. 허공 속에 피어난 바람꽃이 시공을 넘어 춤사위를 펼치니 순간이 바람이고 순간이 꽃이다.

285. It is not easy that you and I unite into one while distinguishing between a green light and a red light in life. You must stop, and I must go. However, we return to the origin, walking hand in hand if light is put out.

286. If one pursues something, one ought to lose something. Even though one gets something like that, it is life to return to dust, leaving everything in the end. Nevertheless, it is a life not to become possessed with discretion until seeing oneself standing like a bare tree after returning to the origin, before one is aware while living a lifetime as one day.

287. A body is caught in a spatiotemporal trap. The trap of space is set between people confined in body, and the memory of the past and the illusion of the future suppress a life with the trap of time. A body dreams of me and pretends to be the whole, but I don't exist primarily, and a body is only a shape. The past and the future dream of all eternity and pretend to continue, but there is no way to find the serene sky inside the cocoon losing a moment. The body caught in the trap does not bloom as a flower until casting its skin at last while struggling for survival. Once a windflower bloomed in the void, it performs a dance beyond time and space. A moment is a wind, and a moment is a flower.

288. 일상 속에 펼쳐진 여러 가지 현상들과 변화, 그것을 바라보는 마음이 내가 아닌 것이 나인 양 스스로 껍질을 만들고 격리되어 외부에 대한 저항감을 불러일으킨다. 껍질 속에 갇힌 유한성과 그 속에 격리되어 생기는 이원성, 껍질을 지탱하려는 수고로움과 껍질을 넓힐수록 좁혀오는 긴장감이 스스로를 왜곡시킨다. 나에 대한 집착으로부터 한순간 놓여나면 긴장 속에 대치하고 있던 현상계가 왜곡된 억압에서 풀려나고 그 순간 자유와 신생이 도처에서 펼쳐진다. 이 얼마나 풍요로움인가! 거울 속에 갇혀있던 나는 너울을 벗고 거울 밖으로 되살아난다. 맑은 하늘에 찬란한 햇살이 부서지고 거리마다 꽃들이 일체감을 이룬다. 바람꽃은 제각기 다양한 모습으로 춤을 춘다. 나는 없는 것이다. 나는 당초에 없었고 지금도 없으며 잠시 드리워진 육체의 그림자는 언젠가 사라져버릴 것이 분명하다. 언젠가 벗어질 거죽으로 가상의 공간 속에 나를 가둬본들 무슨 소용 있으랴! 애당초 없었던 내가 어디 있는가? 나라는 환상이 나를 꿈꾸고 그림자가 나인 양 가상의 껍질을 드리우고 바람 속 그물처럼 착각을 일으킨다. 꿈속에 쌓인 껍질이 나이려니 하는 잘못된 생각이 삶을 왜곡시킨다. 한번 꿈에서 깨어나면 꿈과 함께 나는 사라지고 억압된 모든 것이 본래의 모습으로 되살아난다. 거기에는 나도 없고 나로 인한 착각도 없고 생사의 모순도 없다. 나도 없고 너도 없고 그들도 없다. 가상의 껍질에서 왜곡된 나를 해방시킬 수 있는 것은 오직 나라는 꿈에서 깨어나는 것뿐이다. 한 껍질 벗고 나면 세상은 있는 그대로 천국이다.

288. The mind looking at the various phenomena and their changes spread in daily life raises a sense of resistance to the exterior while isolated by a cocoon made for myself, as if the thing that is not me seems to be me. The limitedness confined in a cocoon, the duality raised in the isolation of a cocoon, efforts to maintain a cocoon, and tension becoming closer by trying to widen a cocoon—those distort myself. If I get free from the attachment to myself at a moment, the phenomenal world that confronted with tension is released from distorted suppression, and a freedom and a new life are spread everywhere at the same time. What an affluence it is! I who was confined in the mirror take off a veil, then revive out of the mirror. The sunlight shines in the serene sky, and flowers bloom with a sense of unity in every street. Each windflower dances with various features. I am not to be. I didn't exist primarily, don't exist even now, and it is obvious that the shadow of a body hanging down transiently will disappear someday. What a meaning it is even to confine myself in a virtual space with the appearance taken off someday! Where am I, who didn't exist from the first? An illusion by the name of me dreams of me, and makes the mistake like a net in the wind, hanging down an imaginary cocoon as if a shadow seems to be me. The mistaken thought that the cocoon spun in a dream might be me distorts life. After awakening from a dream once, I disappear together with a dream, and all suppressed things revive as the original appearance. There are not me, no mistake caused by me, and no discrepancy between life and death. Neither I nor you nor they also exist. Those that can set me free from the imaginary cocoon, are only to awake from the dream by the name of me. The world is heaven as is, if the cocoon is taken off.

289. 수컷 사마귀는 잡아먹힐 각오를 하고 자기보다 덩치 큰 암컷에게 접근하여 필사적인 교미를 시도한다. 거의 대부분 수컷은 교미 후 암컷에 잡아먹히고 만다. 종의 진화과정에서 후손을 남기고 죽는 것이 후손도 남기지 못하고 죽는 것보다는 낫다는 전략이다. 나는 죽지만 후손을 통해 우리를 기약할 수 있는 것이다. 우리가 곧 나라고 하는 생각이 나의 죽음을 긍정적으로 받아들이게 한다. 우리를 통한 나의 확장이다.

290. 개인주의가 발달된 사회에서는 나의 의미가 강하지만 집단주의가 발달된 사회에서는 나보다는 우리라는 의미가 강렬하다. 개미사회가 대표적인 집단주의 사회다. 개개인은 미약하지만 집단을 이루면 거대한 힘을 발휘한다. 문명의 발달과 함께 현대 인류사회는 개인주의가 발달되어 개인적인 죽음에서 공포와 고독을 체험한다. 동시대를 살면서도 저개발 국가의 사람들은 가족단위의 연대의식이 발달되어 개인의 죽음이나 고독을 효과적으로 극복한다. 나라고 하는 개인적인 생각은 매우 일시적이고 제한적인 개념이다. 나라고 하는 것은 하나의 생물학적인 개체와 주변 환경을 인지하는 능력이 결합된 한시적인 존재다.

291. 본디 여기 산 것도 늘 살 것도 아니기에 삶이라는 꿈에서 깨어나 몸과 맘의 집착을 끊고 무엇이 되려거나 구하는 바 없이 소유하지 않는 사랑으로 지금 순간을 자유하며 있는 그대로 참 나를 깨달음으로 일체의 근원이자 영원한 생명인 허공과 하나가 되리라.

289. A male mantis dares to be preyed upon, approaching a female mantis bigger than it, and desperately attempts to mate with the female. Most male mantises are preyed on by a female after mating. It is a strategy—to die after leaving descendants is better than to die without descendants—in the course of the evolution of species. Even though I die, we can be expected through our descendants. The thought that we are just me makes me accept my death positively. That is to expand me through us.

290. The meaning of me is strong in the society developed with individualism, but the meaning of us rather than me is strong in the society developed with collectivism. A society of ants is a representative society of collectivism. Each individual is weak, but they show mighty power if they form a group. As individualism developed in modern human society, with the advance of civilization, the individual began to experience fear and loneliness in death. Even though people in developing countries live in the same age, they effectively overcome individual death and loneliness by the sense of solidarity of their family unit. The thought of an individual as me is a very temporary, limited concept. A thing called me is a transient existence combined with a biological individual and an ability to perceive its surroundings.

291. Unite with the void as an original source of all things as well as an eternal life by realizing my true self as is, while freeing every moment with nonpossessed love, from a desire either to become someone or to pursue something after breaking off attachment from a body and a mind, by awaking from a dream by the name of life because I neither have ever lived here primarily nor will live forever.

292. (시 50)

일본인은 차별 그대로 평등이요
형상과 실체는 불일불이라 하고
한국인은 하나로 시작해서 하나로 돌아가니
순간순간이 곧 끝이다 하고
중국인은 도라 하면 이미 도가 아니요
하는 바 없이 아니함이 없다 하고
인도인은 마음이 사라지면 일체가 사라지니
있는 그대로라 한다.
태어남은 하나요 태어나니 둘이라
육신으로 태어나서 마음이 일어나고
마음과 함께 세상이 열리니
거울 속의 눈동자는 거울 밖을 바라보고
삶 속에서 꿈꾸고 꿈속에서 살며
없다가 있고 있다가 없는 듯이
하나가 둘이 되고 둘이 하나가 되었다.

292. (Poem 50)

A Japanese says that distinction itself is even,

and a figure and an essence are neither one nor two.

A Korean says that a moment to a moment is just the end,

for all things start from one and returns to one.

A Chinese says that it is already not the way if it is called the way,

and there is nothing not to be done without doing.

An Indian says that everything is as it is,

for everything disappear if a mind disappears.

It is one thing to be born, and it is two things after being born.

A mind arises as a body is born,

then the world is open with a mind.

A pupil inside a mirror looks at the outside of the mirror,

while dreaming in a life, and living in a dream,

as if not to be from to be, and to be from not to be.

One became two, and two became one.

293. (시 51)
너를 잊고 이름 없이 오라.
하늘도 별도 너를 맞으리라.

너를 벗고 알몸으로 오라.
산도 들도 너를 맞으리라.

짐 다 벗고 노래하며 오라.
새소리 바람 소리 너를 반기리라.
온갖 꽃이 친구 되어 반기리라.

너는 이제 외롭지 않으리.
모두가 너와 함께 노래 불러라.

네 목소리 주위에 생명을 불러오고
네 몸짓은 신선한 바람 되어 오리라.

순간에서 영원으로 함께하리니
너는 우리의 모두이어라.

너의 노래 너의 몸짓에
하늘 바다 별 바람 모두 다 춤추리라.

293. (Poem 51)
Come without a name, forgetting you.
So the firmament as well as the stars will receive you.

Come with a naked body, taking off you.
So the mountains as well as the plains will receive you.

Come singing after being relieved of all burden.
So the sound of birds and the wind will welcome you,
and all flowers will welcome you, forming a friendship.

You will never feel lonely anymore.
And all sing together with you.

Your voice put life in your surroundings,
and your gesture becomes fresh with the wind.

As you are together from a moment to eternity,
you are everything to us.

With your song and your gesture,
the firmament, the sea, the stars, as well as the wind dance
together.

294. (시 52)
몸이 나인가? 마음이 나인가?
꿈속의 나인가? 꿈꾸는 나인가?
마음이 사라지니 꿈도 사라진다.
몸도 없고 나도 없다.
하나가 둘인 것은 하나이기 위함이니
텅 빔이 하나고 일체다.
없이 있는 그대로가 참이다.
마음이 사라지니 바람꽃이 피어난다.
소유되지도 소유하지도 않으니
일체가 지복이다.

295. (시 53)
내가 되기까지 산마루에 꽃은 피고
바람은 소리 없이 스쳐 갔다.

말 못 하던 언어가 까닭 없이 열리고
어미를 그리워하는 아이처럼

별빛을 바라보고 또 하루를 보내며
나의 어리석음을 되새기면서

조각 난 빛과 그림자 사이로
내가 된 까닭을 삼키고 있었다.

294. (Poem 52)

Is a body me, or is a mind me?
Is that me in a dream or a dreaming me?
Once a mind disappears, a dream also disappears.
Neither my body nor I exist.
It is for being one that one is two.
To be void is one as well as the whole.
To be as not to be is the true as is.
Once a mind disappears, a windflower blooms.
As it is neither to be possessed nor to possess anything,
all things are the supreme bliss.

295. (Poem 53)

In order to becomes me, a flower bloomed in the ridge,
and the wind silently blew by.

The language that couldn't be spoken was open without any reason,
like the child who misses his mother.

Looking at starlight and spending another day,
while ruminating on my ignorance,

between the light and shadow split,
I was bearing why it became me.

296. (시 54)
언제부터인가
무조건한 내가

얼굴도 이름도 아닌 것이
어느덧 내가 되어

변해가는 육체인 듯
그물에 바람인 듯

잡힐 듯 잡히지 않고
보일 듯 보이지 않는

전부인 듯 하나인 듯
아무것도 아닌 듯

순간의 티끌인 듯
영원한 침묵인 듯

불가사의한 것이
내가 아닌 내가 되어

삶인 듯
꿈인 듯하여라.

296. (Poem 54)
From one day
I who was unconditional⋯.

Those that were neither a face nor a name
became me before I was aware,

as if it was a changing body,
or the wind in a net.

Not to be caught as if it can be caught,
and not to be shown as if it can be shown⋯.

Like the whole, like the only one,
rather like nothing⋯.

Like a dust in a moment,
or like an eternal silence⋯.

As the mysterious thing
becomes me who am not me⋯.

Like life,
or like a dream is it.

297. (시 55)
거울 속으로
다가서는 너를 바라보며
나는 서 있다.

오감의 분별이
거울 앞에 흔들리고

언제부터인지
너와 나는 메아리 되어

너는 나인 양
나는 너인 양
거울 속에서 그리고 거울 밖에서
함께 살고 있다.

297. (Poem 55)
Into the mirror,
looking at you approaching,
I stand.

The distinction of the five senses
wavers in front of the mirror.

From time unknown,
you and me become an echo···.

As if you are me,
and as if I am you,
inside the mirror and outside the mirror,
we are living together.

298. (시 56)
거울을 바라본다.

거울 속에 비친 눈동자
그 속에 비친 모습을 본다.

세상은 너보고 나라고 한다.
너를 통해 나는 살고 있다.

너는 시간 속에 살고
나는 시간 밖에 산다.

너는 나의 그림자
너를 통해 나는 깨우친다.

너는 나의 친구.

너 없이 나는 아무것도 아니고
너를 통해 나는 비워진다.

298. (Poem 56)
I look at the mirror.

The pupil reflected in the mirror···.
I look at the feature mirrored in it.

In the world you are called as me.
I am living through you.

You live with time,
and I live beyond time.

You are my shadow,
and I am awakened from you.

You are my friend.

I am nothing without you,
and I am emptied out of you.

299. (시 57)

밤바다 열리는 동녘으로
새로울 것 없는 하루를 헤치고
벌거벗은 해가 솟아오른다.

소금밭에 백야는 흔들리고
잃어버린 전설을 찾아서
순간은 영원을 엮어 가는데

선문을 넘고 넘어도
육신은 마음 안에 머무니
마침내 해는 서산에 기울고

찾으려 헤매던 것은
그물에 걸리지 않는 바람이라
차라리 허공이었구나.

299. (Poem 57)
From the east where the sea by night is open,
breaking through a routine day,
the naked sun is rising.

The midnight sun in the salt field shakes,
seeking the forgotten legend,
a moment weaves an eternity.

Though a question and answer is exchanged,
as a body stays inside a mind,
at last the sun sets in the western hill.

As the one who wandered to seek
is the wind not to be caught in a net,
it is rather the void.

300. (시 58)
언제부터인지 동쪽 문에 영혼이 있고
서쪽 문에 육체가 있다 하여

영혼을 부를 때면 동쪽 문을 통하고
육체를 찾을 때는 서쪽 문을 통하곤 하였다.

양쪽 문이 따로 있어 그렇듯
영혼을 부르고 육체를 노래하다가

어느 날 한쪽 문을 통하여
영혼도 육체도 함께 해보니 더없이 행복하다.

그렇게 단순한 삶을 분별하느라
한평생이 흘러갔다.

300. (Poem 58)
As said that there is a soul in the eastern gateway,
and a body in the western gateway from time unknown,

I used to pass through the eastern gateway when calling a soul,
and the western gateway when seeking a body.

As both gateways were separated like that,
I used to call a soul and sing with a body for a while.

One day, by passing through one gateway,
getting both a soul and a body, so I am happy supremely.

While I distinguished such a simple life,
a lifetime flew.

301. (시 59)
빈 잔을 정갈히 하니 탐욕이 사라지고
허공을 마시니 정기가 맑다.

나를 바라보고 세상을 바라보고
무애인 듯 침묵인 듯하여라.

어느 곳에나 있고
어느 곳에도 머물지 않는 바람처럼

소유할 수 없고
소유되지 않는 것이 나일지니

작위함이 없이
만물은 그대로 온전하고

육체가 벗어지듯 마음도 그러하니
사라진 마음에 생사가 없구나.

301. (Poem 59)
As an empty cup is kept clean, greed disappears.
As the void is inhaled, a spirit is fine.

Looking at me, and looking at the world,
it seems infinite and silent.

Like the wind to be everywhere,
and not to stay anywhere,

the one who cannot possess,
and cannot be possessed is me.

Without performing a task,
all things as is are sound.

As if a body comes off, even a mind disappears.
In the disappeared mind there is neither life nor death.

302. (시 60)
순하고 힘센 짐승을 찾아서
아이가 길을 떠나니

산 넘고 물 건너 온종일 헤매다가
햇살 아래 곤한 몸 잠이 들고

짐승 울음소리에 깨어보니
발자국소리 멀어진다.

지나온 길을 되돌아보니
아이는 간데없고
낯선 노인이 짐승을 몰고 간다.

303. (시 61)
나를 벗으니
만물이 새롭고

차 향기에
하루가 그윽하다.

평상심에
생사는 간데없고

잔잔한 미소는
바람이어라.

302. (Poem 60)
To look for a meek, strong beast,
as a child starts on a journey,

wandering over a hill and crossing a river all day,
a tired body falls asleep under the sunlight.

On waking up at the cry of a beast,
footsteps fade away in the distance.

On looking back upon the way passed,
the child is missing,
and a strange old man is driving a beast.

303. (Poem 61)
Once I get off myself,
all things are fresh.

With the scent of tea,
a day is profound.

With presence of mind,
life and death disappear.

To smile serenely,
it might be the wind.

11. 죽음이란 무엇인가?

죽어서 어찌 될지 묻기 전에 왜 태어났는지를 먼저 물어라.

304. 촛불을 밝히는 것은 마음이 일어남이며 마음의 불꽃이 꺼졌을 때 비로소 어둠 속에 적멸의 순간이 찾아온다.

305. 아직 살아있다면 완전한 삶을 이룬 것이 아니다. 죽음으로써 완전한 삶을 이룬 것이다.

11. What Is Death?

Ask why you were born before asking what will happen after dying.

304. To light up a candle is that a mind appears, and a moment of death comes from the darkness when a flaming mind is extinguished at last.

305. If you are still alive, it is not that you've achieved a complete life. Only after dying can you achieve a complete life.

306. 삶과 죽음은 동전의 양면과 같이 분리되지 않는 하나다. 살아있기 때문에 죽는 것이고 죽을 수 있기 때문에 살아있는 것이다. 산 것이 죽는 것은 없던 것이 태어났기 때문이고 없던 것이 태어났기 때문에 태어난 것이 없어지는 것이다. 삶과 죽음은 하나로서 이미 온전한 것이니 삶과 죽음을 여러 번 반복한들 하나와 다를 것이 무엇이며 하나보다 나을 것이 무엇인가? 결국 삶과 죽음 아닌가? 탄생은 태어나는 것이고 부활은 죽은 자가 다시 태어나는 것이고 윤회는 죽고 태어나는 것을 반복하는 것이니, 태어나는 것이나 다시 태어나는 것이나 반복해서 태어나는 것이나 모두 다 삶과 죽음을 경험함에 있어서 결국 같은 것이니 지금 살고 있는 생명이 부활하여 태어날 생명이나 윤회하여 태어날 생명보다 못할 바 없다.

307. 과거의 추억 속의 나, 지금 여기 있는 나, 미래에 있을 나를 바라본다. 현실, 꿈, 게임을 바라본다. 생과 사, 있음과 없음을 바라본다. 이 모든 것들을 연관해 보면 하나로 연결되어 있다. 과거의 추억 속에 있는 나도, 지금 여기 있는 나도, 미래에 있을 나도 하나다. 현실도 꿈도 게임도 생과 사도 있음과 없음도 꼬리에 꼬리를 물고 얽혀 있다. 꿈에서 깨고 나면 지금이 깨어 있는 현실이고 깨어나기 전을 꿈이라고 생각하지만 깨어나기 전의 꿈속에서는 꿈이 현실이 된다. 게임이 시작되기 전에는 게임이라 생각하지만 게임이 시작되면 게임이 곧 현실이 된다. 게임이 끝나고 나서 현실로 돌아오면 그제야 게임이라 생각한다. 지나간 추억 속의 나는 마치 꿈속의 나처럼 느껴지고 다가올 미래의 나는 마치 게임을 시작하려는 나처럼 느껴진다. 꿈과 현실과 게임을 애써 구별할 필요가 없다. 꿈도 현실에 기초하고 게임도 현실에 기초하기 때문에 이 모든 것이 결국은 하나다. 생과 사를 구별하는 것도 어리석다. 왜 태어났는지 묻지 않고 살았듯이 죽어 어찌 될지 물을 필요도 없다. 생사는 동전의 양면과 같아서 대치적이면서 동시에 서로

306. Life and death are one thing, not to be separated like two sides of the same coin. A man dies because he is alive, and he is alive because he can die. A living thing dies because a thing that used to be nonexistent was born, and the thing born disappears because the thing that used to be nonexistent was born. Since life and death are already sound as one, what is different and better than one though they are reborn several times? It is life and death after all, isn't it? As a birth is to be born, a rebirth is for a dead man to be reborn, and transmigration is to repeat life and death. So a birth, a rebirth, and transmigration are the same in view of experiencing life and death. Therefore, a life at present is not inferior to a life to be reborn or a life to be born through transmigration.

307. I look at me in my memories of the past, me being here in the present, and me expected in the future. I look at reality, a dream, and a game. I look at life and death as well as to be and not to be. Considering their relationships, all of them are connected into one. I in memories of the past, I being here in the present, as well as I expected in the future am one. The reality, a dream, a game, life, death, to be as well as not to be—they get entangled one after another. Once I wake from a dream, I think that the present is the awakening reality, and the status before waking is a dream; however, a dream becomes the reality in the dream before waking. I think that it is a game before starting a game, but a game becomes just the reality if a game is started. Once I come back to reality after finishing a game, then I think that it was a game. I in memories of the past feel as me in a dream, and I in the future feel as me just about to start a game. It is not necessary to distinguish between a dream, reality, and a game. Since a dream as well as a game is based on reality, all of them are one after all. It is foolish even to distinguish life and death. As people live without questioning why they were born, it is not necessary to ask what will happen after dying. As life and death are like both sides of the

가 서로를 있게 한다. 동전의 양면을 분리할 수 없는 것처럼 삶과 죽음은 분리할 수 없는 하나다. 과거, 현재, 미래도 하나고 꿈과 현실과 게임도 하나고 삶과 죽음도 하나다. 모든 것이 하나다.

308. 무생물은 죽지 않지만 모든 생물들은 살아 있기 때문에 죽는다. 바위나 강물처럼 무생물이라면 죽을 필요가 없다. 살았으니까 죽는 것이라 생각하면 명쾌하다. 죽지 않는다면 그것은 산 것이 아니다. 살아있는 것은 죽어야만 산 것이다. 동전이 공중에 던져졌으면 땅에 떨어져야지 계속 솟구쳐 있을 수 없다. 죽는다는 것은 없던 것이 잠시 있다가 다시없어지는 것이다. 오래전부터 살고 있었다고 착각하기 때문에 죽는 것이 낯 설게 느껴지지만 원래 없었던 것이 잠시 소풍 나왔다가 원래대로 돌아가는 것이라 생각하면 보다 자연스럽다.

309. 영속성에 얽매이지 않아야 삶이 자유롭다. 순간순간이 자유로우면 죽고 사는 것이 하나같이 자유롭다. 우리가 아침에 날기 시작해서 저녁에 죽는 하루살이라면 이미 수천 번 죽고 살고 죽고 살고 한 것이다. 순간순간이 영원하고 그러기에 우리는 영원한 지금을 살고 있다. 사는 동안 나로 인해 누군가가 행복했으면 그것으로 족하다. 누구 하나 죽었다고 해서 그것이 무슨 의미가 있는가? 이미 사는 동안에 하루하루를 통하여 수없이 죽고 또 죽은 것이다. 또한 죽는 것이 고통스럽다고 하지만 살아있기에 고통스러운 것이지 죽으면 고통도 함께 사라진다. 나라는 별개의 존재는 주관적이고 한시적인 것으로 객관적으로 보면 본래 없는 것이다. 만물 모든 것들이 형상을 바꿔가며 잠시 함께하는 것이라 생각하면 굳이 영원을 추구하고 죽음을 피하려는 망상과 굴레에서 놓여나게 된다.

same coin, they not only confront but also depend on each other simultaneously. Life and death are one, not to be separated, like how two sides of the same coin cannot be separated. The past, the present, as well as the future are one. A dream, reality, as well as a game are one. And life as well as death are one. Everything is one.

308. A lifeless thing does not die, but all living things should die because they are alive. Lifeless things like rocks and rivers don't need to die. It is clear if you think that things die because they are alive. If they don't die, they are not alive. Those who are alive should die, to complete their lives. If a coin is tossed up in the air, it should fall to the ground. It cannot soar continuously. Dying means that nonexistent thing disappears again after being for a while. It feels unfamiliar to die because people misunderstand as if they have lived since old times, but it is more natural to think that a primarily nonexistent thing goes home after enjoying a picnic for a while.

309. Life is free if it is not bound by perpetuity. Life and death are free as ever if every moment is free. If we are mayflies dying at dusk after flying at dawn, we are already born and have died several thousand times. Every moment is perpetual, so we are living in the everlasting present. It is enough for life if somebody was happy while living because of me. What does it mean when a certain person dies? We are already dead countlessly through our daily lives while living. In addition, it is said that dying is painful, but it is only painful because one is still alive. If one dies, the pain also disappears. As a special existence called me is subjective and transient, I am not primarily when viewed objectively. If we think that all things are temporarily together while changing their shapes, we can free ourselves from restrains and our delusions to pursue perpetuity and avoid death firmly.

310. 죽음은 예고된 것이지만 아무도 의식하려고 하지 않는다. 하루의 태양 아래 모든 것을 맡기고 오직 살아있음을 의식한다. 하지만 육신이 바람과 꽃이 되어 춤출 수 있는 것은 죽음과 삶이 서로 껴안으며 사랑하고 존중하기 때문이다.

311. 생명체는 유전적인 분화과정을 통하여 대대로 삶과 죽음을 반복하며 진화해 왔다. 생명체의 구성은 세분화되고 정교해지면 그만큼 취약해진다. 쇠는 수백도의 변화에도 견디지만 생명은 불과 몇 도의 변화에도 생사를 오간다. 생명체가 진화과정에서 정교해질수록 더욱 취약해지는 것이라면 생명체의 진화는 죽음과 더욱 가까워지는 것이 아닌가? 의문에 상관없이 생명의 흐름은 대대로 이어져가고 있다. 개체마다 한시적인 미학과 신념을 가정해놓고 거기에 진선미를 부여하고 생사의 수레바퀴를 굴린다. 할아버지의 손자가 이제는 할아버지가 되어 손자를 바라본다. 그것이 대를 이어가는 것이라 생각하고 삶과 죽음을 넘어서 또 다른 삶을 기대한다. 개체의 죽음을 전체로 극복하려는 것이다. 생사의 수레바퀴가 굴러가는 가운데 개체는 죽고 주검을 바라보는 의식만이 남겨진다. 시작도 끝도 없이 생사의 춤사위가 허공 속에 펼쳐진다.

310. Death is fateful, but nobody wants to be conscious of that. We are conscious only of survival, leaving everything under the sun. However, a body can dance, becoming the wind and a flower, because death and life hug. They love and respect each other.

311. Creatures have evolved, repeating life and death from generation to generation through the course of genetic specialization. The constitution of creatures becomes weak as much as specialized and accurate. Iron withstands a change in temperature by the hundred degrees, but a creature hovers between life and death when the temperature changes even by only a few degrees. If creatures become weak as much as they have become accurate in the course of evolution, it would seem that the evolution of creatures has only brought them closer to death, doesn't it? Regardless of the question, the flow of life continues from generation to generation. Each individual assumes transient aesthetics and beliefs, applying the truth, the good, and the beautiful to them, rolling the wheel of life and death. The grandchild of a grandfather becomes a grandfather now, and he looks at the grandchild. He thinks that it is to continue from generation to generation and expects another life beyond life and death. It is expected that the whole overcomes an individual death. An individual dies while the wheel of life and death rolls, and only the consciousness looking at the death remains. The dance of life and death is performed in the void without beginning and end.

312. 이른 아침부터 밖이 소란스럽다. 농장을 돌보는 노인이 돌연사했다는 것이다. 사람들이 시신처리에 급히 농장으로 달려갔다. 그렇게 어수선한 가운데 점심시간이 가까워지자 또 사람이 죽었다는 소식이다. 웬 사람이 두 번씩이나 죽느냐고 하니 이번에는 사업부지 환경영향평가를 담당했던 공무원이 심장마비로 급사했다는 것이다. 한편에서는 사업승인을 받기 위해 사람들이 분주한데 다른 한편에서는 두 사람이 연달아 세상을 등지고 떠난 것이다. 죽은 자는 삶을 다 놓고 가지만 산 자에게 죽음은 단지 삶의 일부로 받아들여진다.

313. 연어는 태평양을 돌아다니다가 산란을 위해 태어난 강으로 돌아와서 죽는다. 사람도 성장하고 나면 태어난 곳을 그리워한다. 사람이나 동물이나 회귀본능이 있기는 마찬가지다. 태어난 곳은 생명의 출발점이자 자신의 현재 모습을 있게 한 근원이다. 모든 생명은 자신의 뿌리를 찾고 싶어 한다. 나무들이 태양과 바람을 즐기지만 그 뿌리는 햇빛이 닿지 않는 땅속에서 어둠을 품고 사는 것과 같다. 지금에 살고 있지만 과거를 품어 안고 살고 있다. 과거는 지금의 뿌리이자 회귀본능의 근원이다. 삶과 죽음이 연결되어 있는 것도 회귀본능과 무관하지 않다. 지금에 살면서도 지난날을 그리워하는 것은 과거를 통해서 지금을 확인할 수 있기 때문이다. 뿐만 아니라 과거로의 회기는 다가올 미래를 보여주기도 한다. 연어는 회귀하여 알을 낳고 죽음으로써 새로 태어날 생명을 기약한다. 과거를 통해서 미래를 보는 것이다.

312. The outdoors was noisy early in the morning. Someone said that the old man who used to take care of the farm died suddenly. A few people went hurriedly to the farm to treat the dead body. When it got closer to noon while being disordered like that, again a notification was sent out that someone died. It was asked how in the world a person can die two times. They said that a public official in charge of environmental assessment died of a heart attack this time. On the one hand, the staff members were busy getting governmental approval for a business. On the other hand, two persons left this world in succession. The persons passed away, leaving all of their life, while the living accepts their deaths as only a part of life.

313. Salmons die after returning to the river where they were born for spawning after traveling all over the Pacific. People also long for their hometown, where they were born, after growing. Humans as well as animals have a homing instinct. A birthplace is the starting point of life as well as the origin of oneself, as is now. All life wants to seek their roots. It is like how the roots of a tree live in darkness under the ground without sunshine even though the tree enjoys itself together with the sun and the wind. Though it is living at present, it is living while holding the past in its arms. The past is the roots of the present as well as the origin of the homing instinct. The fact that life is connected with death is also related to the homing instinct. While living at present, people long for the past because they can confirm the present through the past. In addition, a return to the past also shows the future coming soon. A salmon expects a coming new life by dying after spawning on its return. The future can be seen through the past.

314. 삶은 순간순간 떠오르는 비누방울과 같고, 죽음은 한순간에 사라지는 비누방울과 같다. 이와 같이 삶과 죽음은 결국 같은 것이다.

315. 내가 나 스스로를 잡고 있으니, 내가 나 자신을 버려야 내가 없어지는 것이고, 내가 없어져야 나의 죽음도 없는 것이니, 나 자신을 버리는 것이 곧 죽음을 넘어서는 길이다.

316. 삶이란 태어남과 동시에 너와 나로 둘이 되었다가 죽어서 하나로 돌아가는 것이다. 생명이 죽음에 이르는 것은 스스로를 향한 완성이다. 죽음은 개체가 전체와 하나 됨을 의미한다. 차별 없이 하나 됨은 순수 무구하니 미소 이외에 달리 표현할 길이 없다.

317. 들숨에 하나를 품고 날숨에 둘을 비운다. 길을 걷다가도 일을 하다가도 하나를 품고 둘을 비운다. 그러노라면 결국 텅 빔만이 남게 되고 차별심은 사라진다. 빛과 어둠, 삶과 죽음은 차별심에서 일어나니 차별 없는 하나 됨이 지복이다.

318. 낮과 밤의 조화 속에서 사람들이 산다. 계절의 변화 속에서 삶이 더욱 깊어진다. 그리고 삶과 죽음이 합일하여 인생이 완성된다.

314. Life is like a bubble rising every moment, whereas death is like a bubble disappearing in a moment. Like this, to be and not to be, those are one thing after all.

315. Since I am holding myself, I have to discard myself in order that I can be gone. As my death also disappears when I am gone, it is just a way to overcome death that I discard myself.

316. It is life that two as you and me are born, then return to one after dying. It is the perfection of self that a living thing meets its death. Death means that an individual is uniting with the whole. To become one without distinction is pure, so it cannot be expressed without a smile.

317. One is taken while inhaling, and two are emptied while exhaling. Regardless if you are walking along or taking up work, one is taken, and two are emptied. If so, only the emptiness remains, and a distinct mind disappears after all. It is supreme bliss to unite without distinction because life and death as well as light and darkness rise from a distinct mind.

318. People live in the harmony of day and night. Life becomes deeper in the changing of seasons, and one's life is completed by uniting into one with living and death.

319. (시 62)
나는 없소이다.

이름도 없고 몸도 없고
마음도 없소이다.

빛도 가고 소리도 가고
꿈도 가고

텅 빈 허공만
비어 있는 그대로 남았소이다.

320. (시 63)
하루의 길목에서 만남은
거울 속 세상의 그림자라

꿈같은 한세월 언덕에 쉬고
살아온 길을 되돌아보니

누군가 행복했던 것이라면
그것으로 지족인 것을

무엇을 더 구하리
오갈 것 없는 텅 빔 속에서

319. (Poem 62)
I am not.

A name as well as a body is not.
Even a mind is not.

A light is gone, and a sound is gone.
Even a dream is gone.

Only the empty void as is
remains there.

320. (Poem 63)
A meeting in daily life
is a shadow of the world in the mirror.

While a dreamy tide remains on the hill,
as I look back the way I passed by,

if someone was happy,
I might be contented.

What is wanted more?
In the void without coming and going⋯.

321. (시 64)

허공은만물의어머니용서함도사랑함도지극하여라
외로울때친구가되어줄수있는건허공과바람뿐인데
헤진얼굴들세월에지고체취와온기는가슴에묻었다
생명이빛속에서잉태하니빛은어둠에밀려긴장하고
수많은언어들이칼날위에춤을추며형상을조각한다
지평선너머로그림자기울면침묵은고요히밀려오고
순간은영원을남기지않고바람은허공속에꿈을꾼다
천지에펼쳐진오색의정열은한자락춤사위를펼치고
죽어도또죽어도유혹은시작되어그리움은꽃이되니
비로소불사조는한줄기바람으로허공속을날아간다

321. (Poem 64)

The void is all things' mother, whose forgiveness and love are profound.

Though it is only the void and the wind to become friends when one feels lonely,

the old faces faded in time and tide, then body smell and warmth were cherished in one's heart.

As life becomes pregnant in the light, light becomes tense, pushed into the darkness.

A lot of words carve an image, dancing on the edge of a sword.

When a shadow sinks beyond the horizon, a silence surges serenely,

and a wind dreams in the void while a moment never leaves eternity.

As the passion of five cardinal colors spreading in the heavens and on earth performs a dance in harmony,

temptation begins and a longing becomes a flower even though one dies and dies.

At last a phoenix flies in the void, becoming the wind.

322. (시 65)

한세상 사는 것이 이리도 꿈 같아서

스쳐간 군상들 추억만 남기고

아련히 사라진 멀고도 짧은 세월

남은 것은 거친 호흡과 지친 심장뿐

육신만이 짐이 되어

거울 앞에 다가선 인생이여!

무얼 찾아왔는지

낯선 모습이 가엾기만 하구나.

살아온 길이

선과 악, 죄와 벌 속에 갇혔어도

진정한 네 모습은 그것을 넘으리니

눈뜨면 보이고 눈감으면 사라지는

꿈속의 세상에 걸쳐진 무지개

강 건너 저편으로 열차는 가고 또 온다.

삶이 서러우냐? 죽음이 서러우냐?

삶 속에 혼을 묻고

혼마저 강산에 흩어지면

이름 모를 무덤가에 꽃은 피리니

조상의 자손아!

끝없이 흐르는 강물을 보아라.

바람을 보아라.

머물지 않는다면

네가 너를 떠난다면 무엇이 서러우랴.

타오르는 혼이여!

322. (Poem 65)

As life is so much dreamy,

a crowd of passed people leaves only a memory,

and the short far-off time disappeared dimly.

The remains are only hard breaths and tired hearts.

As a body becomes a burden,

what a life closer to the mirror!

What does it come to look for?

The strange feature is merely pity.

Though the trace of life is confined

in good and evil as well as sin and punishment,

your true self will go beyond that.

In the dreamy world seen on opening eyes, then disappearing on closing eyes,

there is a rainbow connected,

and trains come and go across a river.

Do you sorrow for life, or death?

If the spirit is buried in life,

and even if the spirit is scattered,

a flower will bloom on the nameless grave.

What a descendant of ancestry!

Look at the river flowing endlessly.

Look at the wind.

If you don't stay,

and you leave yourself, what will be so sad?

What a blazing spirit!

By becoming ashes after disappearing,

flow endlessly along the river with the wind.

What a boundless life!

What a life without coming and going!

What a life that is not your own!

사라져 재가 되어
강물 따라 바람 따라 한없이 흘러라.
막힘없는 인생이여!
오갈 것 없는 인생이여!
네가 아닌 인생이여!
꿈이 아닌 꿈이여!
강물이여! 바람이여!
영원하여라.

323. 삶이 무엇인가? 지금 있는 그대로가 삶이다. 생의 수레바퀴는 지면에 붙어 있지도 않고 떨어져 있지도 않고 굴러간다. 혼자 살 수 없으니 서로 어울리지만 어울려도 하나가 될 수 없으니 외롭다. 삶은 죽음 속에서 피고 죽음은 삶 속에서 피어난다. 모든 것은 역설적으로 흐르지만 서로가 서로를 있게 해준다. 꽃이 진다고 아주 지는 것이 아니다. 바람 떠난 침묵 너머에 꽃은 다시 피어난다.

324. 진정한 삶은 막힘이 없다. 죽음으로 막히는 삶이라면 그것은 육신에 매인 삶이다. 애당초 삶이란 내가 되고자 하여 태어난 것도 아니고 원래 없었던 몸이니 그물에 걸림이 없는 바람이다. 삶이라는 꿈속에서 스쳐 가는 바람일 뿐이다. 육체적인 환상이 전부인 양 유혹하여 삶을 착각에 빠지게 한다. 감각기관이 지배하는 세계는 삶과 죽음의 세계이자 이원론적인 세계이다. 이원론적인 세계는 대립과 다툼의 세계이며 상대적인 세계다. 대립과 다툼을 극복하고 삶과 죽음을 하나로 품어 안을 때 진정한 바람꽃이 피어난다. 하나가 되기 위해서 이념과 주의, 신념 등을 버리고 있는 그대로 바라보자. 현상계는 더 이상

What a dream not to be a dream!
What a river, what a wind!
Last forever and ever.

323. What is life? It is life to be as it is now. Life's wheel rolls without stopping and departing from the ground. We accompany each other because it is impossible to live alone, but we are lonely because we cannot become one despite accompanying each other. Life blooms in death, and death blooms in life. Everything is flowing reversely, but they exist with the help of each other. It is not really to be gone that the flowers are gone. A flower blooms again beyond the silence where the wind blew off.

324. There is no barrier in true life. It is a life bound to a body if life is interrupted by death. Life is not to be born primarily by one's will, and a body doesn't exist originally, so it is like the wind flowing freely through the net. It is only a wind passing in the dream called life. Physical illusions tempt us as if they are everything to us, so they let life fall into misunderstanding. The world governed by the sense organs is the world of life and death as well as the dualistic world. The dualistic world is the world of opposition and competition as well as the relative world. When the opposition and competition are overcome and life and death unite into one, a windflower blooms truly. An ideology, a doctrine, a principle, etc., should be discarded, and one should look at everything as is in order to unite them into one. The phenomenal world is not the waves comprised of a top and a bottom but the horizon connected from wave to wave. That is the wind as well as the flower as is.

산과 골로 대립되는 파도가 아니며 파도에서 파도로 이어지는 수평선이다. 있는 그대로 바람이요 꽃이다.

325. 삶은 쳇바퀴처럼 반복되지만 태양은 언제나 새롭기만 하다. 여명이 어둠을 헤치고 삼라만상을 깨우는 순간 이름 모를 죄인은 죽음을 맞이하고 독수리는 황금 햇살을 받으며 창공을 날아간다. 삶과 죽음은 하루해의 꿈이다. 삶은 어디서 와서 어디로 가는가? 지금 황혼에 기우는 그림자를 바라보는가? 지평선에 차오르는 여명을 바라보는가? 인생은 강건해야 팔십 수이거늘 수십억 년 타오르는 태양에 비하면 지상의 세월은 티끌이다. 만물은 황혼과 여명 속에 생멸하지만 태양은 언제나 새롭게 타오른다. 어제의 황혼은 지고 밝아오는 여명은 모든 생명에게 태초의 빛이 되고 있다. 가을 들판에 벼 이삭이 고개를 숙이고, 오수를 즐기던 노인이 고요히 숨을 거두듯이 모든 생명은 서두르거나 멈추지 않고 스스로를 향해서 돌아간다. 삶에서 무엇을 얻고 무엇을 잃으리? 이제 죽어 작별한다고 하여도 사는 동안 한 송이 꽃을 피울 수 있었다면 그것으로 행복이요 기쁨이다.

325. Life repeats itself like a squirrel cage, but the sun is always new. While all things are awakened at dawn, pushing through the darkness, an unknown prisoner meets his death, and an eagle flies away in the sky bright with the morning glow. Life and death are the dream of a day. Where does life come from and go to? Do you look at a shadow declining at dusk, or the horizon glowing at dawn now? Since human lifetime is merely eighty years even if he is healthy, the time and tide of the earth is like dust compared with the sun blazing for billions of years. Though all things are born and then die at dawn and dusk, the sun shines as it is always new. After the dusk fell yesterday, the beginning dawn becomes the first light for all lives. As if the rice plant bows its head in the autumn field and an old person enjoying a nap breathes his last breath calmly, all lives go back to themselves without hurrying or stopping. What are gotten and lost in life? Though you have to say good-bye for death now, you'll have happiness and delight if you made a flower bloom while living.

326. (시 66)
백 년 전에는 있지도 않은
백 년 후에는 있지도 않을
지금 이 순간 인생들이

저마다 세상을 담아내며
아침 이슬처럼 맺혀 있구나.

이제 가면 언제 오려나,
꿈 같은 세월 벗어 놓고
스스로를 향해 돌아가니

없다가 있고
있다가 없는 듯이
가슴마다 피는 꽃이 되었구나.

326. (Poem 66)
As were not a century ago,
and won't be after a century,
such lives at present moment,

bearing the world respectively,
form like a dewdrop in the morning.

If you go now, when will you come back?
Taking off the dreamy time and tide,
as you go back to yourselves,

to be as if not to be,
and not to be as if to be—
that becomes a flower blooming in each heart.

327. (시 67)

삶이여!
죽음 속에 피어난 이슬이여!
위태롭고 경이로운 꽃이여!

육신이여!
허공 속에 쏘아 올린 화살이여!
거울 속에 드리워진 그림자여!

사랑이여!
순간마다 머무는 바탈(性)이여!
나를 벗고 네가 되는 순결이여!

자유여!
가슴속에 타오르는 혼불이여!
재가 되어 흩어지는 바람이여!

죽음이여!
삶을 잉태하는 여신이여!
영원한 침묵의 눈동자여!

327. (Poem 67)
What a life!
What a dewdrop standing on death!
What a dangerous, marvelous flower!

What a body!
What an arrow shot into the void!
What a shadow reflected in the mirror!

What a love!
What a character staying each moment!
What an innocence becoming you from me!

What a freedom!
What a spirit burning in heart!
What a wind scattering with ash!

What a death!
What a goddess bearing life!
What a pupil of the eternal silence!

328. (시 68)

드라이플라워 마른 잎 벽에 걸려 아직도 숨 쉬는가?

장밋빛 영광 어디다 묻고 매혹의 향기 어디로 사라져
그때 그 사람 모두 다 떠난 뒤
쌓여가는 먼지로 늙은 얼굴 분 바르고
아무도 찾지 않는 세월 속에 창백한 그림자 되었는가?

벽에서 걸어 나와 소리 없이 목매던 울음 그치고
앙상한 목 줄기에 숨결 돋우면
퇴바랜 빛깔에 이슬 머금고 한 떨기 꽃으로 피어나리니

사랑스러운 드라이플라워
아스파라 안개꽃 붉은 장미 함께 바람 거닐고
도란도란 속삭임 들리거든 너 다시 살아와 봄에 안겨라.

328. (Poem 68)

Does the petal of a dried flower still breathe hanging on the wall?

As the rosy glory was buried, and the scent of charms was gone somewhere,
after all then people left.
Powdering an old face with collecting dust,
did it become a pale shadow in the time and tide that nobody remembered?

Getting out of the wall and stopping sobs,
when it breathes again through a lean stem,
a flower will bloom, having dew with a faded color.

A lovely dried flower.
An asparagus, a foggy flower, and a red rose walk together in the wind.
When you hear a murmuring whisper, come back to life again, and put yourselves in the spring.

329. (시 69)
아침에 피었다
저녁에 지는 꽃을 보아라.
한낮에 태양을 즐기고
비바람 속에 흔들리다가
노을 저편 어둠이 오면
서두르지도 멈추지도 않고
스스로를 향하여
침묵에서 침묵으로
돌아가는
삶의 여유로움이여!

330. 사람들이 사후세계에 대해서 진실처럼 말하지만 그렇게 말할 수 있는 것은 실제 죽은 자는 말이 없기 때문이다. 더욱 위험스러운 것은 잠시 죽었다가 살아난 자의 증언인데 그것은 가사상태에서 나타난 환상을 말하는 것일 뿐 실제 사후세계를 말하는 것이 아니다. 육체가 죽으면 소멸되어 생명의 근본인 흙으로 돌아가듯이 개체의 혼백도 죽으면 소멸되어 전체의 영혼과 합일한다.

329. (Poem 69)
Look at a dayflower,
falling at dusk after blooming at dawn,
while enjoying the midday sun
and swaying in the rainstorm.
When the sunset glow lapses in the dark,
without hurrying or stopping,
toward itself,
from silence to silence,
returning,
what a presence of life!

330. People speak about the world after death as if they're true, but they can only say so because the truly dead person speaks no more. It is more dangerous that a temporarily dead person testifies about the world after death. That is, only to say about the illusion shown in suspended animation, not the real world after death. Like how a body returns to dust as the origin of life by becoming extinct after death, an individual spirit is also united with the whole soul by becoming extinct after death.

331. 내일 죽을지도 모르면서 오늘을 사는 것이 인생이다. 백 년도 못살면서 천년을 살 것처럼 사는 것이 인생이다. 노인들이 가족과 떨어져서 요양원에 모여 산다. 가족들과 떨어져 살 수밖에 없는 사연이야 여러 가지지만 그들의 여읜 어깨만큼이나 지나온 삶의 무게가 한결같이 공허하다. 그나마 식생활을 스스로 할 수 있는 노인들은 다행이다. 몸 거동이 불편하여도 수발마저 들어줄 사람 없이 힘겹게 삶을 견디다가 소리 없이 죽음을 맞이하는 노인들도 많다. 육신을 입고 태어난 자는 누구나 육신을 벗어야 할 때가 오지만 낡은 거죽을 벗는 것이 힘겨워 죽지도 살지도 못한 채 생사의 문턱을 헤매는 인생들이 너무도 많다. 겨울이 오기 전에 나무들은 무성했던 잎을 다 떨쳐버리고 나목이 되어 벌거벗은 몸으로 스스럼없이 겨울을 맞이하는데 인생들은 왜 삶의 순리를 받아들이기가 이토록 힘겨운 것인가? 원해서 입은 육신도 아니건만 무슨 미련이 있기에 육신을 벗기가 그리도 힘겨운 것인가? 요양원 창밖에 비치는 따스한 햇살은 삶과 죽음을 함께 보듬은 채 휠체어에 앉은 노인과 그것을 밀고 있는 젊은 간병인을 함께 비추고 있다. 늙음을 뒤에서 바라보는 젊음도 머지않아 젊음을 뒤로하고 떠나야 할 늙음인데 천년만년 살 것 같은 착각 속에서 사는 것이 인생이다.

331. It is life that people live today though they don't know whether they will die tomorrow. It is life that people live as if they can live for a thousand years though they cannot live more than a hundred. Old people live together at a sanitarium, far from their families. The reasons why they live far from their families vary, but the dignity of their past life is consistently as hollow as their lean shoulders. The old people able to eat and walk by themselves have good fortune at that. There are so many old people who meet their death silently, bearing a suffering life without a nurse while feeling out of sorts. Everybody born with a body has to face the time when they have to take off said body, but there are so many lives hovering between life and death, having trouble taking off their old bodies. Trees meet the winter freely, becoming bare after tearing luxuriant leaves off before the winter comes. However, why is it hard for people to accept the rationality of life? A body is not what they want to get; however, what kind of lingering affection makes it hard for them to take off their body? There is an old person sitting on a wheelchair and a young nurse pushing it, outside the window of the sanitarium, in the warm sunshine holding life and death together. Though the youth looking at the old will become old soon after leaving his youth, it is life to live under the illusion that they're going to live for a few thousand years.

332. 삶이란 흘러가는 세월 속에서 영원한 것이 아니다. 죽음을 배경으로 삶이 피어있다는 사실을 잊어서는 안 된다. 삶에 대한 고마움이 클수록 죽음에 대한 고마움도 크다. 대소변조차 혼자 가누지 못하고 하루하루의 호흡을 간신히 이어가는 생명들을 볼 때 죽음의 미학이 새삼스러운 의미를 갖는다. 재래시장에 가면 노점상 할머니가 야채를 팔다가 그만 잠이 들었는지 오수에 빠져있는 모습을 보게 되는데 평화로운 모습 그대로 오수를 즐기듯이 삶의 마지막 고개를 넘을 수 있다면 얼마나 행복한 것인가? 요양원 병실에서 반송장의 모습으로 죽음의 문턱을 넘기 어려워 애태우는 모습에 비한다면 가히 행복한 죽음이다.

간혹 어떤 시민은 마라톤에 참가하여 달리다가 도중에 쓰러져 그대로 숨지는 경우도 있는데 대소변을 못 가린 채 생명의 문턱을 넘기 버거워하는 삶에 비한다면 달리는 가운데 죽음을 맞이할 수 있다는 것은 역설적이지만 건강하게 삶을 마감하는 한 방법일 수도 있다. 그 이외에도 어느 수도승처럼 앉은 자세로 입적하는 경우도 있으리라. 삶이란 곧 죽음 위에 핀 꽃이요, 죽음으로 돌아가는 것은 새로운 삶의 시작이니 오늘 결혼하는 한 쌍의 축복이 장례식의 슬픔과 결코 동떨어진 것이 아니다. 죽음은 삶과 결부되어 있을 때만 진정한 의미를 지닌다. 삶과 분리되어버린 죽음은 이미 죽음이 아니다. 인간이 삶의 연장선에서 죽음을 바라보고 자신이 외부로부터 타 존재에 의해서 붕괴되는 것이 아니라 육체라는 일시적인 감옥으로부터 해방되어 전체와 하나 되는 것임을 깨닫는다면 죽음은 이미 죽음이 아닌 것이다. 바람은 꽃이 되고 꽃은 바람이 되니 생사의 흐름도 그와 같다.

332. Life is not eternal in the time and tide flowing. It should not be forgotten that life blooms with the background of death. The greater the favor of life is, the greater the favor of death is. Considering that lives continue to breathe hardly without relieving themselves, the aesthetics of death has a meaning all over again. As we can see, an old woman is taking a nap while selling vegetables at a stall in a conventional market—how happy it is to depart from this world while enjoying a nap with a peaceful figure as is. That is really a happy death compared with the half-dead figure that finds it hard to depart from this world in the sanitarium ward.

A certain citizen participates in a marathon race and dies after collapsing once after a long while. It may seem paradoxical, but it is another case of life finishing healthily—to die running—compared with the lives that find it hard to depart from this world without relieving themselves. In addition to the above cases, there are cases when people pass away while sitting, like a certain monk. As life is the flower blooming upon death, and returning to death is the beginning of a new life, the blessing for a couple marrying today is not different from the sorrow at a funeral. Death has a real meaning only when it connects with life. Death separated from life is already not death. If humans look at death as the extension of life, realizing that they are not collapsed by others from outside but united with the whole by being set free from the temporary prison called a body, death is already not death. As the wind becomes a flower and a flower becomes the wind, the stream of life and death is also like that.

333. 개별적인 세계를 일컬어 이승이라 하고 전체적인 세계를 일컬어 저승이라 하는데 사람들은 이승을 떠나기가 아쉽고 저승이 낯설어서 죽음을 두려워 하지만 전체와 하나가 되는 것이라 생각하면 두려움은 사라진다. 한 개체의 생사를 놓고 이승과 저승이 구분되는 것이지 전체를 놓고 보면 이승과 저승은 같은 것이다.

334. 무에서 유는 시작이요 유에서 무는 끝이니, 시작이 끝이요 끝이 시작이다. 점에서 원이 시작되고 원에서 점이 끝을 맺으니 시작도 끝도 없는 순환 속에 만물은 생멸한다. 삶 속에 죽음이 있고 죽음 속에 삶이 있으니 삶과 죽음은 오고 간다. 수컷이 암컷을 먹겠다고 하나 수고로움뿐이고 실상은 암컷에게 먹히고 암컷은 수컷을 먹고 번식하다가 암컷 자신도 자손을 남기고 텅 빈 껍질만 남긴 채 스러져 간다. 생명의 끝은 바람이 스쳐 간 들판에 시작을 묻는 것이니 봄의 새싹이 하얀 속살을 드러우고 해골을 품는 격이다. 산 자와 죽은 자가 함께 무덤에 왔다가 잠시 헤어지는 것과 같다. 삶과 죽음을 동시에 받아들일 수 있는가? 삶을 지극히 음미해 보면 죽음과 삶이 대립적인 것이 아니라 동시적인 것임을 깨닫게 되고, 죽음을 삶의 일부로 받아들이게 될 때 삶과 죽음 사이에 경계가 없어진다. 죽음이 곧 삶이다. 우연한 존재라면 없어져도 될 것이며 필연적인 존재라면 어떤 형태로든 있을 터이니 죽어도 새로울 것은 없지 않은가?

335. 행복한 삶이 행복한 죽음을 이루는 것이니 행복하게 살아라.

333. Since the individual world is called this world, and the whole world is called the other world, people are afraid of death because they are not only reluctant to leave this world but also unfamiliar with the other world, but this fear disappears when they think that death is for uniting with the whole. This world and the other world can be distinguished in the aspect of an individual death, but this world and the other world are the same in the whole aspect.

334. As a being out of nothing is a beginning and nothing out of a being is an end, a beginning is an end, and an end is a beginning. As a circle begins with a dot and a dot ends with a circle, all things are born and then die in an endless cycle. As death is in the life and life is in the death, life and death come and go. A male wants to eat a female, but that is nothing but laborious work. Actually, a male is eaten by a female. Propagating itself by eating a male, even a female itself disappears, leaving only its cast-off skin after leaving its descendants. As the end of life is to bury a beginning in the plains passed by the wind, the sprout of the spring seems to hold a skeleton while showing its white skin under clothes. It is like the living and the dead are temporarily parted, coming together to the grave. Is it possible to accept life and death simultaneously? Reviewing life deeply, people can realize that death and life are not opposite but simultaneous, and there is no boundary between life and death when death is accepted as a part of life. Death is just life. It is acceptable that you will disappear if you are an accidental being, and no matter what you become, you will exist if you are an inevitable being. So it is nothing new even if you die, isn't it?

335. A happy life completes a happy death, so live happily.

336. 하나가 둘인 듯이 너와 나로 갈리고 생과 사로 헤어지니 산 자는 죽은 자를 기억하고 죽은 자는 산 자의 모습으로 기억된다.

337. 사람들은 살아가는 과정도 문제지만 그에 못지않게 장례에도 지대한 관심을 갖는다. 한평생 살아온 몸이니 장례에 소홀히 할 수 없는 일이다. 동서고금 문화에 따라 장례는 매장, 화장, 수장, 풍장 등 여러 가지가 있다. 심지어 어느 부족은 가족의 시신을 귀하게 여겨 유족들이 시신을 먹는 풍습도 있으니 장례하는 방법은 다양하다. 묘지를 택할 때 풍수지리를 논하고 동서남북을 논하고 화장한 유골에 대해서는 유골함에 보관할지 바람에 날릴지 강물에 뿌릴지 등등 이미 끝나버린 주검에 대한 처리가 삶보다 더 복잡하다. 그것은 산 자들이 주검을 삶의 연장선상에 이어보려는 각별한 관심과 미혹의 소산이다. 주위에 혐오감을 주지 않고 환경적으로 건전한 방법이라면 장례는 단순하고 소박한 것일수록 좋다. 바람처럼 살아온 인생이라면 남겨진 주검의 거처에 대해서 별스러움 없이 마음속 고향이면 어디든 상관없지 않은가?

338. 남극의 혹한 속에서도 수십여 종의 생명체가 생존하고 있는 것은 무엇을 의미하는가? 살아있다는 것은 그토록 질기고 모진 것이다. 어두운 삶을 부지하고 사는 도심 속의 빈민가는 문명의 거울 속에 드리워진 그림자다. 기쁠 것도 슬플 것도 없는 무너진 존재의 잔해가 방황하는 유령처럼 도심의 뒷골목을 배회한다. 바람꽃은 어디로 갔는가? 슬픈 미소마저 추억이 돼버린 태중의 전설처럼 한 호흡 한 호흡마다 각혈이 고인다. 하지만 무엇이 그리 서럽겠는가? 삶을 비추는 죽음의 거울 앞에서 모두 다 평등하지 않은가?

336. Since you and I are divided into life and death as if one is two, the living remembers the dead, and the dead is remembered through the figure of the living.

337. People have trouble while living; however, they are interested in funerals no less than living. Funerals cannot be treated lightly because a body has lived during its lifetime. According to the cultures of all ages and countries, there are burials, cremations, water burials, aerial burials, etc., as part of funeral rites. There is even a custom wherein the bereaved family of a certain tribe eats a dead body in respect for the dead. Indeed funeral rites are varied. Topography as well as the four cardinal directions are debated when a graveyard is decided, and it's taken into account whether the cremated ashes would be placed in an urn, blown into the air, or scattered over a river. Like this, the treatment for the already dead body is more complicated than life. This results from the particular concern and delusion that the living tries to connect death with life. The more simple and humble a funeral is, the better, as long as it is environmentally sound, not causing hatred to the surroundings. If life has lived like a wind, it doesn't matter to the dead where he is buried, as long as it is a place adopted in his mind. Does it?

338. Why are several kinds of creatures living even in the severe cold of the Antarctic? To be alive is very tough and harsh. The slums enduring a gloomy life downtown is the shadow reflected on the mirror of civilization. The wreckage of collapsed existence, without joy as well as sorrow, wanders along the backstreet like a lost ghost. Where does a windflower go? Blood is spat out every moment of breathing, like a legend of the womb, that even a sad smile becomes a memory. However, what will be so sad? We are

339. 지구상의 온갖 생물들은 탄생과 죽음을 통하여 종족을 이어가고 있다. 수많은 생물들은 긴 세월 동안 다양하게 분화하기도 하고 진화하기도 하고 퇴화하기도 한다. 그 과정에서 탄생과 죽음은 생물들이 종을 이어나가는 필수사항이다. 바위나 강물도 오랜 세월을 거치면서 모습을 바꾸지만 이를 두고 탄생과 죽음이라고 하지 않는다. 한 생물의 개체가 없다가 나타난 것이 탄생이고 있다가 없어진 것이 죽음이다. 생물 종은 불연속적인 개체의 탄생과 죽음을 통하여 종족을 이어간다. 한 개체의 탄생과 죽음은 종족을 연속적으로 이어나가기 위한 것으로 전체 입장에서 보면 하루의 일출과 일몰처럼 일상적인 것이다. 탄생과 죽음이 개체의 입장에서 보면 절대적이지만 전체 입장에서 보면 긴 세월 속을 스쳐 가는 하룻밤의 꿈이다.

340. 사람들은 불사조, 불사신이라는 가상의 존재로 신화를 만들고 게임이나 흥행물 속에 죽지 않는 인물을 등장 시켜 불사를 대리 만족한다. 어찌 보면 한시적인 삶을 살고 있는 사람들에게 죽지 않는다는 것은 매력일지도 모른다. 그러나 푸르른 여름이 지나고 나면 가을이 오고 가을이 끝날 무렵이면 나무들은 모든 잎을 떨치고 나목으로 겨울을 맞이한다. 겨울이 깊어 가는 계절에 아직 떨어지지 못한 잎이 앙상한 나뭇가지에 매달린 채 창백한 모습으로 삭풍에 흩날리고 있다면 그것이 과연 불사의 모습일까? 가을이 깊어지면 낙엽이 되고 봄에 새싹을 돋우는 거름이 되는 것이 자연의 순리에 따라 불사를 이어가는 참모습이 아닌가? 산소마스크에 의지하고 대소변을 남에게 의지해야 하는 처지라면 그것은 불사의 매력이라기보다 불사로 인한 고통이다. 사람마다 차이는 있지만 육십 세까지는 노력과 의지만 있다면 주위에 도움을 베풀면서 살 수 있다. 육십 넘어 팔십 세에 이르면 겨우 주변

all equal before the mirror of death reflecting life, aren't we?

339. All creatures on earth are continuing their species through birth and death. A lot of creatures become variously specialized, evolve, or degrade for a long time. During that time, birth and death are essential for creatures to continue their species. A rock and a river also change their figures, but we cannot call it birth and death. It is through birth that a creature appears from nothing, and it is with death that a creature disappears from being. Species continue their family through the birth and death of a discontinuous individual. The birth and death of an individual are for continuing his species endlessly, so those are daily happenings, like dawn and dusk in the whole aspect. Birth and death are absolute in view of an individual, but those are only a dream of a night passing by, a long period of time, in view of the whole.

340. People create myths with imaginary existence, like a phoenix and a dauntless spirit, and are satisfied by proxy with the immortality of these characters, never dying in a game or performance. In some point of view, it may be an enormous attraction for people living with limited life not to die. But the autumn comes after a green summer, and most trees greet the winter with their naked features—from falling leaves at the end of autumn. If a leaf not fallen from the tree yet is swaying with the north wind of winter, is it an immortal feature? It is a real feature, succeeding immortality by the rationality of nature, for leaves to fall in autumn and become the compost for buds in spring, isn't it? If people have to breathe through oxygen masks and relieve themselves with other people's help, that is an immortal agony rather than an attraction of immortality. There is a difference according to each individual's situation, but people can live supporting others until they're sixty years old. If they make efforts

신세를 면할 수 있고 팔십 세가 넘으면 주위로부터 신세를 지고 살아야 하는 것이 육신의 처지이고 보면 행복한 죽음이 어떤 것인지 헤아려야 한다.

341. 태양 아래 사막 속에서 수천 년의 세월 동안 잠들어 있던 파라오의 무덤. 그곳을 파헤친 자들의 죽음과 파라오의 저주가 세월의 의미를 되새기게 한다. 현대문명과 고대문명이 어느 날 갑자기 만나면서 마음속 심연에 잠들어 있던 무의식을 일깨운다. 소년 미라의 황금마스크 너머에는 수천 년의 세월이 신비를 간직한 채 무덤의 입구에 비문을 남기고 있다. "이곳을 넘는 자는 죽으리라!" 황금미라는 죽어도 죽지 않는 모습으로 침묵을 가르치고 있다. 황금미라는 죽음을 넘어서고자 하는 삶의 의지를 상징한다. 주검을 보며 삶과의 단절을 용납할 수 없는 것이 사람들의 마음이다. 사람들은 순간을 살면서 영원을 꿈꾼다. 죽음을 죽음 이상으로 보려는 것은 삶에서 오는 환상이다. 태양이 바람을 일으키면 사막에는 모래폭풍이 불고 모래들은 지평선 위로 비상할 것이지만 그것들은 결국 사막에 또 다른 지평선을 이룬다. 역사는 사막의 지평선과 같다. 열사에 휘날리는 무수한 모래알들은 부서진 바위의 파편이자 세월 속에 사라져 간 수많은 주검들이다. 이제 그러한 주검과 주검이 사막의 지평선을 이루고 수많은 무덤들이 모래폭풍 속에 묻힌 채로 태양 아래 침묵한다. 작열하는 태양마저 저물고 모든 사념들이 사라져 버린 열사의 지평에 어둠이 나리면 별들은 차가운 밤하늘을 반짝이며 하룻밤의 영광을 또다시 꿈꾸리라.

and have a will, they can live without others' help from sixty to eighty years old, and they have to live while receiving assistance from people if they are more than eighty years old. That is the human situation of living together with a body, so people have to consider what a happy death is.

341. The tomb of Pharaoh slept in the desert of the sun for a few thousand years. The death of people violating the tomb and the curse of Pharaoh have made us ruminate on the meaning of the time and tide. One day modern civilization and ancient civilization met each other suddenly, which awakened the unconscious sleeping in the abyss of mind. A few thousand years beyond the golden mask of a boy's mummy leaves an epitaph inscribed, "Those who go over this place will die!" at the entrance of the tomb while veiling a mystery. The mummy of the golden mask is teaching the silence with the immortal feature even if it was dead. The mummy of the golden mask symbolizes the will of life to overcome death. It is the nature of a human mind not to accept interruption in life while looking at death. People dream about eternity while living in the moment. It is an illusion coming from life, to think of death as being beyond death. If the sun raises the wind, a sandstorm blows up in the desert, and sands fly over the horizon. Then that makes another horizon in the desert. History is like the horizon in the desert. The innumerable grains of sand scattering in the burning desert are fragments of a broken rock as well as numerous corpses disappeared with the lapse of time. Now such a corpse and corpse form the horizon of the desert, and numerous graves are silent in the sun while buried in a sandstorm. If even the scorching sun sets and it grows dark beyond the burning horizon such that all thoughts disappear, the stars will dream of the glory of a night again, twinkling in the cold night sky.

342. (시 70)

언제부터인지 닫힌 사원에 석상 하나 외로이 혼자 서 있고
주위에는 꽃들이 피었습니다.

축제 때면 찾아오는 사람들마다 한결같이 석상을 바라보면서
행복스러운 모습이라 하였습니다.

그럴 때면 아니라고 대답하여도 그들은 알아듣지 못했습니다.

발아래 드리우는 그림자 따라 종일토록 오가는 일상 속에서
똑같은 하루하루를 보냈습니다.

세월이 흘러서 자란 석상은 처음으로 담장 밖을 바라봅니다.

굽이굽이 감싸 도는 돌담 아래로 시냇물 속삭임이 들려옵니다.

바람 따라 나르는 산새 이야기 계절 따라 바뀌는 숲속 이야기
남김없이 실어 와서 들려줍니다.

바깥이 이제는 그리워지고 지난 삶이 시리도록 서러워져서
그믐달 깊은 밤 남모른 밤에 석상은 담장을 넘어봅니다

한 걸음 두 걸음 넘기도 전에 무너져 산산이 흙이 돼버린
자신의 주검을 바라보다가 새벽 종소리에 깨었습니다.

342. (Poem 70)
From time unknown, a stone statue stood alone in a closed temple,
and flowers bloomed in the surroundings.

Whenever people visited there during the festival,
looking at the stone statue, they said his features seemed happy.

He gave a negative answer whenever they said something like that,
but they could not hear him.

In daily life, coming and going with the shadow hanging down to
his feet,
he spent day by day as a matter of routine.

As time passed by, the grown stone statue looks over a wall for the
first time.

The murmur of a brook meandering along the stone wall is heard.

It tells the story of a mountain bird flying with the wind and the
story of woods changing in the season, carrying all together.

Longing for the outside now and feeling sad about his past life, the
stone statue tries to go over the wall secretly at the dead of night in
an old moon.

Looking at his own death collapsed to dust before going over step
by step, he is awakened by the sound of a daybreak bell.

343. (시 71)

벽에 걸린 사진 속에
먼저 떠난 사람도
아직 남은 사람도 함께 있다.

백 년도 못 되어 사라질 얼굴들
사진 밖을 서성이며
가버린 이름을 그리워하는 것은

오고가는 세월 속에
모두가 하나임을
잊고 살기 때문이다.

344. (시 72)

바람에 꽃이 지니
꽃은 바람이 되련다.

어디서 온 지 묻지 않았듯이
어디로 가는지도 묻지 않으리라.

언젠가 모두 떠나야 할 길목에서
돌아보지도 않으리라.

바람 같은 흔적일랑
흩날리는 꽃잎으로 족하리니

343. (Poem 71)
In the picture hanging on the wall,
not only people passed away
but still-living people are also together.

The features that will disappear within a hundred years,
hovering outside the picture,
long for a name that passed away.

In the time and tide coming and going,
all is one,
for they live forgetting that.

344. (Poem 72)
Once a flower falls with the wind,
it seems to return to the wind.

As not asked where it comes from,
it will not ask where to go.

On the way that all have to leave someday,
it will not even look back.

Because the scattering petals are
enough to be traces like the wind.

345. (시 73)

하늘이 열리고

잔잔한 미소가
노을 지던 날

한 호흡 찰나에
빈 거죽 벗고

공산을 넘어서
궁극에 이르니

허공에 피어나는
바람꽃이여!

346. 죽음이 삶을 감싸고 있기에 이를 극복하려고 사랑이 있는 것이다. 그러면 왜 죽음이 있는 것인가? 사랑을 깨우쳐주기 위하여 죽음이 있는 것이다. 죽지 않는 목숨에 무슨 애틋함이 있으며 사랑이 있겠는가?

345. (Poem 73)
The heavens open

on the day aglow
with the smile of serenity.

At a moment taking a breath,
getting out of a hollow skin⋯.

Beyond an empty hill,
on reaching the ultimate⋯.

Blooming in the void,
what a windflower!

346. There is love to overcome death because life is shrouded
by death. If so, why is death in life? It is for humans to be awake
to love. How in the world can love as well as affection be in the
immortal life?

347. 먹이사냥에 동료와 협동하지만 언젠가는 사냥한 먹이를 놓고 동료와 싸워야 한다는 것을 깨닫는다. 재물의 많고 적음은 허허실실하여 얻은 재물은 다시 잃을 수 있다는 것도 깨닫는다. 꿈에서 깨고 나면 현실이듯이 이성에 대한 사랑도 그와 같은 것임을 깨닫는다. 그리고 흐르는 세월과 함께 늙고 추해지기 쉽다는 것도 깨닫는다. 일상의 체험을 통하여 인생이 철이 들고 동료와 재물과 이성과 늙음이라는 일상의 덫에서 놓여날 때쯤이면 창가에 햇빛이 기운다. 진정한 휴식이 어둠과 함께 시작된다.

348. 죽음의 의미는 모든 것들이 죽음을 통해서 완전히 없어지는 것이 아니라 형상이 바뀌는 것이며 언제나 그 빈자리에는 새로운 것이 함께한다는 것이다. 기성 종교에서 말하는 내세나 윤회는 죽은 후 보다 나은 환경에서 살 것이라는 것으로 현세에서 고통받는 자들에게 위로와 희망을 주려고 그렇게 표현하지만 그런 믿음은 나에 대한 집착을 강화시킬 뿐이다. 나라는 집착에서 벗어나면 이미 죽고 없는 나에게 미련을 둘 필요가 없게 된다. 그리고 내가 죽고 난 빈자리에 새로운 것이 함께한다는 믿음이 보다 신선하다. 모든 것은 없어지는 것이 아니라 새롭게 변하는 것이다. 죽어도 죽은 것이 아니니 허망할 것이 없다.

347. People realize that they have to fight with their fellows for the prey someday, even if they help each other when hunting. They realize that they can lose their gained fortune again because said fortune is of truth and falsehood in amount. As if they know the reality after awaking from a dream, they also realize that their love of the opposite sex is like that. In addition, they realize that it is easy for them to become old and ugly with the changing time and tide. When they mature in life by their daily experience and get free from the usual traps—such as fellows, fortune, the opposite sex, and old age—the sun sinks down outside the window. The real rest starts together with the dark.

348. The meaning of death is that all things do not disappear completely, but their shapes are changed through death, and the new things are always together in the empty space. According to the next world and the transmigration asserted by the existing religion, people will live in better circumstances after dying. They express the next world like that in order to console and give hope to people suffering in this world, but such kind of faith only reinforces an attachment to my own. On getting out of an attachment to my own, I do not need to have a lingering affection for my already dead self. It is a fresher belief that the new things are together in the empty space where I die. All things do not disappear but change to a new thing. Even if one dies, one is not dead, so there is no falsehood.

349. 모든 생명체는 혼이 있고 혼은 생기를 뜻하는바 생기가 떠나면 죽는 것이고 생기를 불어넣으면 살아나는 것이다. 가뭄 끝에 비가 내려 나무에 생기가 솟는 것은 무생물인 비가 생명으로 변화됨을 보여주는 것이니 생명이 귀하다 하여 무생물보다 우월할 것도 없는 것이다. 오히려 생명은 무생물보다 불안정하여 이를 극복하기 위하여 대를 이어나가는 것이니 그 과정에서 생명은 사랑과 죽음을 깨우치게 된다.

350. 삶과 대치되는 죽음은 가상의 죽음이며 산 자가 말할 수 있는 죽음이 아니다. 산 자가 말할 수 있는 죽음은 삶의 일부로서의 죽음이다. 삶이 깊어질수록 죽음은 더욱 가까이 다가서는 반려자이다. 죽음은 사랑을 통하여 내가 너로 확장되고 무리와 하나가 됨으로써 전체와 합일할 수 있게 한다. 죽음은 개체를 넘어서 전체로 확장되어 나가는 과정에서 스스로 깨닫게 되는 체험이다. 어느 누구도 스스로를 탈피하기 전에는 온전한 사랑을 말할 수 없다. 내가 죽어 너로 부활하는 것만이 삶의 마지막 불꽃이며 온전한 사랑이다. 그러한 사랑의 꽃이 피기 전에 누가 진정 죽음을 말할 수 있으랴? 죽음은 사랑의 지극함 속에서 피어나는 바람꽃이자 삶의 완성이다.

349. All creatures have a spirit. As a spirit means vigor, a creature dies if it is out of vigor, and it comes to life again if it is inspired with vigor. Accordingly, as it rains after a long drought, trees are inspired with vigor. This shows that lifeless rain changes into a creature, so a creature is not much superior to a lifeless thing even if that creature is precious. On the contrary, a creature is less stable than a lifeless thing, so it succeeds from generation to generation to overcome its weakness, during which time the creature awakes to love and death.

350. The death confronting life is an imaginary death, and it is not the death that a living person can comment. The kind of death that a living person can comment is death as a part of life. The deeper life is, the closer death is as a companion. Death lets me unite with the whole as I expand into you through love, becoming one with a crowd of people. Death is an experience realized for oneself in the course of expanding to the whole beyond an individual. Nobody can comment on the sound love before breaking from himself. Only to revive you with my death is the last flame of life as well as the entire love. Who can truly say death before such a love of flower blooms? Death is not only a windflower blooming with the utmost love but also the completion of life.

12. 사랑이란 무엇인가?

351. (시 74)

거짓말을 해도 듣고 있는 것은
사랑하는 마음을 알기 때문에
하지만 해가 가고 달이 지도록
거짓말로 이어진다면….

12. What Is Love?

351. (Poem 74)

When you tell a lie, I just listen to you because I know that you love me.

But until the sun sets and the moon rises, if you tell a lie continuously···.

비록 화낼까 봐
실망할까 봐 그랬다 해도
어머니가 가르쳐주고
형제자매가 그랬다 해도

누구나 거짓말을 할 수 있지만
거짓으로 끝날 수는 없어
꼭 잡은 손길 따뜻한 체온이
거짓으로 끝날 수는 없어

해가 가고 달이 지도록
거짓말로 이어진다면
차라리 더 이상 묻지 않으리
거짓말을 하지 않도록….

Though you did like that not to make me angry and not to disappoint me, and you did like that because a mother taught you, and siblings did like that.

Everybody can tell a lie, but we cannot end like that because it is not false to hold hands and feel warm temperature each other.

Until the sun sets and the moon rises, if you tell a lie continuously, I'd rather not ask you any more in order for you not to tell a lie···.

352. (시 75)
사무치게 그리운 것이
사랑이고
너랑 나랑 함께라면
죽어도 좋은 것이 사랑이다.

사랑에는 잣대가 없으니
추녀가 미인이 되고
거지가 부자가 되는 것이
사랑이다.

사랑은 요지경 속이다.
전부인 듯하다가
꿈에서 깨고 나면
아무것도 아닌 것이 사랑이다.

사랑에 눈먼 자여!
지금 "사랑한다." 말하지 마라.
죽고 나서도 사랑하거든
그때 "사랑한다." 말하여라.

352. (Poem 75)
To long for thy heart and soul,
it is love.
And if thou and me are together,
we can die; that is love.

As there is no rule in love,
the ugly becomes a beauty,
and the poor becomes rich.
That is love.

Love is kaleidoscopic.
It looks like the whole.
But after awakening from a dream,
it comes to nothing; that is love.

Thou blinded with love!
Don't say now, "I love thee."
If thou love ever after death,
say then, "I love thee."

353. (시 76)
점 하나 찍고 가는 인생이고
허공에 점 하나 찍어본들
아무것도 없는 것이니
얼마나 홀가분한 인생인가!
누군가를 한때 사랑했고
그로 인해 행복했으면
그것으로 족한 것이지.

354. 빛은 어둠 속에 뿌려진 춤사위다. 그리고 사람들은 춤사위에 울고 웃으며 순간을 사랑한다.

355. 사랑은 주는 것이며 아무것도 구하지 않는 것이다. 사랑은 물질과 육체를 넘어서는 자유로운 정신에 있다. 사랑은 나를 벗고 전체와 하나 되는 것이다.

356. 사랑은 정글의 법칙하에 벌어지는 치열한 경쟁 속에서 고독한 생존으로부터 긴장을 이완시키고 개체가 전체로 확장되는 즐거움을 안겨준다.

357. 생명은 때가 되면 스스로 흩어져 대자연의 품으로 돌아간다. 그리고 해체된 생명은 또 다른 생명으로 부활한다. 수없이 많은 내가 죽어 수없이 많은 너로 부활하는 것이 사랑이다. 사랑은 순간 속에 피고 지는 생사의 리듬이니 거기에 소유와 지속이란 없다.

353. (Poem 76)
It is life to leave after putting a dot,
even if it is to put a dot in the void,
as there is nothing.
What a load off life it is!
If you loved someone at one time,
and it made someone happy,
that might be enough.

354. Light is a dance spread into the darkness, and people love a moment while laughing and crying according to the spreading dance.

355. Love is to give something and not to pursue anything. Love is in the free spirit, getting over matter and body. Love is to unite with the whole by breaking from myself.

356. Love releases the tension from the solitary survival in the keen competition under the law of the jungle, and it satisfies the pleasure that an individual is enlarged into the whole.

357. Life returns to the bosom of nature in time, scattering by itself, and then the scattered life is revived into another life. It is love to revive a lot of you by perishing a lot of myself. As love is the rhythm of life and death, blooming and falling at a moment, there is no possession and continuance in love.

358. 정글의 법칙과 사랑의 법칙은 모순되지만 현실 속에서 엄연히 공존한다. 먹이를 잡아먹는 쪽과 잡아먹히는 쪽이 분명 다르지만 두 개체가 하나가 되는 순간 모순은 사랑으로 극복된다. 수컷 사마귀가 교미 후 암컷 사마귀에 잡아먹히는 자연 현상은 희생을 통한 나의 확장이며 정글의 법칙 속에서 사랑을 실현하는 것이다. 수컷 사마귀를 무자비하게 잡아먹은 암컷 사마귀도 마침내 알을 낳는 데 축적된 영양분을 다 소진해버리고 껍질만 남은 채 흩날리는 바람결에 낙엽처럼 쓰러져 간다. 도시의 정글 속에 살면서 지금 잡아먹었다 하여 잡아먹은 것이 아니고 잡아먹혔다 하여 잡아먹힌 것이 아니다. 각자 거죽을 벗고 때가 되면 자신의 모든 것을 자연에 되돌려주고 가야 하는 것이 삶이다. 삶이란 희생을 통한 나의 확장이며 사랑의 신비를 배우는 과정이다. 빵 한 조각 베푸는 사랑은 사랑이 아니다. 소유하려는 사랑은 더욱 사랑이 아니다. 주는 것도 받는 것도 사랑이 아니다. 사랑이라 생각하면 그것은 이미 사랑이 아니다. 소리 없이 찾아와서 소리 없이 가버리는 바람처럼 내가 죽어 너로 부활하는 것이 진정한 사랑이다.

358. Even if there is a contradiction between the law of the jungle and the law of love, they coexist with each other in reality. There is a discrepancy between eating and being eaten, but the contradiction is overcome with love at the moment when two individuals unite into one. The natural phenomenon when a male mantis is caught by a female mantis after mating shows me to expand myself through my sacrifice as well as to realize love in the law of the jungle. The female mantis that preyed on the male mantis brutally also disappears like a fallen leaf, scattering in the wind at last after consuming all nutriment to lay eggs and leaving its cast-off skin. While living in the urban jungle, people realize it is not to catch and eat if one catches and eats now, and it is not to be caught and eaten if one is caught and eaten. It is life to leave after returning all of oneself to nature while casting off each surface in time. Life is to expand myself through my sacrifice and to learn the mystery of love. It is not love to share a slice of bread. Furthermore, it is not love to possess, and it is not love to give and take. It is already not love to think that it is love. It is real love to revive with you through my death, like the wind coming and going silently.

359. 생존의 양대 축은 식과 성이다. 생존을 위한 일차적인 에너지는 식에 의한 것이고 성은 이차적으로 추구되는 것임에도 불구하고 성이 삶의 중심에 깊이 자리 잡고 있다. 모든 문학과 철학과 예술의 저변에 는 성이 사랑과 결부되어 똬리를 틀고 있다. 성은 종족 간의 유전자 교환을 통하여 우성의 진화를 위하여 발달된 것이지만 이제 성은 본 래 목적 이상의 가치를 추구한다. 성행위는 하나의 죽음과 하나의 탄 생을 순환하는 행위이다. 성을 통하여 종족의 진화를 추구해나가지만 동시에 진화는 앞서간 죽음 위에서 피어난다. 적자생존이나 약육강식 속에서 생명체 간에 서로 경쟁하고 배고픔이 해결된 후에 성을 추구 한다. 식을 해결함에 있어서는 개체 간에 차이가 없다. 그러나 성의 해 결 양상은 강자와 약자 간에 큰 격차를 보인다. 대부분 무리를 지어 사는 동물들의 경우에 성행위는 무리의 우두머리에게만 주어지는 특 권이다. 약자에게는 성행위 할 기회가 극히 제한적으로 위축되어 있거 나 불가능하다. 종족의 진화를 위한 우생학적 자연법칙인 것이다. 성 은 사랑을 배경으로 한다. 성은 육체적이고 사랑은 정신적인 것으로 이해되지만 대부분의 경우 이들 간에 복합적으로 작용한다. 개체는 순간적이고 종족은 영속적이기 때문에 성은 사랑을 필요로 한다.

359. The two axes of survival are food and sex. Though the primary energy for survival comes from food and sex is pursued only secondarily, sex lies deeply in the center of life. Sex is situated at the bottom of all literature, philosophy, and art while still connected with love. Though sex is developed for the evolution of the dominant, by the exchange of genes between the species, sex pursues more value than its original purpose. Sex is the act circulating between one's death and one's birth. The evolution of species progresses through sex, but this evolution is simultaneously achieved by death that has gone ahead. Creatures compete with each other in the survival of the fittest or in the right of the strongest, and they pursue sex after solving hunger. There is no difference between individuals when having food, but there is a big difference between the strong and the weak when having sex. In the case of most animals forming a group, sex is a privilege given only to the head of the group. The chance of sex is strictly restrained or not allowed among the weak. It is eugenically the natural law for the evolution of species. Sex is based on love. Though it is understood that sex is physical and love is spiritual, in most cases they react compositely. Since an individual is momentary and species is everlasting, sex has need of love.

360. (시 77)
봄 나비 날던 시절
꿈속의 하늘가

밀고 당기던 입술
노을에 타오르고

알몸으로 부둥키던
여름밤의 숨결이

너와 나의 속삭임
흐르는 냇물 되어

이제는 가을마저
텅 빔 속으로

너 지금 내 곁을
떠나 있어도

꽃잎은
바람결에 흩날린다.

361. 인생을 사랑할지라도 기대하지 말고 애달파하지도 마라. 다가가서 얻으려 애쓰지도 말고 다가오는 것을 소중히 보듬어라. 만나는 인연마다 모두 소중한 것이다.

360. (Poem 77)
In the season that a butterfly flutters,
on the edge of the heavens in a dream,

the giving and taking lips
glow with the setting sun.

Hugging with a nude body,
a breath of summer night.

A whisper between you and me
becomes a flowing stream.

Even fall now
disappears into the void.

Though you at present
are far away from me,

petals are scattering
on the wind.

361. Don't expect or feel sorrow in life even though you love life.
Don't exert yourself to get something by going ahead, but welcome
whatever is coming to you. Each tie met in life is precious.

362. 남자는 여자를 갖고 싶어 한다. 여자는 그러한 남자의 마음을 안다. 우선 마음이 열려야 몸을 섞지, 라고 여자는 남자를 가르친다. 그러한 여자의 마음을 열려고 남자는 온갖 노력을 동원한다. 숲속의 작은 새들을 보아라. 수컷이 암컷을 위하여 노래를 부르고 그 노랫소리에도 암컷이 반응이 없으면 수컷은 나뭇가지와 허공을 번갈아 오가며 온갖 날갯짓으로 암컷을 유혹한다. 마침내 암컷이 수컷의 노래와 율동에 관심을 보이면 수컷은 정성 들여 마련해놓은 둥지로 암컷을 유인한다. 암컷은 수컷이 마련한 둥지를 살펴보고 마음에 들면 둥지에 머물기로 작정하고 수컷에게 몸을 허락한다. 수컷은 피나는 노력 끝에 드디어 짝짓기에 성공한다. 여자의 마음을 열려면 무릇 남자들은 건강한 신체와 생활능력과 여자가 마음에 들어 하는 거처가 있어야 한다. 이것이 여자를 갖고 싶어 하는 남자들이 갖춰야 할 조건이다. 여자의 마음이란 단순하다. 남자들이 갖춰야 할 조건들은 대부분 경제력과 관련되어 있으니 "돈 없으면 여자는 꿈도 꾸지 마라."라는 속언이 숲속에 사는 새들에게도 도시 속에 사는 남자들에게도 그대로 적용된다. 수컷이 짝짓기에 성공한 뒤 그 후에 전개되는 상황은 자연의 법칙에 따른다. 수컷은 암컷에게 봉사하다가 죽고 암컷은 새끼 양육에 봉사하다가 죽고 그렇게 종의 진화는 이어져 간다. 현실을 비정하다고 탓하지 마라. 베토벤도 한 여인의 사랑을 얻는 데 실패하였으니 닭의 눈에 다이아몬드보다 보리 한 알이 더 소중하게 보이는 것을 어찌하랴! 모순 속에 피고 지는 것이 바람꽃이 아니던가? 그러나 바람꽃은 그 자체를 즐겨야 하는 생존게임이다. 가엾은 남자들이여! 진화의 덫에 걸려 몸부림치는 바람꽃이여! 오늘 밤도 얼마나 많은 남자들이 잠 못 이루며 여자의 마음을 열기 위해 바닷가 해변을 헤매고 있을까?

362. A man wants to get a woman. The woman knows such a man's mind. The woman teaches the man that she will open her body after he opens her mind first. So the man tries to do everything to open such a woman's mind. Look at little birds in the bush! A male sings a song for a female. If a female does not respond to the song, the male tempts her to love him by flying between trees in turn. Then the male introduces the female into the nest—if she was interested in his song and flying. If satisfied with the nest after looking around it, the female decides to stay there and allows the male to mate with her. At last the male succeeds in mating with the female after trying so many times to satisfy her. If a man wants to open a woman's mind, he should have a sound body, social ability, and a house where she'd like to live. Those are the conditions that a man should meet to get a woman. A woman's mind is simple. Because the conditions that a man should have are related to economic ability, this proverb is fitting: "Don't dream of a woman if you have no money." And it is applicable to males in the bush as well as men in urban areas. After a male succeeds in mating with a female, the developments of the situation follow the laws of nature. The male dies after serving the female, and the female dies after serving baby birds. Like that, the evolution of species progresses. Don't blame reality for being harsh. Even Beethoven also failed to win a woman's love, as it cannot be helped that hens prefer a grain of barley to a diamond. It is for a windflower to bloom and fade in the discrepancy between reality and game, isn't it? But a windflower is a survival game to enjoy itself. What miserable men! What a windflower struggling in the trap of evolution! How many men are wandering along the seaside to open women's minds without sleeping even tonight?

363. 바람에 꽃이 피니 사랑도 하나가 되려는 열망으로 시작된다. 하나이기에 둘이 되어 헤어진 아픔이 이제 하나이고 싶다. 하나이고 싶은 열망이 혼불을 사르고 그리움으로 타올라 고독한 몸부림은 꿈속을 헤맨다. 격정의 어둠이 지나고 밝음이 찾아오면 고요한 피로가 햇살처럼 밀려와 그리움에 피워 올린 한 송이 바람꽃이 창밖에서 속삭인다. 혼돈이 지나고 고요한 평화가 육체의 마디마다 밀물처럼 밀려오고 남모르게 속삭이던 남과 여는 둥지로 돌아와 진화의 꿈을 꾼다. 거울 속의 바람꽃은 꿈을 꾸고 오감으로 타오르는 욕망은 정수리를 타고 열사의 사막을 지나 머나먼 별의 노래가 된다. 지평선을 넘어 산과 골이 여인의 풍만한 곡선을 이룬다. 촉감은 부드럽고 머릿결에 흐르는 살내음은 향기롭다. 입술에 고인 혀는 달콤하고 목소리는 감미롭다. 바람꽃은 오감으로 흩날리고 기나긴 해후 속에 눈물로 전율한다. 하나가 되려는 피와 살의 몸부림이 한판의 춤사위로 흩날리고 바람꽃이 죽어 허공으로 부활하는 꿈을 꾼다. 종의 진화는 사랑을 남기고 바람처럼 떠난다. 너는 내 가슴에 바람꽃이 되고 너와 내가 몸부림치던 오색의 혼돈은 어둠 속에서 침묵한다. 하나가 어찌 둘인 줄 알고 그리도 하나이길 갈망하였던가! 너와 나로 조각난 사랑이여!

363. As a flower blooms on the wind, love starts with the ambition to become one. Now it wishes to become one because of the pain of parting from one to two. The ambition to become one bursts into the flame of the soul, being filled with nostalgia, so it wanders alone in a dream. When the darkness of passion passes by and it becomes light, a calm fatigue surges like the sunlight, and a windflower blooming with affection whispers outside a window. When chaos passes by, and peace surges calmly into each joint of a body like the rising tide, the secretly whispering man and woman dream of evolution, coming back to their nest. A windflower has a dream in the mirror, and the desire blazing with the five senses becomes the song of a star far away, the desert passing through the crown of the head. The peak and valley over the horizon form the curves of a plump woman. It is soft to the touch, impregnated with the fragrance of skin and hair. A tongue and lips and voice are sweet. A windflower scatters with the five senses and shivers with a tear, encountering after a long time of separation. The struggle of blood and flesh to become one scatters with a dance, and a windflower has a dream reviving into the void after dying. The evolution of species goes away like a wind, leaving love. You become a windflower in my heart, and the chaos of the five cardinal colors in which you and me have struggled becomes silent in the dark. What a desire to become one, knowing that one seems to be two! What a love separated as you and me!

364. 음식은 살아있는 생명이 죽어서 이뤄진 것으로 생명의 잔해이자 또 다른 생명을 위하여 바쳐진 헌신이다. 그러니 음식을 어찌 장난하듯이 먹겠는가! 그들이 죽어 너로 태어나는 소중함과 사랑의 실천으로 음식은 무엇보다 귀한 것이다. 오늘 너 앞에 놓인 빵 한 조각은 너에게 내려진 귀한 선물이다. 너는 그 귀한 선물에 감사해야 하고 감사함을 다른 생명에게 되돌려줘야 한다. 생명의 시작은 사랑인데 사랑을 잊고 사랑이 베풀어주는 감사함을 잊고 음식을 대한다면 그것은 생명의 근본을 잊은 것이다. 생명은 바람처럼 자유로운 것이니 축복으로 생의 즐거움을 함께하라. 꽃이 바람을 마시듯이 오늘 식탁에 놓인 음식을 접하라! 생명을 먹고 생명을 되돌리는 귀한 시간 너를 위한 죽음이 헛되지 않도록 있는 그대로 온전하게 하라. 과식은 천벌과 같은 것. 생명을 생명으로 갚지 못하고 귀한 생명을 죽음으로 맞이한다면 어찌 그 생명이 온전하길 바라겠는가? 아직도 굶주리는 자가 무수히 많거늘 하물며 과식이란 더없는 죄악이다. 생명을 생명으로 갚지 못하고 죽음으로 끝을 냈으니 거기에는 부활도 사랑도 없다. 이 모든 생명은 땀에서 일궈지는 것이거늘 생명을 어이 두 번 죽이려 하는가? 네 앞에 주어진 한 끼의 음식에 감사하라. 너를 위해 죽은 자의 은혜가 헛되지 않도록.

364. Since food consists of the death of living things, it is the remains of life as well as devotion to the other life. Accordingly, how in the world can you eat food for fun! Food is the preciousness to be reborn as you after they die and the practice of love, so it is the most valuable thing. A slice of bread in front of you is a precious present given to you. You have to be grateful for the precious present, and this gratefulness has to be returned to another life. If you have a meal without love and a thankful mind, that is to forget the essence of life because the start of life is love. Since life is as free as the wind, take pleasure in the blessed life. Have a meal on the table as flowers meet the wind! Let it be sound as is in order that death for you is not in vain, during the valuable time when a life is created by eating another life. Overeating is like punishment by heaven. If life is not rewarded as life, and life meets death, how can you expect that such life is sound? Overeating is the most serious sin because there are so many people still hungry in the world. There is no resurrection as well as love because life is not rewarded as life, and it ends with death. How can you try to kill life twice since all life comes from sweat? Be thankful for the meal in front of you so that death's favor is not vain.

365. (시 78)
그대 가슴에 촛불을 밝히오니
꺼지지 않는 빛으로 어둠 사르고
바람처럼 오세요.

어둠에 여울지는 촛불이
누구의 숨결인지 묻지 마시고
신부처럼 오세요.

사랑에 흔들리는 그림자여!
살라지는 아픔 안고
흐르는 눈물이여!

또 하나의 그대가
어둠 속에 제 몸 살라
잃어버린 그대를 찾으시거든

서러움을 거두시고
타오르는 촛불을 바라보세요.

그리운 가슴속 영혼 밝혀줄
타오르는 촛불을 바라보세요.

365. (Poem 78)

As a candle is lit up in thy heart,
burning the dark with unextinguished light,
come like the wind.

The candle swaying in the dark,
don't ask whose breath it is,
and come like a bride.

What a shadow swaying to love!
Enduring a burning pain,
what a shedding tear!

Another thou,
burning thy body in the dark,
when it looks for the forgotten thee···.

Stop sorrowing,
and look at the lighting candle.

To brighten a soul in the longed-for heart,
look at the lighting candle.

366. 살다 보면 자연스럽게 사람과 사물들 간에 또는 사람들 간에 이해가 이뤄지고 이해가 깊어지면 서로 사랑하게 되고 사랑하다 보면 서로 기대할 수도 있게 된다. 그러나 기대는 기대일 뿐이며 기대한 것이 예상에서 빗나갈 경우 기대는 실망으로 변한다. 삶을 주의 깊게 관찰해보면 크게 두 가지로 분류된다. 하나는 자연과 인간의 관계를 있는 그대로 이해하는 것이며 다른 하나는 그것으로부터 미지의 것을 기대하는 것이다. 기대는 이뤄질 수도 있고 이뤄지지 않을 수도 있기 때문에 불완전하고 온전하지 못하다. 기대가 빗나가 감정이 격해지면 그동안 쌓아온 이해심도 사라지고 사랑은 증오로 바뀌어 절망에 휩싸이기도 한다. 이해는 주고받음과 상관없이 있는 그대로를 받아들이는 온전한 것이지만 기대는 있는 그대로 이외에 다른 무엇인가를 추구하는 불완전한 것이다. 이해에서 사랑이 싹트고 기대에서 사랑이 사라진다. 진정으로 사랑하고자 한다면 있는 그대로 이해하고 그 이상 기대하지 마라.

366. While people live together, there is naturally understanding between a person and things or between a person and another person. When their comprehension deepens, they love each other, and they can expect each other while loving. However, an expectation is only an expectation, and the expectation changes into disappointment when things fall short. If life is deeply observed, two sorts of things are classified. One is to understand the relationship between nature and humans as is, and the other is to expect the unknown from it. An expectation is imperfect and is not sound because it can be achieved or not. If people are agitated by emotions when things fall short of their expectations, their understanding accumulated for a while disappears, and they fall in despair while love changes into hatred. Understanding is the sound thing, to accept things as is regardless of giving and taking reciprocally, while an expectation is an imperfect thing, pursuing something except as it is. Love disappears when you expect more than it can give, while love sprouts up only when you understand it. If you really want to love, don't expect more but understand it as it is.

367. 동서고금을 막론하고 가장이 가족의 생계를 위하여 일하는 것은 기본적인 것이고 아내가 자식의 양육을 위하여 가사 일을 돌보는 것은 당연한 것으로 받아들여지고 있다. 전쟁터에서 목숨을 바쳐서 보상금으로 가족을 돕는 아들이 있는가 하면, 병든 부모의 목숨을 위하여 콩팥의 일부를 떼어주는 자식들도 있다. 이러한 희생정신은 가족이 곧 자기 자신과 같다는 일체감이 있기에 가능하다. 그러나 가족 간의 관계가 모두 일체감 속에서 사랑만으로 이뤄지는 것은 아니다. 처자식을 상습적으로 폭행하는 포악한 가장이 있는가 하면 병든 남편을 두고 가출해버리는 비정한 아내도 있다. 거처할 데 없는 노부모를 버리는 자식이 있는가 하면 심지어 돈을 안 준다고 살해까지 하는 패륜아도 있다. 이러한 가족관계는 차라리 남만 못하다. 가족이란 일체감으로 상호 신뢰하고 사랑하며 연대의식으로 희생마저 감내할 수 있지만 그렇지 않은 경우도 있다. 효행사상에서는 부모 섬기기를 자식 돌보기보다 더 잘하라고 강조하고 있지만 대부분의 여자들은 부모와 자식이 동시에 위급에 처한 경우 자식을 먼저 구할 것이라고 한다. 자손을 번성시키고 보존하려는 생존본능을 어찌 나무랄 수 있겠는가! 그래서 사랑은 내리사랑이라 한다. 부모가 자식에게 베푸는 사랑은 조건 없는 사랑이다. 종달새도 새끼가 스스로 창공을 날고 먹이를 사냥할 수 있게 되면 미련 없이 새끼를 떠난다. 베푼 사랑을 되돌려 받으려는 것은 사랑이 아니다. 조건 없이 주는 것이 사랑이다.

367. It is fundamental that a husband earns a living, and it is also natural that a wife does housework to bring up their children, across all ages and countries. Not only is a son supposed to help his family with compensation for sacrificing himself in a war, but children are also to share one of their kidneys to their sick parents. Such a spirit of sacrifice is possible because of the son's sense of unity, that his family is the same as himself. However, a family relationship is not constituted only with love in the sense of unity. There is a ruthless husband who assaults his wife and children habitually, as well as a heartless wife who runs away after leaving a sick husband. Not only is there a child who discards his old parents without shelter, but there is also an immoral person capable of even killing his parents for not giving him money. These kinds of family relationships are worse than others. A family counts on each other, loves in the sense of unity, and endures even a sacrifice in the sense of solidarity, but there are some other cases that are not like that. They say that serving parents is more important than taking care of children in the filial piety thought, but most women say that they will rescue their children first if parents and children are simultaneously in an emergency. How can they be blamed for their instinct to survive—to bring up and preserve their posterity! Therefore, love is called a handed-down love. The love that parents give their children is unconditional love. Even a lark leaves its baby birds without attachment when they fly and catch a prey by themselves. To get a reward for given love is not love. To give unconditionally is love.

368. (시 79)

심연에서 꺼질 듯 이어지는 숨결은
한줄기 사랑이고 싶다.

애타는 그리움에 지쳐 울던
못다 한 사랑 찾고 싶어

간밤의 추위에 떨던 날개에
찾아드는 햇살이 되고 싶어

절망하기엔 삶의 향기 잊지 못하고
육신 흩어지기엔 심장 멈추지 못해
침묵 속으로 메아리치는 사랑이고 싶다.

어둠이 앞을 가려 볼 수 없어도
꿈결 같은 사랑은 빛을 찾아 흐르고

혼과 육이 광야에서 헤맬지라도
한 줄기 생명은 사랑이고 싶다.

368. (Poem 79)

A breath continuing ceaselessly in the abyss
wanna be a stream of love.

Looking for unfulfilled love,
weeping endlessly from longing···.

And for becoming the sunlight warming
the wing shivering last night···.

Not to forget the scent of life rather than despair,
and not to let a heart stop beating before a body scatters,
that wanna be love echoing in silence.

Though the dark disturbs a sight,
a dreamy love flows toward the light.

Though a soul and a body wander in the wild plains,
a stream of life wanna be love.

369. (시 80)
고독할 때 기다려지는 그리움을
사랑이라 부르지 마라.

모두 다 떠나버린 폐허에서
어둠을 사르는 등불처럼

너를 향한 그리움에 죽을지라도
사랑이라 부르지 마라.

사랑은 흔적을 남기지 않고
사랑은 사랑이라 부르지도 않고

너와 나 사이에 강물이 되어
언제나 가슴속에 흐르고 있나니.

370. 예전에 그린 그림들이 숙소에 여러 점 걸려 있는데 어느 날 찾아
온 친지가 이를 보고 물었다. "그림 중에 여자 가슴을 그린 것이 여러
점인데 특별한 이유가 있습니까?"
갑작스러운 질문에 한동안 할 말을 잊고 있다가 이렇게 대답하였다.
"그것은 생명의 젖줄일 뿐만 아니라 둥근 모습이 편안하다는 생각이
듭니다." 아마도 그 편안함이 사람들을 사랑하게 하는 것이리라.

369. (Poem 80)
The longing when you feel lonely,
never call it love.

In the desert where everyone departs,
like a lamplight keeping the darkness⋯.

Though you die due to longing,
never call it love.

Love leaves no trace behind,
and love does not call it love.

Like a river between you and me,
it is always flowing in our hearts.

370. Since there were several pictures that I drew long ago hanging on the wall in my abode, one day an acquaintance asked me, looking at the pictures, "Is there any special reason why there are several pictures in which women's bosoms are drawn among your paintings?"
I could not answer the surprise question for a while, then replied after thinking it over and over again, "Not only is that the milk of life, but the round shape of bosoms also sets my mind at ease." Perhaps such comfort seems to make people love.

371. (시 81)
하염없이 성을 쌓고
무너지면 또 쌓던 기억 속으로

외로운 짐승은 해를 찾아
오늘도 호숫가에서 꿈을 꾼다.

허공이 숲을 외롭게 하고
한 줄기 바람으로 돌아갈 새

사랑은 부분으로 다가와서
어느새 전부가 되었다.

372. 젊음이란 무엇인가? 시간의 비롯에 서 있는 것이 젊음이다. 늙음이란 무엇인가? 시간의 마침에 누워있는 것이 늙음이다. 젊은이는 미지의 세계에 대한 꿈과 열정을 갖고 앞을 향해 달린다. 젊은이는 죽음을 두려워하지 않고 산다. 늙은이는 추억을 동경하며 과거의 틀에 안주한 채 산다. 죽음을 두려워하지 않는 자는 나이가 많아도 늙은이가 아니다. 과거의 틀에 안주하며 사는 자는 나이가 젊어도 젊은이가 아니다. 시간과 함께 달리는 자는 항상 새로운 시간 속에서 젊게 산다. 시간에 뒤처져서 사는 자는 앞서가는 시간을 바라보며 스스로 늙었다고 생각한다. 젊음과 늙음은 상대적이다. 어떻게 느끼고 어떻게 보느냐에 따라서 시간은 다르게 흐른다. 스스로 시간을 창조하는 자는 항상 인생을 젊게 산다. 벗이여! 살아 있다는 그것만으로도 이미 젊은 것이다. 왜 지금을 사랑하지 않는가?

371. (Poem 81)

In the memory that a castle was built endlessly,
and built again if collapsed,

a desolate beast dreams on the shore of a lake,
looking for the sun even today.

While the void is gone with the wind,
making woods lonely,

love approached as a part,
and became the whole in no time.

372. What is youth? To stand at the start of time is youth. What is old age? To lie down at the end of time is old age. The young runs forward, having a dream and passion for the unknown world. The young lives, not being afraid of death. The old lives, longing for a memory and settling down into the pattern of the past. Those who are not afraid of death are not the old, though their ages are old. Those who live settling down into the pattern of the past are not the young, though their age are young. Those who run together with time live youthfully in the always new time. Those who live behind time think that they are old while looking at the time flying ahead. Youth and old age are relative. Time flies differently according to the view—how to feel and how to see. Those who create time by themselves always live youthfully. What a companion! Only to be alive is enough to be young. Why don't you love the present?

373. 하나가 되면 그 이상 바랄 게 없다. 사랑하고 결혼하고 하는 것도 하나 되기 위함이다. 푸른 들녘에 펼쳐진 하늘과 땅은 서로 입맞춤하며 하나 되고자 지평선을 껴안는다. 거친 파도의 추억은 이제 고요한 바다가 된다. 비움은 내가 너를 받아들이는 것이고 사랑하는 것이고 하나 되는 것이다. 사랑의 미완성은 충족되지 않는 아름다움이며 여유로움이다. 여유로움 속에 육체는 지치지 않고 정신은 맑고 모든 것을 배려할 수 있다. 만월은 오만이자 기울음의 시작이다. 비어 있는 여유로움에는 두려움도 없고 기다림도 없다. 너도 없고 나도 없다. 그대로가 하나이고 그대로가 지복이다. 항상 여유를 갖고 살아라. 그러면 언제나 충만한 삶을 즐길 수 있다. 자만하지도 않을 것이며 자신감도 잃지 않을 것이다. 그러한 여유로움을 보듬어서 상대에게 나누어라. 그리고 또 하나의 내가 되어가는 과정을 즐겨라. 나를 주는 것 그리고 또 하나의 나를 갖는 것. 그래서 너와 내가 하나 되는 것이 사랑의 비밀이다. 먹는 것이 결국 먹히는 것임을 삼라만상의 변화 속에서 깨닫지 않았던가? 주어라. 그리고 사랑해라. 주는 것은 즐거움이요 확장이요 죽음이자 부활이다. 부활한 너는 나를 위해 또다시 살 터이니 그 속에서 나를 즐기고 너를 만나리라.

374. 이해는 그대로 받아들이는 것이요, 기대는 그 너머를 얻으려는 것이요, 사랑은 그 너머를 받아들이는 것이니, 개체가 전체와 하나 됨은 이해도 아니요 기대도 아니요 오직 사랑이다. 사랑은 믿음이자 깨달음이기에.

373. It is the best if united into one. It is also for becoming one to love and get married. Heaven and earth hug the horizon, spreading over the green field, giving a kiss to each other, to unite into one. The memory of a rough wave becomes a calm sea now. To empty is that I accept you, love you, and unite with you into one. Incompletion of love is unfilled beauty as well as presence of mind. A body is not tired, a spirit is clear, and all things can be taken care of in a composed mind. A full moon is the arrogance as well as the beginning of an eclipse. There is no fear as well as an expectation in a composed mind having room. You as well as I are also no more. Itself is one, and itself is the supreme bliss. Live always with presence of mind. If so, you can always enjoy a fulfilled life. You will not be conceited and will not lose confidence. Share something extra with a partner with presence of mind, and enjoy the course becoming another me. Giving me, taking another me, and so uniting into one with you and me—those are the secrets of love. Didn't you realize that to eat was the same as to be eaten, after all, in the change of all nature? Give and love. To give is pleasure, enlargement, death, as well as resurrection. I will meet you, enjoying myself inside you because you will live again for me after resurrecting.

374. Understanding is to accept something as is, expectation is to pursue something beyond what it is, and love is to accept something beyond what it is, so it is through neither understanding nor expectation but love that an individual unites with the whole, because love is an awakening as well as faith.

375. (시 82)
나목이 아름다운 것은
홀 벗었기 때문만은 아니다.

나목이 아름다운 것은
고요하기 때문만은 아니다.

겨울 안개 흐르는 호숫가에서
하염없이 기다리는 것은

새로울 것 없는 알몸으로
부활하는 봄을 꿈꾸기 때문이다.

376. 삶의 5대 불가사의를 돌이켜 보면 신과 모든 존재와 나는 각기 개별적인 개념에서 출발하였지만 서로가 서로를 있게 하는 것으로 이들 간에 죽음과 사랑이 함께하여 이들을 분리시키기도 하고 새롭게 결합시키기도 한다. 죽음이 있기에 결합된 것이 분리되고 사랑이 있기에 분리된 것이 새롭게 결합된다. 나의 믿음 속에 신이 있고 신의 온전함 속에 모든 존재가 있고 모든 존재 속에 내가 있어 죽음이나 사랑에 의해 분리되기도 하고 새롭게 결합되기도 하니 결국 신과 모든 존재와 나는 별개의 것이 아니고 사랑과 죽음과 함께 하나로 어우러진 것이다. 삶의 5대 불가사의는 제각기 바라보면 불가사의였지만 전체를 하나로 엮어서 보면 서로가 서로를 하나되게 하니 더 이상 불가사의한 것이 아니다. 이제 삶의 5대 불가사의는 비밀의 문을 열고 나와 우리와 함께한다.

375. (Poem 82)

It is not only due its naked shape that a bare tree is beautiful.

It is not only due to the silence that a bare tree is beautiful.

To await endlessly on the shore of a lake covered with winter fog⋯.

That's because it dreams of the spring, revived with the nude as usual.

376. In retrospect, regarding the five mysteries of life, even though God, all existence, and I start from an individual concept, respectively, they support each other as to be themselves. Furthermore, death and love are together with them, so death and love not only separate them but also unite them freshly. The united thing is separated by death, and the separated things are united by love. Since God is in my faith, all existence is in God's soundness, and I am in all existence. They are either separated or united by death or love. God, all existence, and I are not to be separated but united into one together with death and love after all. In retrospect, the five mysteries of life are indeed mysterious, but they are no more mysterious from an overall view because they support each other to become one. Now the five mysteries of life are together with us by getting out of the secret door.

377. 개체에서 전체로 나아가는 것이 나요, 그 길을 함께 가는 것이 신이요, 그렇게 오고 가는 것이 만물이요, 오고 감이 죽음이자 사랑이다.

378. (시 83)
처음도 끝도 없이
바람에 꽃은 피어

하나 되는 그리움이
하늘을 벗 삼아

있을 듯 없는 나를
넘어서려니

홀로히 스러져도
온누리 함께하여

너로 다시 움터나는
사랑이어라.

377. It is me to enlarge from an indivitual to the whole, it is God to go with me on the same way. Things coming and going like that are all existence, and the coming and going are death as well as love.

378. (Poem 83)
Without beginning and end,
a flower blooms with the wind.

God becomes a companion in faith,
for all things in one.

As I get out of the surface
not to be as if to be,

though an individual disappears,
it is always present with the whole.

Thus to revive with you,
that is love.

379. (시 84)
모두가 하나인 것을…

지평선을 껴안고
하늘과 땅이 입마춤하니
온갖 것은 하나가 되고,

있는가 하면 없고
없는가 하면 있으니
천지 그대로 허공이라.

부풀은 꿈은
비누방울 무지개 되어
창공에 사라지고,

합장하는 두손에
피와 땀은 흘러서
구름이 되려니,

그리움은
넋이 되어
노을에 물들련다.

무엇을
귀하고 천하다 하리?
무엇을
진실이고 거짓이라 하리?

379. (Poem 84)
Now that all things are one...

Hugging the horizon,
heaven and earth kiss each other,
so all creatures become one.

As it is not if it is,
and it is if not,
everywhere is the void as is.

An inflated dream,
becoming a rainbow of bubbles,
disappears into the sky.

On two hands joining together,
blood and sweat flow,
and turn into the clouds.

Longing,
that becomes a soul,
is tinged with the setting sun.

What can be called noble,
or vulgar?
What can be called true,
or false?

To become one,
as it is,
that is life as well as dream.

하나 되어
그대로
삶이요 꿈인 것을…

꽃이 아름다운 건
어둠을 지켜온
뿌리 때문 아니런가?

홀로 살 수 없고
홀로 죽을 수 없어
휘도는 바람 아니런가?

아기가 태중에서
생명을 얻고
믿음을 깨우칠 새,

하나가 둘이 되고
둘이 하나 되어
바람과 꽃이 어우르니,

어찌 둘 인줄 알고
그리도 하나이길
갈망했던가!

내가 죽어
너로 부활하는
사랑의 신비여!

Flowers are beautiful,
isn't it thanks to the roots,
enduring in darkness?

As one cannot live alone,
and die alone,
isn't the wind swirling?

While a baby gets life,
in the womb,
and realizes faith,

as one becomes two,
and two become one,
the wind and flowers are in harmony.

What a desire,
to become one
as if one is two!

What a mystery of love,
reviving with you
through my death!

꽃이 되어

모든 존재를 나무에 비유하면 빛은 나무에서 피어난 꽃이다. 존재와 빛의 관계는 나무와 꽃의 관계와 같다. 빛은 존재의 일부이면서 동시에 존재의 빛깔을 보여주는 존재의 꽃이다. 어미가 자식을 낳으므로 자식이 어미의 사랑에 보답하듯이 존재는 빛을 통해 존재의 배경이 되어준 어둠의 침묵을 밝혀준다. 그러나 빛을 분별할 수 있는 것은 오직 생명뿐이니 생명이야말로 존재의 꽃을 더욱 아름답게 느끼게 하는 향기라 할 것이다. 이렇듯이 생명은 우연한 것이 아니라 존재의 정점에서 이뤄낸 향기다. 비록 생명이 운명의 수레바퀴에 매여 있지만 생명이 있기에 삼라만상 천지가 향기로운 것이니 이보다 더 귀한 것이 무엇이며 더 바랄 것이 무엇이 있겠는가?

Becoming a Flower

Metaphorically comparing all existence with a tree, light is a flower blooming on this tree. All existence is to light as the tree is to the flower. Light is not only a part of all existence but also a flower of existence showing the color of existence. As a child returns a mother's love because she gave birth to him, existence makes the silence of the dark—serving as the background of existence—bright by means of light. However, only life is able to distinguish light, so life is really the fragrance making the flower of existence more beautiful. In this way, life is not an accident but the fragrance of existence achieved at the zenith of said existence. Though life hangs on fortune's wheel, heaven and earth are fragrant due to life. Therefore, what is more precious

바람과 꽃 속에 숨겨진 비밀은 이젠 더 이상 비밀이 아니다. 돌아서 보면 삶은 단순하고 끝은 시작일 뿐이다. 이제 독자들의 가슴마다 한 송이 꽃이 피어나서 모두의 삶이 향기로울 수 있다면 이보다 더한 기쁨이 없겠다.

and more desirable than life?

Now the secrets hidden in the wind and the flower are no more. In retrospect, life is simple, and the end is a mere beginning. It will be my pleasure if all life can be fragrant accordingly as a flower blooms in each reader's heart from now on.

희망과 기쁨이 사라지면 아무것도 아닌 것이 인생이다.
꿈을 꾸어라. 그리고 웃어라. 영원한 지금 속에서···.

If hope and joy disappear, life is nothing.
Dream and smile in the everlasting present.